ENDURANCE

ENDURANCE

Shackleton's Incredible Voyage

Alfred Lansing

Introduction by Nathaniel Philbrick

BASIC BOOKS
A Member of the Perseus Books Group
New York

Published in 2014 by Basic Books,
A Member of the Perseus Books Group

First published by Carroll & Graf in 1986
Published by arrangement with Mrs. Alfred Lansing

Basic Books are available at special discounts for bulk purchases in the
United States by corporations, institutions, and other organizations. For more
information, please contact the Special Markets Department at the Perseus
Books Group, 2300 Chestnut Street, Suite 200, Philadelphia, PA 19103, or
call (800) 255-1514, ext. 5000, or e-mail special.markets@perseusbooks.com.

Book design in Garamond by Cynthia Young.

Library of Congress Cataloging-in-Publication Data

Lansing, Alfred.
    Endurance : Shackleton's incredible voyage / Alfred Lansing.
      pages   cm
    ISBN 978-0-465-05878-5 (hardback)—ISBN 978-0-465-05879-2 (e-book)
  1. Shackleton, Ernest Henry, Sir, 1874–1922—Travel—Antarctica.
2. Endurance (Ship) 3. Imperial Trans-Antarctic Expedition (1914–1917)
4. Antarctica—Discovery and exploration—British. I. Title.
G850 1914 .S53 L36 2014
919.89—dc23

                                                              2014005005

ISBN (paperback): 978-0-465-06288-1

10 9 8 7 6 5

Introduction

Today, more than fifty years after its publication, Alfred Lansing's *Endurance* is recognized as the definitive account of Ernest Shackleton's doomed attempt to cross the Antarctic continent on foot. When his ship the *Endurance* became trapped and was eventually crushed by the pack ice of the Weddell Sea in October 1915, Shackleton's focus shifted from conquering a continent to getting his twenty-seven-man crew to safety. Unfortunately, more than twelve hundred miles lay between them and the nearest outpost of civilization. If they were to survive, they must ride the drifting ice floes to the north and then, once the ice had begun to melt, take to their tiny lifeboats and sail hundreds of miles across the forbidding Drake Passage, one of the stormiest pieces of open water on the planet. What followed was a yearlong, almost impossible-to-believe ordeal during which Shackleton displayed the skills that have earned him a well-deserved reputation as one of the greatest leaders of all time.

Certainly, the story of Shackleton and the *Endurance* contains all the elements of a rip-roaring good yarn. But Lansing's book is more than a well-executed rendering of an amazing real-life adventure. While remaining rigorously true to the documentary record, Lansing has crafted a narrative that immerses the reader in the sensory world of his characters. By the time we've finished *Endurance,* we know what it is like to watch an ice floe crumble and crack around us, we've felt the needlelike sting of the freezing salt spray as the men cling to their wave-tossed cockleshells, and, finally, we've experienced the exaltation of knowing, after months of deprivation and despair, what it is like to be saved.

A half century after its publication, Lansing's masterpiece has a loyal and devoted readership. But it was not always this way. When *Endurance* was first published in 1959, the book did not appear on the *New York Times* best-seller list and quickly fell out of print. Not until 1986, more than a decade after the author's death, did the book finally find the large popular audience it enjoys today. What follows is the story of how a young midwesterner named Alfred Lansing came to write this classic tale of survival and the sea and how, after decades of languishing in relative obscurity, Lansing's *Endurance* came to be so enthusiastically embraced by a new generation of readers.

Alfred Lansing was born in Chicago, Illinois, in 1921. In 1941 he joined the US Navy and, like many new recruits, was captivated by the just-published *Delilah,* an energetically written novel about a World War I–era destroyer and its crew by screenwriter Marcus Goodrich. Although little read today, *Delilah* was hugely popular among naval recruits in the 1940s; future novelist James Michener, who joined the navy about the same time as Lansing, later recalled that *Delilah* was "so powerful, so uncompromising in its depiction of what happens in a fighting ship that I was stunned by its brilliance." Whether or not *Delilah* inspired Lansing to one day become a writer, his wife, Barbara, later remembered him as being "obsessed" with the book, and, as we shall see, Goodrich's novel may have served as a source of inspiration for Lansing more than fifteen years later when he began to write about the Shackleton expedition.

Lansing served for five years in the navy, earning a purple heart (Barbara remembers that his arms were badly scarred from the burns he suffered after his ship was hit), and eventually majored in journalism at Northwestern. For a time he edited a weekly newspaper in Illinois and eventually joined the United Press, after which he moved to New York City to work as a staff writer at *Collier's*. Wanting to "get away from Manhattan," Lansing moved to the village of Sea Cliff, New York, on the north shore of Long Island, where he met Barbara, who was working at a drugstore. She describes him at this time as "tall, wiry, and enthusiastic—very active and adventurous, a typical writer who wanted to go off into the woods and write." Money was tight, but that didn't prevent them from getting married and buying a dilapidated house that Lansing attempted to renovate between assignments as a freelance journalist.

At some point soon after their marriage, Barbara remembers, Lansing "read something that sparked his interest" in Shackleton and the *Endurance*. Up until that point, the only significant book about the expedition had been Shackleton's own *South* (1919), a ghostwritten account that harks back to the Edwardian era of heroic exploration. "We had pierced the veneer of outside things," Shackleton intones after describing how he and two others survived the unforgettable slide down the icy side of a near-vertical peak that delivers them to the outskirts of a whaling station on South Georgia Island. "We had seen God in His splendors, we had heard the text that Nature renders. We had reached the naked soul of man." Clearly, after two world wars and the emergence of Ernest Hemingway, it was time to free the story of the *Endurance* expedition from this sarcophagus of stilted prose.

By 1957 Lansing had made several important contacts in Great Britain, including Alexander Macklin, one of the five surviving participants in the expedition, as well as writers Margery and James Fisher, whose biography of Shackleton appeared that year. Lansing realized that if he were to write a book about the expedition, he must travel to England and interview the survivors. By this time Barbara was pregnant with their first child, and Lansing decided to postpone his eagerly anticipated research trip until after the birth of their son, whose name was inspired, Barbara reports, by the sobriquet with which Margery Fisher signed her letters, "Angus."

Once in Britain, Lansing crisscrossed the country conducting interviews. Much of his time was spent in Aberdeenshire, Scotland, speaking extensively with Macklin, the expedition's surgeon and Shackleton's close friend. He also visited the Scott Polar Research Institute in Cambridge, where he consulted several logbooks from the expedition. In the preface to *Endurance,* Lansing speaks of how important the examination of the physical diaries was to his research process, describing them as "a wonderfully strange assortment of documents, smudged with the smoke of blubber oil, wrinkled from being waterlogged and then dried out." But it was the opportunity to speak with the survivors, who, Lansing writes, "submitted to long hours, even days, of interviewing," that allowed him to create "as true a picture of the events as we could collectively produce." For Lansing, the writing of *Endurance* was a collaborative process, and he speaks movingly in the preface of being "extremely proud of my association with [the survivors]."

Once back at their house in Sea Cliff, Lansing started "writing obsessively," Barbara remembers, "for hours and hours." From the beginning, Lansing was determined to avoid the excesses of Shackleton's own account. In a fascinating September 13, 1957, letter to Alexander Macklin, he wrote of how he wanted to tell the story in "the most unimpassioned tone of voice possible. . . . In fact, I think a great deal is lost if you allow any histrionics to creep in." It was his hope to recount the events of the expedition "from the same point of view as you people yourselves had—without heroism or tears or lunatics wildly embracing rocks, and so forth. The end result . . . will be much greater if the reader comes to feel the truth of the situation, that you people were not supermen, defying danger with grim abandon or some such foolishness. Instead, I think, you were all really quite mortal men who found yourselves in rather extraordinary circumstances."

Lansing soon began to realize that the sheer number of journals and interviews he had at his disposal presented something of a challenge, since, he wrote Macklin, "the same men seeing the same event at the same time will often give slightly varying accounts of what actually happened." In the "scores of times" when there were disagreements in the testimony, Lansing had no choice but "to make my own solitary decision as to who was right—or to strike an average, so to speak." This meant that it was likely that Macklin and the other survivors "will see inaccuracies in what I have said. In this regard, my only defense is that I did my best."

One of the biggest challenges for a writer of nonfiction is to avoid using too much of his or her hard-won material. A great and enduring book isn't comprehensive; it is highly, even ruthlessly, selective, zeroing in on the most evocative and illustrative moments while dispensing with the clutter that might prevent the high points from resonating to maximum effect. This is particularly important when it comes to a book's opening scene, and Lansing begins *Endurance* with an extraordinary description of the ship being torn apart by the ice.

In Lansing's hands, the *Endurance* is a dying animal caught by vast remorseless forces made terrifyingly immediate when he recounts Macklin's and Frank Wild's descent into the "black-dark" innards of the twisting ship to retrieve some much-needed lumber. Lansing clearly questioned Macklin closely about every detail of this incident, but he may have also been inspired by the beginning of *Delilah,* the novel he had read in the navy, which starts with a memorable depiction of the destroyer as a living, breathing

thing: "always tense, often atremble . . . a mass of almost terrible power wrapped in a thin and fragile blue-grey skin." Lansing invested the *Endurance* with this same sense of organic, frightening life while avoiding Goodrich's verbal excesses. By thrusting the reader into the middle of this chaotic and unnerving scene, Lansing foreshadows the challenges to come even as he plants the inevitable question: how did these men get into this fix in the first place?

It is only after the ship has been torn apart by the pack ice and the crew have retired to their tents that Lansing introduces the expedition's leader. "Few men have borne the responsibility Shackleton did at that moment," he writes. It was 1915, and without a radio transmitter to broadcast an SOS and with an ever-escalating war in Europe demanding the world's attention, they were on their own. "Thus their plight was naked and terrifying in its simplicity. If they were to get out—they had to get themselves out."

And off we go.

Endurance was published in the spring of 1959 to excellent reviews. Walter Sullivan in the *New York Times Sunday Book Review* described it as "a harrowing, as well as a thrilling, reading experience. One comes out of it with new faith in the resourcefulness of man, his almost indefatigable will to live and above all, his ability to fight back despair." Sullivan, who had authored a book about Antarctic exploration, noted how "remarkable [it] is that we have had to wait for more than forty years for a full, searching and impartial account" of the Shackleton expedition. Orville Prescott in the daily *New York Times* marveled at how Lansing had "packed *Endurance* with [so many] concrete and often horrifying details. Without having been there himself, he makes his readers feel as if they had been." *Newsweek* agreed, claiming that "most readers will almost personally recoil from the attacks of the sea leopards, damn the men who snored so irritatingly at close quarters, and taste the steady diet of seal blubber and penguin hearts," while proclaiming *Endurance* to be "one of the most breath-takingly exciting books of the year." The anonymous reviewer at *Time* mentioned Lansing's journalism background and noted that "he has a good newspaperman's respect for telling in unexcited prose the breathless story of men in peril." The reviewer at the *Times* of London felt that the book's greatest strength was the attention Lansing gave to Shackleton's men. "He does not allow the brooding, complex character of the leader to overshadow the rest. Shackleton, to be sure, is there. But for once, too, the carpenter, the cook and the stowaway emerge as flesh and blood. Perhaps as an American Mr. Lansing does not always understand the English. His judgment of personalities is sometimes harsh. But for all that he makes good use of his magnificent material."

All in all, *Endurance* enjoyed an impressive string of what are known in the publishing industry as "selling" reviews. For a first-time book author, it was quite an accomplishment. However, despite being a Book of the Month Club selection, *Endurance* showed few signs of becoming the perennial best seller that it is today. In 1959, two years after the launch of Sputnik, Americans were not interested in the wilds of the sea or Antarctica; they were interested in the "final frontier" of space.

After the publication of *Endurance*, Lansing supported his growing family (his son was soon joined by a daughter) with a series of journalism jobs that included positions at the book division of Time-Life and Reader's Digest. Several potential topics for another book crossed his desk, but none had, Barbara remembers, "the same pull" as the story of the Shackleton expedition, and as the years passed he grew increasingly "sensitive" about his failure to produce a second book. When asked by the magazine *Contemporary Authors* about his thoughts on the writing life, he responded, "I have a great many opinions about writing, but I'm afraid that all of them are unprintable." In 1975 he was working as the editor of a weekly newspaper in Bethel, Connecticut, when he died at the age of fifty-four.

In 1986 Kent Carroll, publisher and editorial director of the newly established Carroll and Graf, bought the rights to Lansing's *Endurance,* which had been out of print for more than twenty-five years. He remembered having read the book as a boy, and after coming across a copy in a used bookstore, he was newly impressed. "There was this wonderful inspirational quality about it," he remembers.

In the first year, *Endurance* sold a credible four to five thousand copies. But that was just the beginning. Over the course of the next decade, the book climbed onto the *New York Times* paperback best-seller list and ultimately sold an astounding half-million copies. The popularity of this once-forgotten survival tale was part of the trend that also made best sellers out of Sebastian Junger's *The Perfect Storm* and Jon Krakauer's *Into Thin Air,* both published in 1997. In 1998 Caroline Alexander came out with her own lushly illustrated retelling of the Shackleton expedition that enjoyed fifteen weeks on the best-seller list even as it served as the catalog for an exhibit at the American Museum of Natural History in New York that attracted as many as 140,000 visitors.

By the start of the twenty-first century, what a *Wall Street Journal* reporter called "Shackleton mania" was in full swing. Two business books based on "leadership lessons" from the *Endurance* expedition appeared, as well as a documentary, a BBC film starring Kenneth Branagh, and an IMAX film. Although sales of Lansing's book initially suffered due to the appearance of these rival Shackleton books, *Endurance* has since reasserted its rightful place as, in the words of cultural scholar Stephanie Barczewski, "the standard first choice for people when they first hear about

Shackleton or the story of the *Endurance*." As of the fall of 2013, the book was in its forty-ninth printing.

For Lansing's family, the belated popularity of *Endurance* is more than a little bittersweet. Barbara reports that her son, Angus, an infant when his father was working so slavishly on the book and now in his midfifties, is still amazed by the number of people who buttonhole him with testimonials about *Endurance*, especially since no one seemed to be aware of the book's existence when he was growing up in the sixties and seventies. "It's sad," Barbara says of her husband. "He would have been so proud, and yet he never knew."

For an author, posterity is the toughest of proving grounds. Only a handful of books are so firmly connected to the timeless underpinnings of life that they survive into the future. *Endurance*, by Alfred Lansing, is one of those books.

—*Nathaniel Philbrick, November 2013*

My thanks to Barbara Lansing and Kent Carroll for speaking with me about Alfred Lansing and *Endurance*. Thanks to Margot Morrell, coauthor of *Shackleton's Way: Leadership Lessons from the Great Antarctic Explorer* (2001), for reprinting Alfred Lansing's letters to Alexander Macklin on her website, http://leadership lives.com; thanks to Barbara Lansing for granting me permission to quote from those letters. In addition to the books mentioned above, I also consulted Stephanie Barczewski's *Antarctic Destinies: Scott, Shackleton, and the Changing Face of Heroism* (2007).

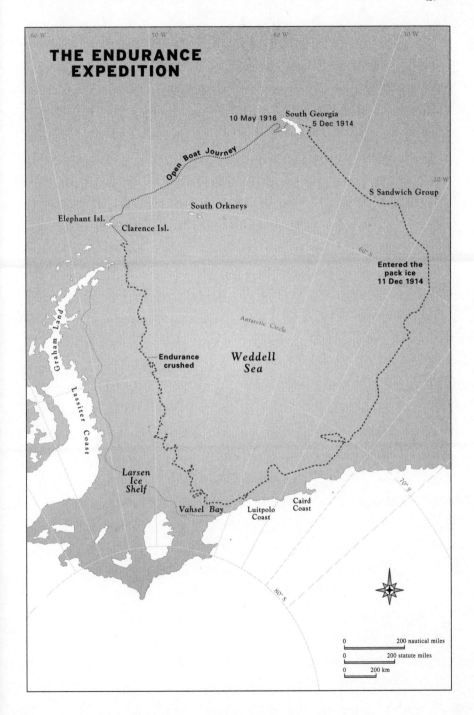

THE ENDURANCE EXPEDITION

60 W   50 W   40 W   30 W

10 May 1916   South Georgia
5 Dec 1914

Open Boat Journey

20 W

S Sandwich Group

South Orkneys

Elephant Isl.

Clarence Isl.

60° S

Entered the
pack ice
11 Dec 1914

Graham Land

Antarctic Circle

Endurance
crushed

Weddell
Sea

Lassiter Coast

70° S

Larsen
Ice
Shelf

Vahsel Bay   Luitpolo
Coast

Caird
Coast

80° S

0   200 nautical miles

0   200 statute miles

0   200 km

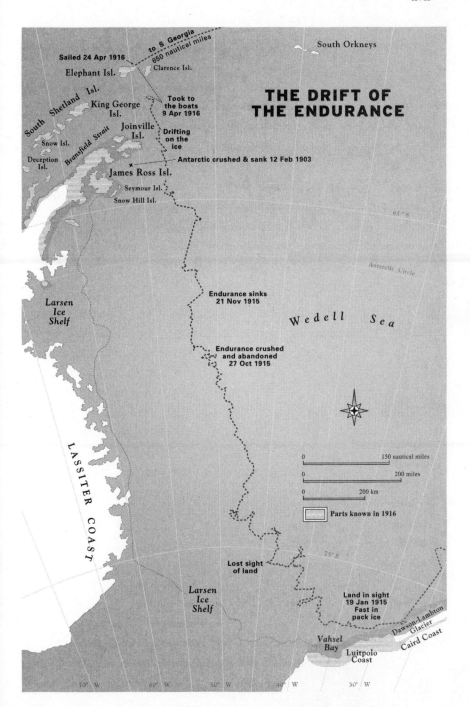

Sailed 24 Apr 1916

to S Georgia
650 nautical miles

South Orkneys

Elephant Isl.

Clarence Isl.

King George Isl.

Took to the boats 9 Apr 1916

THE DRIFT OF THE ENDURANCE

South Shetland Isl.

Snow Isl.

Joinville Isl.

Drifting on the ice

Deception Isl.

Bransfield Strait

James Ross Isl.

Antarctic crushed & sank 12 Feb 1903

Seymour Isl.

Snow Hill Isl.

65 °S

Antarctic Circle

Larsen Ice Shelf

Endurance sinks 21 Nov 1915

W e d e l l   S e a

Endurance crushed and abandoned 27 Oct 1915

0   150 nautical miles

0   200 miles

0   200 km

Parts known in 1916

L A S S I T E R   C O A S T

75 °S

Lost sight of land

Larsen Ice Shelf

Land in sight 19 Jan 1915 Fast in pack ice

Dawson-Lambton Glacier

Vahsel Bay

Luitpolo Coast

Caird Coast

70° W   60° W   50° W   40° W   30° W

Preface

The story that follows is true.

Every effort has been made to portray the events exactly as they occurred, and to record as accurately as possible the reactions of the men who lived them.

For this purpose, a wealth of material has been generously made available to me, most notably the painstakingly detailed diaries of virtually every expedition member who kept one. It is amazing how thorough these diaries are, considering the conditions under which they were kept. In fact, the diaries contain much more information than could be included in this book.

These logs are a wonderfully strange assortment of documents, smudged with the smoke of blubber oil, wrinkled from being waterlogged and then dried out. Some were written in bookkeepers' ledgers in appropriately large handwriting. Others were kept in very small notebooks in tiny script. In all cases, however, the exact language, spelling, and punctuation have been preserved just as they were originally written.

In addition to making these diaries available to me, almost all the surviving members of the expedition submitted to long hours, even days, of interviewing with a courtesy and cooperativeness for which my grateful appreciation is hardly an adequate repayment.

The same patient willingness marked the numerous letters in which these men replied to the many questions which arose.

Thus most of the survivors of this astounding adventure worked with me, graciously and with a remarkable degree of objectivity, to re-create in the pages that follow as true a picture of the events as we could collectively produce. I am extremely proud of my association with them.

However, these men bear no responsibility whatever for what follows. If any inaccuracies or misinterpretations have crept into this story, they are my own and should in no way be attributed to the men who took part in this expedition.

The names of those who helped to make this book possible appear at the back of the book.

A. L.

Members of the
Imperial Trans-Antarctic Expedition

Sir Ernest Shackleton	*leader*
Frank Wild	*second-in-command*
Frank Worsley	*captain*
Lionel Greenstreet	*first officer*
Hubert T. Hudson	*navigator*
Thomas Crean	*second officer*
Alfred Cheetham	*third officer*
Louis Rickinson	*first engineer*
A. J. Kerr	*second engineer*
Dr. Alexander H. Macklin	*surgeon*
Dr. James A. McIlroy	*surgeon*
James M. Wordie	*geologist*
Leonard D. A. Hussey	*meteorologist*
Reginald W. James	*physicist*
Robert S. Clark	*biologist*
James Francis (Frank) Hurley	*official photographer*
George E. Marston	*official artist*
Thomas H. Orde-Lees	*motor expert*
	(*later storekeeper*)
Harry McNeish	*carpenter*
Charles J. Green	*cook*
Walter How	*able seaman*
William Bakewell	*able seaman*
Timothy McCarthy	*able seaman*
Thomas McLeod	*able seaman*
John Vincent	*able seaman*
Ernest Holness	*fireman*
William Stevenson	*fireman*
Perce Blackboro	*stowaway* (*later steward*)

PART I

CHAPTER 1

The order to abandon ship was given at 5 P.M. For most of the men, however, no order was needed because by then everybody knew that the ship was done and that it was time to give up trying to save her. There was no show of fear or even apprehension. They had fought unceasingly for three days and they had lost. They accepted their defeat almost apathetically. They were simply too tired to care.

Frank Wild, the second-in-command, made his way forward along the buckling deck to the crew's quarters. There, two seamen, Walter How and William Bakewell, were lying in the lower bunks. Both were very nearly exhausted from almost three days at the pumps; yet they were unable to sleep because of the sounds the ship was making.

She was being crushed. Not all at once, but slowly, a little at a time. The pressure of ten million tons of ice was driving in against her sides. And dying as she was, she cried in agony. Her frames and planking, her immense timbers, many of them almost a foot thick, screamed as the killing pressure mounted. And when her timbers could no longer stand the strain, they broke with a report like artillery fire.

Most of the forecastle beams had already gone earlier in the day, and the deck was heaved upward and working slowly up and down as the pressure came and went.

Wild put his head inside the crew's quarters. He spoke quietly. "She's going, boys. I think it's time to get off." How and Bakewell rose from their bunks, picked up two pillowcases in which they had stowed some personal gear, and followed Wild back up on deck.

Wild next went down into the ship's tiny engine room. Kerr, the second engineer, was standing at the foot of the ladder, waiting. With him was Rickenson, the chief engineer. They had been below for almost seventy-two hours maintaining steam in the boilers to operate the engine-room pumps. During that time, though they couldn't actually see the ice in motion, they were altogether aware of what it was doing to the ship. Periodically her sides—though they were 2 feet thick in most places—bowed inward 6 inches under the pressure. Simultaneously, the steel floor plates jammed together, screeching where their edges met, then buckling up and suddenly overriding one another with a sharp metallic report.

Wild did not pause long. "Let down your fires," he said. "She's going." Kerr looked relieved.

Wild turned aft to the propeller shaftway. There McNeish, the old ship's carpenter, and McLeod, a seaman, were busy with torn pieces of blankets calking a cofferdam built by McNeish the day before. It had been thrown up in an attempt to stem the flow of water coming into the ship where the rudder and the sternpost had been torn out by the ice. But the water now was almost up to the floor plates, and it was gaining faster than the cofferdam could hold it back and faster than the pumps could carry it away. Whenever the pressure ceased for a moment, there was the sound of the water running forward and filling up the hold.

Wild signaled to the two men to give up. Then he climbed the ladder to the main deck.

Clark, Hussey, James, and Wordie had been at the pumps but they had quit on their own, realizing the futility of what they were doing. Now they sat on cases of stores or on the deck itself, and leaned against the bulwarks. Their faces showed the unspeakable toil of the past three days at the pumps.

Farther forward, the dog-team drivers had attached a large piece of canvas to the port rail and made it into a sort of chute down to the ice alongside the ship. They took the forty-nine huskies from their kennels and slid each one down to other men waiting below. Ordinarily, any activity of this sort would have driven the dogs mad with excitement, but somehow they seemed to sense that something very extraordinary was going on. Not one fight broke out among them, and not a single dog attempted to break away.

It was, perhaps, the attitude of the men. They worked with a deliberate urgency, hardly speaking to one another. There was no display of alarm, however. In fact, apart from the movement of the ice and the sounds from the ship, the scene was one of relative calm. The temperature was 8½ degrees below zero, and a light southerly wind was blowing. Overhead, the twilight sky was clear.

But somewhere, far away to the south, a gale was blowing toward them. Though it probably wouldn't reach their position for at least two days, its approach was suggested by the movement of the ice, which stretched as far as the eye could see, and for hundreds of miles beyond that. So immense was the pack, and so tight, that though the gale had not yet reached them, the distant pressure of its winds was already crushing the floes together.

The whole surface of the ice was a chaos of movement. It looked like an enormous jigsaw puzzle, the pieces stretching away to infinity and being shoved and crunched together by some invisible but irresistible force. The impression of its titanic power was heightened by the unhurried deliberateness of the motion. Wherever two thick floes came together, their edges butted and ground against one another for a time. Then, when neither of them showed signs of yielding, they rose, slowly and often quiveringly, driven by the implacable power behind them. Sometimes they would stop abruptly as the unseen force affecting the ice appeared mysteriously to lose interest. More frequently, though, the two floes—often 10 feet thick or more—would continue to rise, tenting up, until one or both of them broke and toppled over, creating a pressure ridge.

There were the sounds of the pack in movement—the basic noises, the grunting and whining of the floes, along with an occasional thud as a heavy block collapsed. But in addition, the pack under compression seemed to have an almost limitless repertoire of other sounds, many of which seemed strangely unrelated to the noise of ice undergoing pressure. Sometimes there was a sound like a gigantic train with squeaky axles being shunted roughly about with a great deal of bumping and clattering. At the same time a huge ship's whistle blew, mingling with the crowing of roosters, the roar of a distant surf, the soft throb of an engine far away, and the moaning cries of an old woman. In the rare periods of calm, when the movement of the pack subsided for a moment, the muffled rolling of drums drifted across the air.

In this universe of ice, nowhere was the movement greater or the pressure more intense than in the floes that were attacking the ship. Nor could her position have been worse. One floe was jammed solidly against her starboard bow, and another held her on the same side aft. A third floe drove squarely in on her port beam opposite. Thus the ice was working to break her in half, directly amidships. On several occasions she bowed to starboard along her entire length.

Forward, where the worst of the onslaught was concentrated, the ice was inundating her. It piled higher and higher against her bows as she repelled each new wave, until gradually it mounted to her bulwarks, then crashed across the deck, overwhelming her with a crushing load that pushed her head down even deeper. Thus held, she was even more at the mercy of the floes driving against her flanks.

The ship reacted to each fresh wave of pressure in a different way. Sometimes she simply quivered briefly as a human being might wince if seized by a single, stabbing pain. Other times she retched in a series of convulsive jerks accompanied by anguished outcries. On these occasions her three masts whipped violently back and forth as the rigging tightened like harpstrings. But most agonizing for the men were the times when she seemed a huge creature suffocating and gasping for breath, her sides heaving against the strangling pressure.

More than any other single impression in those final hours, all the men were struck, almost to the point of horror, by the way the ship behaved like a giant beast in its death agonies.

By 7 P.M., all essential gear had been transferred to the ice, and a camp of sorts had been established on a solid floe a short distance to starboard. The lifeboats had been lowered the night before. As they went over the side onto the ice, most of the men felt immense relief at being away from the doomed ship, and few if any of them would have returned to her voluntarily.

However, a few unfortunate souls were ordered back to retrieve various items. One was Alexander Macklin, a stocky young physician, who also happened to be the driver of a dog team. He had just tethered his dogs at the camp when he was told to go with Wild to get some lumber out of the ship's forehold.

The two men started out and had just reached the ship when a great shout went up from the campsite. The floe on which the tents were pitched was itself breaking up. Wild and Macklin rushed back. The teams were harnessed and the tents, stores, sledges, and all the gear were hurriedly moved to another floe a hundred yards farther from the ship.

By the time the transfer was completed, the ship seemed on the point of going under, so the two men hurried to get aboard. They picked their way among the blocks of ice littering the forecastle, then lifted a hatch leading down into the forepeak. The ladder had been wrenched from its supports and had fallen to one side. To get down, they had to lower themselves hand over hand into the darkness.

The noise inside was indescribable. The half-empty compartment, like a giant sounding box, amplified every snapping bolt and splintering timber. From where they stood, the sides of the ship were only a few feet away, and they could hear the ice outside battering to break through.

They waited for a moment until their eyes grew accustomed to the gloom, and what they saw then was terrifying. The uprights were caving in and the cross members overhead were on the verge of going. It looked as if some giant vise were being applied to the ship and slowly tightened until she could no longer hold out against its pressure.

The lumber they were after was stored in the black-dark recesses of the side pockets in the very bow of the ship. To reach it, they had to crawl through a thwartships bulkhead, and they could see that the bulkhead itself bulged outward as if it might burst at any moment, causing the whole forecastle to collapse around them.

Macklin hesitated for just a moment, and Wild, sensing the other's fear, shouted to him above the noise of the ship to stay where he was. Then Wild plunged through the opening and a few minutes later began passing boards out to Macklin.

The two men worked with feverish speed, but even so the job seemed interminable. Macklin was sure they would never get the last board out in time. But finally Wild's head reappeared through the opening. They hoisted the lumber up on deck, climbed out, and stood for a long moment without speaking, savoring the exquisite feeling of safety. Later, to the privacy of his diary, Macklin confided: "I do not think I have ever had such a horrible sickening sensation of fear as I had whilst in the hold of that breaking ship."

Within an hour after the last man was off, the ice pierced her sides. Sharp spears drove through first, opening wounds that let in whole blocks and chunks of floes. Everything from midships forward was now submerged. The entire starboard side of the deckhouse had been crushed by the ice with such force that some empty gasoline cans stacked on deck had been shoved through the deckhouse wall and halfway across to the other side, carrying before them a large framed picture that had hung on the wall. Somehow, the glass on its front had not broken.

Later, after things had settled down at the camp, a few men returned to look at the derelict that had been their ship. But not many. Most of them huddled in their tents, cold through and tired, for the time being indifferent to their fate.

The general feeling of relief at being off the ship was not shared by one man—at least not in the larger sense. He was a thickset individual with a wide face and a broad nose, and he spoke with a trace of an Irish brogue. During the hours it took to abandon the ship, he had remained more or less apart as the equipment, dogs, and men were gotten off.

His name was Sir Ernest Shackleton, and the twenty-seven men he had watched so ingloriously leaving their stricken ship were the members of his Imperial Trans-Antarctic Expedition.

The date was October 27, 1915. The name of the ship was *Endurance*. The position was 69°5′ South, 51°30′ West—deep in the icy wasteland of the Antarctic's treacherous Weddell Sea, just about midway between the South Pole and the nearest known outpost of humanity, some 1,200 miles away.

Few men have borne the responsibility Shackleton did at that moment. Though he certainly was aware that their situation was desperate, he could not possibly have imagined then the physical and emotional demands that ultimately would be placed upon them, the rigors they would have to endure, the sufferings to which they would be subjected.

They were for all practical purposes alone in the frozen Antarctic seas. It had been very nearly a year since they had last been in contact with civilization. Nobody in the outside world knew they were in trouble, much less where they were. They had no radio transmitter with which to notify any would-be rescuers, and it is doubtful that any rescuers could have reached them even if they had been able to broadcast an SOS. It was 1915, and there were no helicopters, no Weasels, no Sno-Cats, no suitable planes.

Thus their plight was naked and terrifying in its simplicity. If they were to get out—they had to get themselves out.

Shackleton estimated the shelf ice off the Palmer Peninsula— the nearest known land—to be 182 miles WSW of them. But the land itself was 210 miles away, was inhabited by neither human beings nor animals, and offered nothing in the way of relief or rescue.

The nearest known place where they might at least find food and shelter was tiny Paulet Island, less than a mile and a half in diameter, which lay 346 miles northwest across the heaving pack ice. There, in 1903, twelve years before, the crew of a Swedish ship had spent the winter after their vessel, the *Antarctic*, had been crushed by the Weddell Sea ice. The ship which finally rescued that party deposited its stock of stores on Paulet Island for the use of any later castaways. Ironically, it was Shackleton himself who had been commissioned at the time to purchase those stores—and now, a dozen years later, it was he who needed them.

CHAPTER 2

Shackleton's order to abandon ship, while it signaled the beginning of the greatest of all Antarctic adventures, also sealed the fate of one of the most ambitious of all Antarctic expeditions. The goal of the Imperial Trans-Antarctic Expedition, as its name implies, was to cross the Antarctic continent overland from west to east.

Evidence of the scope of such an undertaking is the fact that after Shackleton's failure, the crossing of the continent remained untried for fully forty-three years—until 1957–1958. Then, as an independent enterprise conducted during the International Geophysical Year, Dr. Vivian E. Fuchs led the Commonwealth Trans-Antarctic Expedition on the trek. And even Fuchs, though his party was equipped with heated, tracked vehicles and powerful radios, and guided by reconnaissance planes and dog teams, was strongly urged to give up. It was only after a tortuous journey lasting nearly four months that Fuchs did in fact achieve what Shackleton set out to do in 1915.

This was Shackleton's third expedition to the Antarctic. He had gone first in 1901 as a member of the National Antarctic Expedition led by Robert F. Scott, the famed British explorer, which drove to 82°15′ South latitude, 745 miles from the Pole—the deepest penetration of the continent at that time.

Then in 1907, Shackleton led the first expedition actually to declare the Pole as its goal. With three companions, Shackleton struggled to within 97 miles of their destination and then had to turn back because of a shortage of food. The return journey was a desperate race with death. But the party finally made it, and Shackleton returned to England a hero of the Empire. He was lionized wherever he went, knighted by his king, and decorated by every major country in the world.

He wrote a book, and he went on a lecture tour which took him all over the British Isles, the United States, Canada, and much of Europe. But even before it was over, his thoughts had returned to the Antarctic.

He had been within 97 miles of the Pole, and he knew better than anyone that it was only a matter of time until some expedition attained the goal that had been denied him. As early as March of 1911, he wrote to his wife, Emily, from Berlin where he was on tour: "I feel that another expedition unless it crosses the continent is not much."

Meanwhile, an American expedition under Robert E. Peary had reached the North Pole in 1909. Then Scott, on his second expedition in late 1911 and early 1912, was raced to the South Pole by the Norwegian, Roald Amundsen—and beaten by a little more than a month. It was disappointing to lose out. But that might have been only a bit of miserable luck—had not Scott and his three companions died as they struggled, weak with scurvy, to return to their base.

When the news of Scott's achievement and the tragic circumstances of his death reached England, the whole nation was saddened. The sense of loss was compounded by the fact that the British, whose record for exploration had been perhaps unparalleled among the nations of the earth, had to take a humiliating second best to Norway.

Throughout these events, Shackleton's own plans for a Trans-Antarctic expedition had been moving rapidly ahead. In an early prospectus designed to solicit funds for the undertaking, Shackleton played heavily on this matter of prestige, making it his primary argument for such an expedition. He wrote:

"From the sentimental point of view, it is the last great Polar journey that can be made. It will be a greater journey than the journey to the Pole and back, and I feel it is up to the British nation to accomplish this, for we have been beaten at the conquest of the North Pole and beaten at the first conquest of the South Pole. There now remains the largest and most striking of all journeys—the crossing of the Continent."

Shackleton's plan was to take a ship into the Weddell Sea and land a sledging party of six men and seventy dogs near Vahsel Bay, approximately 78° South, 36° West. At more or less the same time, a second ship would put into McMurdo Sound in the Ross Sea, almost directly across the continent from the Weddell Sea base. The Ross Sea party was to set down a series of food caches from their base almost to the Pole. While this was being done, the Weddell Sea group would be sledging toward the Pole, living on their own rations. From the Pole they would proceed to the vicinity of the mighty Beardmore Glacier where they would replenish their supplies at the southernmost depot laid down by the Ross Sea party. Other caches of rations along the route would keep them supplied until they arrived at the McMurdo Sound base.

Such was the plan on paper, and it was typical of Shackleton—purposeful, bold, and neat. He had not the slightest doubt that the expedition would achieve its goal.

The whole undertaking was criticized in some circles as being too "audacious." And perhaps it was. But if it hadn't been audacious, it wouldn't have been to Shackleton's liking. He was, above all, an explorer in the classic mold—utterly self-reliant, romantic, and just a little swashbuckling.

He was now forty years old, of medium height and thick of neck, with broad, heavy shoulders a trifle stooped, and dark brown hair parted in the center. He had a wide, sensuous but expressive mouth that could curl into a laugh or tighten into a thin fixed line with equal facility. His jaw was like iron. His gray-blue eyes, like his mouth, could come alight with fun or darken into a steely and frightening gaze. His face was handsome, though it often wore a brooding expression—as if his thoughts were somewhere else—which gave him at times a kind of darkling look. He had small hands, but his grip was strong and confident. He spoke softly and somewhat slowly in an indefinite baritone, with just the recollection of a brogue from his County Kildare birth.

Whatever his mood—whether it was gay and breezy, or dark with rage—he had one pervading characteristic: he was purposeful.

Cynics might justifiably contend that Shackleton's fundamental purpose in undertaking the expedition was simply the greater glory of Ernest Shackleton—and the financial rewards that would accrue to the leader of a successful expedition of this scope. Beyond all doubt, these motives loomed large in Shackleton's mind. He was keenly aware of social position and the important part that money played in it. In fact, the abiding (and unrealistic) dream of his life—at least superficially—was to achieve a status of economic well-being that would last a lifetime. He enjoyed fancying himself as a country gentleman, divorced from the workaday world, with the leisure and wealth to do as he pleased.

Shackleton came from a middle-class background, the son of a moderately successful physician. He joined the British Merchant Navy at the age of sixteen and though he rose steadily through the ranks, this sort of step-by-step advancement grew progressively less appealing to his flamboyant personality.

Then came two important events: the expedition with Scott in 1901, and his marriage to the daughter of a wealthy lawyer. The first introduced him to the Antarctic—and his imagination was immediately captivated. The second increased his desire for wealth. He felt obliged to provide for his wife in the manner to which she was accustomed. The Antarctic and financial security became more or less synonymous in Shackleton's thinking. He felt that success here—some marvelous stroke of daring, a deed which would capture the world's imagination—would open the door to fame, then riches.

Between expeditions, he also pursued this financial masterstroke. He was perennially entranced with new schemes, each of which in turn he was sure would win his fortune. It would be impossible to list them all, but they included an idea to manufacture cigarettes (a sure-fire plan—with his endorsement), a fleet of taxicabs, mining in Bulgaria, a whaling factory—even digging for buried treasure. Most of his ideas never got beyond the talking stage, and those that did were usually unsuccessful.

Shackleton's unwillingness to succumb to the demands of everyday life and his insatiable excitement with unrealistic ventures left him open to the accusation of being basically immature and irresponsible. And very possibly he was—by conventional standards. But the great leaders of historical record—the Napoleons, the Nelsons, the Alexanders—have rarely fitted any conventional mold, and it is perhaps an injustice to evaluate them in ordinary terms. There can be little doubt that Shackleton, in his way, was an extraordinary leader of men.

Nor did the Antarctic represent to Shackleton merely the grubby means to a financial end. In a very real sense he needed it—something so enormous, so demanding, that it provided a touchstone for his monstrous ego and implacable drive. In ordinary situations, Shackleton's tremendous capacity for boldness and daring found almost nothing worthy of its pulling power; he was a Percheron draft horse harnessed to a child's wagon cart. But in the Antarctic—here was a burden which challenged every atom of his strength.

Thus, while Shackleton was undeniably out of place, even inept, in a great many everyday situations, he had a talent—a genius, even—that he shared with only a handful of men throughout history—genuine leadership. He was, as one of his men put it, "the greatest leader that ever came on God's earth, bar none." For all his blind spots and inadequacies, Shackleton merited this tribute:

> For scientific leadership give me Scott; for swift and efficient travel, Amundsen; but when you are in a hopeless situation, when there seems no way out, get down on your knees and pray for Shackleton.

This, then, was the man who developed the idea of crossing the Antarctic continent—on foot.

The largest items needed for the expedition were the ships that would carry the two parties to the Antarctic. From Sir Douglas Mawson, the famous Australian explorer, Shackleton bought the *Aurora*, a stoutly built ship of the type then used for sealing. The *Aurora* had already been on two Antarctic expeditions. She was to carry the Ross Sea party, under the command of Lieutenant Aeneas Mackintosh, who had served aboard the *Nimrod* on Shackleton's 1907–1909 expedition.

Shackleton himself would command the actual transcontinental party, operating from the Weddell Sea side of the continent. To obtain a ship for his group, Shackleton arranged to purchase from Lars Christensen, the Norwegian whaling magnate, a ship that Christensen had ordered built to carry polar-bear hunting parties to the Arctic. Such parties were then becoming increasingly popular with the well-to-do.

Christensen had had a partner in this would-be enterprise, M. le Baron de Gerlache. He was a Belgian who had been the leader of an Antarctic expedition in 1897, and was therefore able to contribute many helpful ideas concerning the construction of the ship. However, during the building of the vessel, de Gerlache ran into financial difficulties and was forced to back out.

Thus deprived of his partner, Christensen was pleased when Shackleton offered to buy the ship. The final selling price of $67,000 was less than Christensen had paid to have the ship built, but he was willing to take the loss in order to further the plans of an explorer of Shackleton's stature.

The ship had been named the *Polaris.* After the sale, Shackleton rechristened her *Endurance,* in keeping with the motto of his family, *Fortitudine vincimus*—"By endurance we conquer."

As with all such private expeditions, finances for the Imperial Trans-Antarctic Expedition were perhaps the primary headache. Shackleton spent the better part of two years lining up financial aid. The blessings of the government and of various scientific societies had to be obtained in order to justify the expedition as a serious scientific endeavor. And Shackleton, whose interest in science could hardly be compared with his love of exploration, went out of his way to play up this side of the undertaking. This was hypocrisy in a sense. Nevertheless, a capable staff of researchers was to go with the expedition.

But despite all of his personal charm and persuasiveness, which was considerable, Shackleton was disappointed time after time by promised grants of financial aid which failed to materialize. He finally obtained some $120,000 from Sir James Caird, a wealthy Scottish jute manufacturer. And the government voted him a sum equal to about $50,000, while the Royal Geographical Society contributed a token $5,000 to signify its general, though by no means complete, approval of the expedition. Lesser gifts were obtained from Dudley Docker and Miss Janet Stancomb-Wills, plus literally hundreds of other, smaller contributions from persons all over the world.

As was the custom, Shackleton also mortgaged the expedition, in a sense, by selling in advance the rights to whatever commercial properties the expedition might produce. He promised to write a book later about the trip. He sold the rights to the motion pictures and still photographs that would be taken, and he agreed to give a long lecture series on his return. In all these arrangements, there was one basic assumption—that Shackleton would survive.

In contrast to the difficulties in obtaining sufficient financial backing, finding volunteers to take part in the expedition proved simple. When Shackleton announced his plans he was deluged by more than five thousand applications from persons (including three girls) who asked to go along.

Almost without exception, these volunteers were motivated solely by the spirit of adventure, for the salaries offered were little more than token payments for the services expected. They ranged from about $240 a year for an able seaman to $750 a year for the most experienced scientists. And even this, in many cases, was not to be paid until the end of the expedition. Shackleton felt that the privilege of being taken along was itself almost compensation enough, especially for the scientists for whom the undertaking offered an unmatched opportunity for research in their fields.

Shackleton built the crew list around a nucleus of tested veterans. The top post as second-in-command went to Frank Wild, a very small but powerfully built man whose thin, mousy hair was rapidly disappearing altogether. Wild was a soft-spoken and easy-going individual on the surface, but he had a kind of inner toughness. He had been one of Shackleton's three companions in the race for the Pole in 1908 and 1909, and Shackleton had developed a tremendous respect and personal liking for him. The two men, in fact, formed a well-matched team. Wild's loyalty to Shackleton was beyond question, and his quiet, somewhat unimaginative disposition was a perfect balance for Shackleton's often whimsical and occasionally explosive nature.

The berth of second officer aboard the *Endurance* was given to Thomas Crean, a tall, row-boned, plain-spoken Irishman whose long service in the Royal Navy had taught him the ways of unquestioning discipline. Crean had served with Shackleton on Scott's 1901 expedition, and he had also been a crewman aboard the *Terra Nova,* which had carried Scott's ill-fated 1910–1913 group to the Antarctic. Because of Crean's experience and strength, Shackleton planned to have him as the driver of a sledge team in the six-man transcontinental party.

Alfred Cheetham, who shipped aboard as third officer, was Crean's opposite in appearance. He was a tiny man, even shorter than Wild, with an unassuming, pleasant disposition. Shackleton spoke of Cheetham as "the veteran of Antarctic," since he had already been on three expeditions, including one with Shackleton and one with Scott.

Then there was George Marston, the expedition's thirty-two-year-old artist. Marston, a boyish-faced, chubby man, had done outstanding work on Shackleton's 1907–1909 trek. Unlike most of the others, he was a married man with children.

The nucleus of veterans was completed when Thomas McLeod, a member of the 1907–1909 expedition, was signed on the *Endurance* as a seaman.

In the matter of selecting newcomers, Shackleton's methods would appear to have been almost capricious. If he liked the look of a man, he was accepted. If he didn't, the matter was closed. And these decisions were made with lightning speed. There is no record of any interview that Shackleton conducted with a prospective expedition member lasting much more than five minutes.

Leonard Hussey, an irrepressible, peppery little individual, was signed on as meteorologist even though he had practically no qualifications for the position at the time. Shackleton simply thought Hussey "looked funny," and the fact that he had recently returned from an expedition (as an anthropologist) to the torrid Sudan appealed to Shackleton's sense of whimsy. Hussey immediately took an intensive course in meteorology and later proved to be very proficient.

Dr. Alexander Macklin, one of the two surgeons, caught Shackleton's fancy by replying, when Shackleton asked him why he was wearing glasses: "Many a wise face would look foolish without spectacles." And Reginald James was signed on as physicist after Shackleton inquired about the state of his teeth, whether he suffered from varicose veins, if he was good-tempered—and if he could sing. At this last question, James looked puzzled.

"Oh, I don't mean any Caruso stuff," Shackleton reassured him, "but I suppose you can shout a bit with the boys?"

Despite the instantaneous nature of these decisions, Shackleton's intuition for selecting compatible men rarely failed.

The early months of 1914 were spent acquiring the countless items of equipment, stores, and gear that would be needed. Sledges were designed and tested in the snow-covered mountains of Norway. A new type of rations intended to prevent scurvy was tried out, as were specially designed tents.

By the end of July, 1914, however, everything had been collected, tested, and stowed aboard the *Endurance*. She sailed from London's East India Docks on August 1.

But the tragic political events of these dramatic days not only eclipsed the departure of the *Endurance,* but even threatened the whole venture. Archduke Ferdinand of Austria had been assassinated on June 28, and exactly one month later Austria-Hungary declared war on Serbia. The powder trail was lighted. While the *Endurance* lay anchored at the mouth of the Thames River, Germany declared war on France.

Then, on the very day that George V presented Shackleton with the Union Jack to carry on the expedition, Britain declared war on Germany. Shackleton's position could hardly have been worse. He was damned if he did, and damned if he didn't. He was just about to leave on an expedition he had dreamed about and worked toward for almost four years. Vast sums of money, much of it involving future commitments, had been spent, and countless hours had gone into planning and preparation. At the same time, he felt very strongly about doing his part in the war.

He spent long hours debating what to do, and he discussed the matter with several advisers, notably his principal backers. Finally he reached a decision.

He mustered the crew and explained that he wanted their approval to telegraph the Admiralty, placing the entire expedition at the disposal of the government. All hands agreed, and the wire was sent. The reply was a one-word telegram: "Proceed." Two hours later there was a longer wire from Winston Churchill, then First Lord of the Admiralty, stating that the government desired the expedition to go on.

The *Endurance* sailed from Plymouth five days later. She set a course for Buenos Aires, leaving Shackleton and Wild behind to attend to last-minute financial arrangements. They were to follow later by faster commercial liner and meet the ship in Argentina.

The trip across the Atlantic amounted to a shakedown cruise. For the ship, it was her first major voyage since her completion in Norway the year before; and for many of those on board, it was their first experience in sail.

In appearance, the *Endurance* was beautiful by any standards. She was a barkentine—three masts, of which the forward one was square-rigged, while the after two carried fore-and-aft sails, like a schooner. She was powered by a coal-fired, 350-hp steam engine, capable of driving her at speeds up to 10.2 knots. She measured 144 feet over-all, with a 25-foot beam, which was not overbig, but big enough. And though her sleek black hull looked from the outside like that of any other vessel of a comparable size, it was not.

Her keel members were four pieces of solid oak, one above the other, adding up to a total thickness of 7 feet, 1 inch. Her sides were made from oak and Norwegian mountain fir, and they varied in thickness from about 18 inches to more than 2½ feet. Outside this planking, to keep her from being chafed by the ice, there was a sheathing from stem to stern of greenheart, a wood so heavy it weighs more than solid iron and so tough that it cannot be worked with ordinary tools. Her frames were not only double-thick, ranging from 9¼ to 11 inches, but they were double in number, compared with a conventional vessel.

Her bow, where she would meet the ice head-on, had received special attention. Each of the timbers there had been fashioned from a single oak tree especially selected so that its natural growth followed the curve of her design. When assembled, these pieces had a total thickness of 4 feet, 4 inches.

But more than simple ruggedness was incorporated into the *Endurance*. She was built in Sandefjord, Norway, by the Framnaes shipyard, the famous polar shipbuilding firm which for years had been constructing vessels for whaling and sealing in the Arctic and Antarctic. However, when the builders came to the *Endurance,* they realized that she might well be the last of her kind—as indeed she was—and the ship became the yard's pet project.*

---

*Though Shackleton bought the *Endurance* for $67,000, the Framnaes shipyard today would not undertake to build a similar vessel for less than $700,000—and the cost might well run to $1,000,000, they estimate.

She was designed by Aanderud Larsen so that every joint and every fitting cross-braced something else for the maximum strength. Her construction was meticulously supervised by a master wood shipbuilder, Christian Jacobsen, who insisted on employing men who were not only skilled shipwrights, but had been to sea themselves in whaling and sealing ships. They took a proprietary interest in the smallest details of the *Endurance's* construction. They selected each timber and plank individually with great care, and fitted each to the closest tolerance. For luck, when they put the mast in her, the superstitious shipwrights placed the traditional copper kroner under each one to insure against its breaking.

By the time she was launched on December 17, 1912, she was the strongest wooden ship ever built in Norway—and probably anywhere else—with the possible exception of the *Fram*, the vessel used by Fridtjof Nansen, and later by Amundsen.

However, there was one major difference between the two ships. The *Fram* was rather bowl-bottomed so that if the ice closed in against her she would be squeezed up and out of the pressure. But since the *Endurance* was designed to operate in relatively loose pack ice she was not constructed so as to rise out of pressure to any great extent. She was comparatively wall-sided, much the way conventional ships are.

However, on the trip from London to Buenos Aires, her hull was altogether too rounded for most of those on board her. At least half the scientists were seasick, and strapping young Lionel Greenstreet, the outspoken First Officer, who had long experience in sailing ships, declared that she behaved in a "most abominable way."

The trip across the Atlantic took more than two months. During the voyage the *Endurance* was under the command of Frank Worsley, a New Zealander who had been to sea since he was sixteen.

Worsley was now forty-two years old, though he looked much younger. He was a deep-chested man of slightly less than average height with a coarse-featured yet handsome face which had a built-in mischievous expression. It was very difficult for Worsley to look stern, even when he wanted to.

He was a sensitive, fanciful individual, and the manner in which he claimed to have joined the expedition, whether it was true or not, characterized him perfectly. As he told it, he was ashore in London, staying at a hotel, when one night he had a dream in which he pictured Burlington Street, in the fashionable West End section, as being filled with blocks of ice through which he was navigating a ship.

Early the next morning, he hurried over to Burlington Street. As he was walking along he saw a nameplate on a door. It read: "Imperial Trans-Antarctic Expedition." (The expedition's London office was, in fact, at 4 New Burlington Street.)

Inside he found Shackleton. The two men were immediately drawn to one another, and Worsley hardly had to mention that he wanted to join the expedition.

"You're engaged," Shackleton said after a brief conversation. "Join your ship until I wire for you. I'll let you know all the details as soon as possible. Good morning."

With that he shook Worsley's hand and the interview, if that is what it was, had ended.

Worsley had thus been appointed captain of the *Endurance*. That is, he was put in charge of the physical running of the ship under the over-all command of Shackleton, as leader of the entire expedition.

Temperamentally, Shackleton and Worsley had some of the same characteristics. Both were energetic, imaginative, romantic men who thirsted for adventure. But while Shackleton's nature drove him always to be the leader, Worsley had no such inclinations. He was fundamentally light-hearted, given to bursts of excitement and unpredictable enthusiasms. The mantle of leadership which fell to him on the trip across the Atlantic did not rest too comfortably on his shoulders. He felt it was his duty to play the part of commander, but he was woefully out of place in the role. His tendency to indulge his moods became obvious one Sunday morning, when a church service was being held. After some appropriately reverent prayers, the idea struck him to sing a few hymns—and he broke up the proceedings by clapping his hands and demanding impetuously, "Where's the ruddy band?"

By the time the *Endurance* reached Buenos Aires on October 9, 1914, Worsley's lack of discipline had let morale slip to a sorry state. But Shackleton and Wild had arrived from London, and they applied a firm hand.

The cook, who had been an indifferent worker on the trip over, came aboard drunk and was immediately paid off. Amazingly, twenty men applied to fill the vacancy. The job went to a squeaky-voiced man by the name of Charles J. Green, who was a different sort of person altogether, conscientious almost to the point of being single-minded.

Later, two of the seamen, after a stormy night ashore, tangled with Greenstreet and were similarly let go. It was decided that the complement would be adequate with only one replacement. The berth went to William Bakewell, a twenty-six-year-old Canadian who had lost his ship in nearby Montevideo, Uruguay. He arrived with a stocky eighteen-year-old shipmate, Perce Blackboro, who was hired temporarily as the cook's helper during the *Endurance's* stay in Buenos Aires.

Meanwhile, Frank Hurley, the official photographer, had arrived from Australia. Hurley had been on Sir Douglas Mawson's last expedition to the Antarctic, and Shackleton had hired him solely on the basis of the reputation he had achieved as a result of his work there.

Finally, the last official members of the expedition came on board—sixty-nine sledge dogs that had been purchased in Canada and shipped to Buenos Aires. They were kenneled in stalls built along the main deck amidships.

The *Endurance* sailed from Buenos Aires at 10:30 A.M. on October 26 for her last port of call, the desolate island of South Georgia off the southern tip of South America. She proceeded out the ever-widening mouth of the River Platte, and dropped her pilot the next morning at the Recalada Lightship. By sunset the land had dropped from sight.

CHAPTER 3

They were on their way at last, really on their way, and Shackleton was immensely relieved. The long years of preparation were over . . . the begging, the hypocrisy, the finagling, all were finished. The simple act of sailing had carried him beyond the world of reversals, frustrations, and inanities. And in the space of a few short hours, life had been reduced from a highly complex existence, with a thousand petty problems, to one of the barest simplicity in which only one real task remained—the achievement of the goal.

In his diary that night, Shackleton summed up his feelings: " . . . now comes the actual work itself . . . the fight will be good."

Among some men in the forecastle, however, there was more a mounting air of tension than of relief. The crew list carried the names of twenty-seven men, including Shackleton. Actually there were twenty-eight men on board. Bakewell, the seaman who had joined the *Endurance* at Buenos Aires, had conspired with Walter How and Thomas McLeod to smuggle his pal, Perce Blackboro, on board. As the *Endurance* rose to the increasing swell from the open ocean, Blackboro half crouched behind the oilskins in Bakewell's locker. Fortunately, there was a great deal to be done on deck, so that most of the forecastle hands were employed elsewhere and Bakewell could periodically slip below to give Blackboro a bite of food or a drink of water.

Early the next morning, the three conspirators decided their time had come; the ship was too far from land to turn back. So Blackboro, who by now was severely cramped, was transferred to the locker assigned to Ernest Holness, a fireman who was due to come off watch shortly. Holness arrived, opened his locker, saw two feet protruding from under his oilskins, and hurried back to the quarterdeck. He found Wild on watch and told him of his discovery. Wild immediately went forward and hauled Blackboro out of the locker. He was brought before Shackleton.

Few men could be more forbidding than Ernest Shackleton in a rage, and now, squarely facing Blackboro, his huge shoulders hunched, Shackleton berated the young Welsh stowaway mercilessly. Blackboro was terrified. Bakewell, How, and McLeod, standing helplessly by, never had expected anything of this nature. But then, at the height of his tirade, Shackleton paused abruptly and put his face up close to Blackboro's. "Finally," he thundered, "if we run out of food and anyone has to be eaten, you will be first. Do you understand?"

A smile slowly spread over Blackboro's round, boyish face, and he nodded. Shackleton turned to Worsley and suggested that he assign Blackboro to help Green in the galley.

The *Endurance* arrived at the Grytviken whaling station on South Georgia on November 5, 1914. Depressing news was waiting. Ice conditions in the Weddell Sea, while never good, were the worst they had ever been in the memory of the Norwegian whaling skippers operating in the area. Several of them predicted it would be impossible to get through, and some even tried to dissuade Shackleton from trying until the following season. Shackleton decided to remain at South Georgia for a time in the hope that the situation would improve.

The whalers were especially interested in the expedition, because their first-hand knowledge of the Antarctic seas gave them a very real appreciation of the problems Shackleton faced. Moreover, the arrival of the *Endurance* was an occasion at South Georgia; ordinarily there was very little in the way of diversion at this southernmost outpost of civilization. There were a number of parties on board the ship, and the whalers reciprocated with gatherings of their own ashore.

Most of the crew were entertained at the home of Fridtjof Jacobsen, the manager of the Grytviken whaling station, and Shackleton even made a fifteen-mile trip to Stromness where he was the guest of Anton Andersen, the off-season factory manager there.

While Shackleton was at Stromness, the regular factory manager, Thoralf Sørlle, returned from his vacation in Norway. Sørlle was a powerfully built man of thirty-eight, with dark hair and a handsome handlebar mustache. In his sea-going days, Sørlle had been perhaps the best harpooner in all the Norwegian whaling fleet, and he had vast knowledge of polar ice navigation. During the following month, Shackleton drew upon the experience of Sørlle and many of the whaling captains to form an overall picture of the movements of ice in the Weddell Sea. In the end, this is what he had learned:

The Weddell Sea was roughly circular in shape, hemmed in by three land masses: the Antarctic continent itself, the Palmer Peninsula, and the islands of the South Sandwich group. Consequently much of the ice that formed in the Weddell Sea was held there, prevented by the encircling land from escaping into the open ocean where it might have melted. The winds in the area were light, by Antarctic standards, and not only failed to drive the ice away, but even allowed new ice to form at all seasons of the year, even summer. Finally, a strong prevailing current moving in a clockwise direction tended to drive the ice in an immense semicircle, packing it tightly against the arm of the Palmer Peninsula on the western side of the sea.

But their destination was Vahsel Bay, more or less on the opposite shore. There was thus reason to hope that the ice might be carried away from that particular stretch of coast by the prevailing winds and currents. With luck, they might slip in behind the worst of the ice along this lee shore.

Shackleton decided to skirt the northeast perimeter of the Weddell Sea and its evil pack and hope that they would find the coast in the vicinity of Vahsel Bay ice-free.

They waited through December 4, hoping that the supply ship for the whaling station would arrive with the last mail from home before they sailed. But it didn't, so at 8:45 A.M. on December 5, 1914, the *Endurance* weighed anchor and proceeded slowly out of Cumberland Bay. When she had cleared Barff Point, the command "Sail stations!" rang out. The mizzen, main, and foresails were set, then the fore topsail and royalsail were braced before the freshening northwest wind. A raw, numbing mixture of drizzle, sleet, and snow was driving across the leaden sea. Shackleton ordered Worsley to set an easterly course for the South Sandwich group. Two hours after the *Endurance* had sailed, the supply ship arrived with their mail on board.

The *Endurance* skirted the coast of South Georgia, running before a high following sea. The ship herself presented an appalling sight. Sixty-nine quarrelsome huskies were tied forward; several tons of coal were heaped on the deck midships; and up in the rigging hung a ton of whale meat for use as dog food. It dripped blood constantly, spattering the deck and keeping the dogs in a near frenzy of anticipation hoping a piece would fall.

The first land sighted was Saunders Island in the South Sandwich group, and at 6 P.M. on December 7, the *Endurance* passed between it and the Candlemas Volcano. There, for the first time, she encountered the enemy.

It was only a small patch of light stream ice which the ship negotiated without difficulty. But two hours later they came up against a band of heavy pack ice several feet thick and a half mile wide. Clear water was visible on the other side, but it would have been extremely dangerous to push into the pack with the heavy swell that was running.

So for more than twelve hours they searched along the edge of it until, at nine o'clock the next morning, they found what appeared to be a safe passage, and they started through, with the engines at dead slow. Several times the *Endurance* smashed head-on into floes, but no damage was done.

Like most of the others on board, Worsley had never seen polar pack ice before, and he was tremendously impressed by it, especially the excitement of dodging large floes.

They passed a number of very large bergs, some of them more than a mile square, which presented a majestic sight as they rode the swell with the seas breaking against their sides and leaping high into the air, like surf pounding against cliffs. The action of the sea had worn huge ice caverns in many of the bergs, and each breaking wave produced a deep booming sound as it rolled into one of these ice-blue caves. Also, there was the hoarse, rhythmic wash of the seas bursting against the graceful, undulating pack as it rode the steep swell.

For two days they sailed east, skirting the edge of the pack, before they were finally able to turn south toward Vahsel Bay at midnight on December 11.

The *Endurance* twisted and squirmed her way through the pack for nearly two weeks, but it was progress of a stop-and-go sort. Frequently she was barely able to push her way through, and sometimes she was stopped altogether, and had to heave to until the ice loosened.

In an open sea she could make 10 to 11 knots without the aid of sails, and could easily have covered 200 miles a day. But by midnight of December 24, her average daily run was less than 30 miles.

Before leaving South Georgia, Shackleton had estimated that they would be ashore by the end of December. But they had not yet even crossed the Antarctic Circle, though the summer had already officially begun. It was now light twenty-four hours a day; the sun disappeared only briefly near midnight, leaving prolonged, magnificent twilight. Often during this period, the phenomenon of an "ice shower," caused by the moisture in the air freezing and settling to earth, lent a fairyland atmosphere to the scene. Millions of delicate crystals, frequently thin and needlelike in shape, descended in sparkling beauty through the twilight air.

And though the pack in every direction appeared to stretch in endless desolation, it abounded with life. Finner, humpback, and huge blue whales, some of them a hundred feet long, surfaced and sported in the leads of open water between the floes. There were killer whales, too, who thrust their ugly, pointed snouts above the surface of the ice to look for whatever prey they might upset into the water. Overhead, giant albatross, and several species of petrels, fulmars, and terns wheeled and dipped. On the ice itself, Weddell and crabeater seals were a common sight as they lay sleeping.

And there were penguins, of course. Formal, stiff-necked emperors, who watched in dignified silence as the ship sailed past them. But there was nothing dignified about the little Adélies. They were so friendly they would flop down on their bellies and toboggan along, pushing with their feet and croaking what sounded like "Clark! Clark!" . . . especially, it seemed, if Robert Clark, the gaunt and taciturn Scottish biologist, happened to be at the wheel.

In spite of the disappointing progress, they celebrated Christmas festively. The wardroom was decorated with bunting, and they had an excellent dinner of soup, herring, jugged hare, plum pudding, and sweets, washed down with stout and rum. Afterward there was a hearty songfest, with Hussey playing a one-stringed violin he had made himself. That night before he turned in, Greenstreet recorded the day's events in his diary, concluding the entry with these words:

"Here endeth another Christmas Day. I wonder how and under what circumstances our next one will be spent. Temperature 30 degrees."

He would have been shocked could he have guessed.

But the coming of the New Year of 1915 brought some changes in the pack. Sometimes they were hemmed in on all sides by dense, hummocky old floes. Yet more and more often they found only brittle young ice in their path, and they raced ahead, hardly even slowed by it.

At 11:30 A.M. on January 9, they passed close to a berg so magnificent they gave it a name: The Rampart Berg. It towered 150 feet into the air, more than twice the height of the *Endurance's* mainmast. So close did they come to it that looking down into the indigo water they saw it stretching away beneath them, 40 feet below the keel of the ship, and going ever deeper, a thousand feet beneath them, Worsley estimated, becoming bluer and bluer until they could see it no more. And just beyond it was the dark, rolling, ice-free ocean, stretching to the horizon. They were through the pack.

"We feel," said Worsley, "as pleased as Balboa when, having burst through the forest of the Isthmus of Darien [Panama], he beheld the Pacific."

They set a course of south by east and ran at full speed for 100 carefree miles through open water with whales sporting and blowing on all sides. At 5 P.M. on January 10, they sighted land which Shackleton named the Caird Coast in honor of the expedition's principal backer. By midnight they were steaming west in the twilight 500 feet off a succession of 1,000-foot ice cliffs, collectively termed "the barrier."

The *Endurance* was now about 400 miles northeast of Vahsel Bay, and Shackleton headed her in that direction. For five days they ran parallel with the barrier, and their progress was excellent. By January 15, they were within 200 miles of Vahsel Bay.

At about 8 A.M. on the sixteenth, heavy pack was sighted ahead from the masthead. They reached it at eight-thirty, and saw that it was kept from moving by a number of giant bergs that were grounded on a shoal. They furled sail and proceeded under steam along the edge of the pack looking for a way through, but none could be found. Toward noon, the wind freshened from the ENE, and by mid-afternoon was blowing a gale. At 8 P.M., when they saw that no real progress could be made, they took shelter under the lee of a large grounded berg.

The gale continued on the seventeenth, and even increased in intensity. Though the sky overhead was blue, clear, dense clouds of snow driven off the land filled the air. The *Endurance* dodged back and forth, keeping under the sheltering protection of the berg.

The northeast gale began to moderate about 6 A.M. on January 18, so they set the topsail and proceeded south with the engines at slow. Most of the pack had blown away to the southwest leaving only a small amount trapped by the stranded bergs. They made their way through it for about 10 miles until at 3 P.M., they ran into the main body of the pack once more, stretching from the face of the barrier away to the northwest as far as could be seen. But dead ahead the dark streak of a so-called water sky held promise of a large patch of open ocean. They decided to work through the pack, and the *Endurance* entered it at 5 P.M.

Almost immediately they realized that this was a different sort of ice from anything encountered before. The floes were thick but very soft, and consisted mostly of snow. They floated in a soupy sea of mushy brash ice composed of ground-up floes and lumps of snow. The mass of it closed in around the ship like pudding.

At 7 P.M., Greenstreet headed the *Endurance* between two large floes toward a pool of open water. Halfway along, the ship got mired in the brash and then another floe closed in behind her. Even with the engines at full speed ahead, it took her two hours to push her way through. What seemed like a routine decision was recorded in Worsley's log: "We therefore lie to for a while to see if the Pack opens at all when this N.E. wind ceases."

But it was six cold, cloudy days until, on January 24, the north-easterly gale dropped off. By then, the ice was packed snugly around the *Endurance* in every direction as far as the eye could see.

And Worsley wrote in his log: "We must possess ourselves in patience till a Southerly gale occurs, or the ice opens of its own sweet will."

But no southerly gale occurred—nor did the ice open of its own sweet will. At midnight on January 24, a crack 15 feet wide appeared about 50 yards ahead of the ship. By mid-morning the crack was a quarter of a mile across. A full head of steam was raised, all sails set, and the engines put full speed ahead in an attempt to break through to the crack. For three hours the ship leaned against the ice with all her might—and never moved a foot.

The *Endurance* was beset. As Orde-Lees, the storekeeper, put it, "frozen, like an almond in the middle of a chocolate bar."

CHAPTER 4

What had happened was simple enough. The northerly gale had compressed and crowded the whole Weddell Sea pack against the face of the land, and no force on earth could open up the ice again—except another gale from the opposite direction. But instead of southerly gales, there were only very moderate winds. Worsley's diary tells the story of day after day of waiting for the gale that never came: "Light SW breeze." . . . "Mod. East'ly breeze." . . . "Gentle SW breeze." . . . "Calm and light airs." . . . "Light West'ly breezes."

It was a chance, a freak. A hard northerly gale—then quiet cold.

Among the men the realization that the *Endurance* was really beset for good came very slowly—like a kind of creeping resignation—a bad dream from which there was no waking. Anxiously they watched each day, but the face of the pack remained substantially unchanged.

The story again was told in their diaries. Dour old Chippy McNeish, the carpenter, wrote at the end of the gale on January 24:

"Still fast & no sign of any opening. The pressure is still a serious business & if we don't get out of it soon I would not give much chance of ever getting away from here. . . . "

On the twenty-fifth: "Still fast. We tried to cut away the ice to relieve the ship, but it was no use. . . . "

On the twenty-sixth: "Still fast. The water has opened out a bit ahead of us, but the floe we are in is still as sound as ever. . . . "

The twenty-seventh: "Still fast. We had another trial to break the ice . . . gave it up."

The twenty-eighth: "Temperature 6°. Very cold. Still fast & no signs of any change."

The twenty-ninth: "Still fast . . . no signs of any change."

The thirtieth: "Still fast. . . . "

The thirty-first: "Still fast. . . . "

Nevertheless, full watches were maintained, and the ship's business was carried out as ever. On January 31, they made the first attempt to use their radio. It was a battery-powered affair, capable only of receiving spark transmission messages in Morse code. Its intended function was to pick up time checks for the chronometers and news programs which were to be broadcast to them on the first of each month from the Falkland Islands, now 1,650 miles away.

In view of the distance to the transmitter, Hubert Hudson, the navigator, and Reginald James, the expedition's academic-minded young physicist, did all they could to increase the range of the set. They attached an extra 180 feet of wire to the antenna, and soldered all the joints to improve the connections.

At three-twenty the following morning, a small group of men gathered around the receiver in the wardroom. They fussed with the dials for more than an hour, but as everyone expected, all they heard was static. There was, in fact, a notable lack of interest in the radio, primarily because it was considered not only a novelty but an unserviceable one. In 1914, radio was barely out of the infant stage, at least as far as long distance reception was concerned. Nobody on board the *Endurance* expected very much of it, and they were neither surprised nor disappointed when their expectations were realized. Had the radio included a transmitter so that they could have broadcast news of their plight and position, the attitude of the crew might have been very different.

Two or three times early in February they tried to free the ship when cracks developed reasonably close to her, but these attempts failed completely. Then, on February 14, an excellent lead of water opened a quarter of a mile ahead of the ship. Steam was hurriedly raised and all hands were ordered onto the ice with saws, chisels, picks, and any other tools that could be used to cut a lane through the floes.

The *Endurance* lay in a pool of young ice only about a foot or two thick. This was systematically sawed and rafted away to give the ship room to batter at the floes ahead. The crew started work at 8:40 A.M., and worked throughout the day. By midnight they had carved out a channel about 150 yards long.

Early the next morning, the men resumed the effort, working more desperately to reach the lane of water before it closed. The ship was eased astern as far as she would go, then thrown full speed ahead toward the floes. A V-shaped slot had been sawed in the ice so that the bow of the ship might split the floe more easily.

Again and again, she slammed into the ice, throwing a wave of water up over the floe, then staggered and rolled and slipped backward. Each time she bit off a little more. The crew on the ice hurriedly threw wire hawsers around each chunk, some of them weighing more than 20 tons, and the *Endurance,* going full speed astern, dragged them back and away in preparation for another run. But she never had a really good crack at the floes ahead. There was always too much loose ice floating around her and freezing up. It slowed her repeated onslaughts and softened all her blows.

At 3 P.M., after she had smashed one-third of the way through the 600-yard ice field leading to the open water, it was decided that the expenditure of coal and effort was useless. The remaining

400 yards of ice was 12 to 18 feet thick, and Shackleton, abandoning hope of getting through, ordered the fires let down.

Still the crew refused to give up and during their watches turned out on the ice to continue cutting away at it. Even frail Charlie Green, the cook, hurried through his bread-making to join his shipmates trying to saw the ship clear.

But by midnight the volunteers themselves could no longer deny the hopelessness of the task, and they returned to the ship. Green made hot porridge for all hands to warm them up before they turned in. The temperature was 2 degrees above zero.

Greenstreet, always plain-spoken and never one to dodge the issue, summed up the general feeling in his diary that night. In a tired hand, he wrote: "Anyway, if we do get jambed here for the winter we shall have the satisfaction of knowing that we did our darnest to try & get out."

Their time was running out. They noticed the approaching end of the Antarctic summer on February 17 when the sun, which had shone twenty-four hours a day for two months, dipped beneath the horizon for the first time at midnight.

At last on February 24 Shackleton admitted that the possibility of getting free could no longer be seriously considered. The sea watches were canceled and a system of night watchmen was instituted.

Shackleton's order merely made official what long before they had all come to accept: they would have to winter on board the ship—with whatever that might bring. Word of Shackleton's decision was passed along routinely by Wild—and if anything, it was almost welcome. The end of sea watches meant that at least the men could sleep all night.

For Shackleton, however, it was another matter. He was tormented by thoughts, both of what had happened and of what might happen. Hindsight now told him that if he had landed the transcontinental party on one of the places they had passed along the barrier, they would at least have been ashore, ready to strike out for the Pole the next spring. But no one could have foreseen the disastrous chain of events that had brought them to their present predicament—unseasonable northerly gales, then calms and subzero temperatures.

Nor was there now any chance of landing the party that was to cross the continent. The drift of the pack since the *Endurance* was beset had carried them to within about 60 miles of Vahsel Bay—a tantalizingly short distance, it would seem. But 60 miles over hummocky ice with God knows how many impassable tracks of open water in between, carrying at least a year's supply of rations and equipment, plus the lumber for a hut—and all this behind sledges drawn by ill-conditioned and untrained dogs. No, 60 miles could be a very long way, indeed.

Even had there been no obstacle to putting the transcontinental party ashore, this was hardly the time for the leader of an expedition to forsake his ship and leave others to see her through—assuming she would get through. She would drift— to the west, probably, under the prevailing winds and currents. But how far? And to where? And what would happen when the break-up came in the spring? Clearly, Shackleton's duty lay aboard the *Endurance*. But that realization did not lessen the bitterness of the fact that the Imperial Trans-Antarctic Expedition's chances of succeeding, while always uncertain, were now a thousand times more problematical.

He was careful, however, not to betray his disappointment to the men, and he cheerfully supervised the routine of readying the ship for the long winter's night ahead.

The dogs were removed to the floes and individual "dogloos" built for them of blocks of ice and snow. Warm winter clothing was issued to all hands, and work was begun to transfer the officers and scientists from their regular wardroom area in the deck-house to warmer quarters in the between-deck storage area. They moved in early in March and christened their new quarters "The Ritz."

The conversion of the *Endurance* from a ship into a kind of floating shore station brought with it a marked slowdown in the tempo of life. There simply wasn't much for the men to do. The winter schedule required of them only about three hours' work a day, and the rest of the time they were free to do what they wanted.

Their only really vital task was to lay in a large supply of meat and blubber. The meat was needed to feed both men and dogs over the winter, the blubber to be used as fuel to make up for the overexpenditure of coal on the trip south.

During February it was easy. The floes in every direction teemed with life. Sometimes they could see as many as 200 seals from the masthead, and it was simple to harvest the number needed. Approached quietly, the seals rarely attempted to get away. Like the penguins, they were devoid of fear when on the ice since the only enemies they knew—sea leopards and killer whales—were creatures of the sea.

However, with the coming of March, when the days grew shorter, the number of animals dropped off noticeably as the seals and penguins migrated north, following the sun. Toward the end of the month, only an occasional maverick seal could be seen— and sharp eyes were needed for that.

Frank Worsley, now universally called "Wuzzles," had those sharp eyes. He became the chief game spotter because his remarkable vision enabled him to pick out seals at distances up to three and a half miles from the crow's nest. To help him at his task, he accumulated a collection of equipment which he hung around his perch aloft—telescopes, binoculars, a megaphone, and a large flag for use in signaling the direction of the quarry or to warn the hunting parties if there were killer whales near them. Little Frank Wild was usually the executioner. Following Worsley's directions, he walked or skied out to where the seal was lying and shot it in the head.

The hardest part of the operation was getting the seal back to the ship, since many of them weighed 400 pounds and more. But there was always a struggle to get the job done as quickly as possible so that the seal wouldn't cool off before it arrived. While the flesh was warm, the men who skinned and butchered the carcass didn't get their hands frostbitten.

During this period the physical condition of the dogs caused considerable anxiety. One after another of them fell sick and wasted away. On April 6, a dog named Bristol had to be shot, bringing to fifteen the total number of dogs lost since they sailed from South Georgia. Of the original sixty-nine, only fifty-four remained, and several of these were in a bad way.

The two doctors—young Macklin and McIlroy, the senior surgeon—performed post mortems on each dog and discovered that the majority of them suffered from huge red worms, often a foot or more long, in their intestines. Furthermore, there was nothing that could be done to cure the sick animals. One of the few items the expedition had failed to bring from England was worm powder.

The loss of the fifteen dogs had been partly made up, in numbers if not in pulling power, by the arrival of two litters of puppies. Eight of the newcomers survived, and it soon became apparent that they were as nondescript as their parents—though considerably more good-natured.

The older dogs were vicious—toward each other, toward their drivers, and especially toward any seals or penguins they might meet on a training run. They were not pure-bred huskies in the present day sense. Rather they were a rag-tag collection of short-haired, long-haired, snubby-nosed, pointed-nosed beasts. Born in the remoter wilds of Canada, they had a basic sledging instinct and a resistance to cold weather, but little else.

In dealing with them, the only technique that seemed to work was a demonstration of physical superiority. On several occasions one dog might have killed another if somebody hadn't stepped in and stopped the fight by a simple show of strength. Macklin, though a gentle individual by nature, developed a technique that was more effective than almost any amount of effort with a whip. He simply struck the aggressor dog a thudding uppercut under the jaw with his mittened fist. No harm was done, and the animal invariably was stunned into letting go its hold.

Early in April, Shackleton decided that permanent dog drivers should be assigned with full responsibility for their teams. These posts were allotted to Macklin, Wild, McIlroy, Crean, Marston, and Hurley.

Once the teams had been parceled out and were training regularly, the whole crew developed a great interest in the dogs. There was keen competition each day for the positions of assistants to the sledge drivers. These training sessions were also put to the practical purpose of sledging seal carcasses back to the ship on the infrequent occasions when seals were killed. But these occasions, unfortunately, were becoming very infrequent indeed.

Nevertheless, by April 10, the party had accumulated 5,000 pounds of meat and blubber. Shackleton calculated that this would last ninety days, and would eliminate the need to dip into their supply of tinned and dried provisions until the middle of the Antarctic night, which was approaching very rapidly. At below-zero temperatures, they had no worries about food spoilage; fresh meat was automatically frozen.

Throughout April, the sun sank lower each day, gradually shortening the hours of light. Though the pack remained generally quiet, their observations showed that the entire mass was on the move as a unit. It began slowly. During February, when they were newly beset, the pack had crept almost imperceptibly westward, parallel with the coast. Early in March, it gradually turned to the wNw and gained speed. In April, it swung due northwest and moved at an average speed for the month of 2½ miles a day. On May 2, their position showed a total northwest drift since the end of February of 130 miles. The *Endurance* was one microcosmic speck, 144 feet long and 25 feet wide, embedded in nearly one million square miles of ice that was slowly being rotated by the irresistible clockwise sweep of the winds and currents of the Weddell Sea.

Early in May the sun appeared over the horizon for the last time, then slowly dropped from sight—and the Antarctic night began. It did not happen all at once; the gradually diminishing dusk grew shorter and less intense each day.

For a time a hazy, deceiving half-light remained, and the stark outline of the ship could be seen against the horizon. But it was difficult to perceive distances. Even the ice underfoot grew strangely indistinct so that walking became hazardous. A man could drop into an unseen hollow or collide with a hummock thinking it was still a dozen yards away.

But before long even the half-light disappeared—and they were left in darkness.

CHAPTER 5

I n all the world there is no desolation more complete than the polar night. It is a return to the Ice Age—no warmth, no life, no movement. Only those who have experienced it can fully appreciate what it means to be without the sun day after day and week after week. Few men unaccustomed to it can fight off its effects altogether, and it has driven some men mad.

By coincidence, the man who had once been a partner in the *Endurance*, M. le Baron de Gerlache, had himself been beset in the Weddell Sea aboard a vessel called the *Belgica* in 1899. With the coming of the night, the *Belgica's* crew became infected with a strange melancholy. As the weeks went by this slowly deepened into depression and then despair. In time they found it almost impossible to concentrate or even to eat. In order to offset the terrifying symptoms of insanity they saw in themselves, they took to walking in a circle around the ship. The route came to be known as "madhouse promenade."

One man died of a heart ailment brought on partly by his unreasoning terror of the darkness. Another was seized with the idea that the rest of the crew intended to kill him, and whenever he slept he squeezed himself into a tiny recess of the ship. Still another gave way to hysteria which left him temporarily deaf and dumb.

But there was very little depression on board the *Endurance*. The coming of the polar night somehow drew the men closer together.

When the *Endurance* sailed from England, there could hardly have been a more heterogeneous collection of individuals. They varied from Cambridge University dons to Yorkshire fishermen. But after nine months of being together almost constantly and living and working in the same close quarters, the men had built up a backlog of shared experiences that offset the vast differences between them. During these nine months, the men on board the *Endurance* had come to know one another very well indeed. And with few exceptions, they had come to like one another, too.

Nobody much thought of Blackboro as a stowaway any more. The stocky dark-haired young Welshman was a regular member of the crew now. Blackboro was an extremely quiet individual but nonetheless quick-witted and well liked, a cheerful, willing shipmate, who helped Green in the galley.

They all knew Bobbie Clark, the biologist, to be a dour, hardworking, almost humorless Scot. But they knew also that he could be counted on to do his share and more whenever all hands were called to duty. He got excited only when the dredge he lowered through the ice each day fetched up a new species of creature for his collection of bottled specimens. The crew once tricked him into great excitement by placing some pieces of cooked spaghetti in one of his jars of formaldehyde. Clark kept his own counsel, and never mentioned to a single man anything about his personal life.

Tom Crean—tall, almost gaunt—was exactly what he appeared to be—a heavy-handed sailorman, forthright and tactless, who spoke with a sailorman's rough vocabulary. He was certainly not a very warm personality, but he knew the sea and he knew his

job, and the others respected him for it. Shackleton was personally quite fond of Crean. He liked the big Irishman's willingness.
Shackleton also put a high value on discipline, and Crean, after
years in the Royal Navy, regarded an order as something to be
obeyed without question. Nor was Crean above giving Shackleton
a bit o' the blarney occasionally.

When it came to Charlie Green, the cook, there was a wide-
spread feeling that he was a little "crackers," or daft, because of
his disorganized and seemingly scatterbrained mannerisms. They
called him Chef or Cookie—or sometimes Doughballs because
of his high, squeaky voice and because he had in fact lost a tes-
ticle in an accident. They poked fun at him on the surface, but
underneath there was a fundamental respect, and a fondness, too.
Few men were more conscientious. While the others worked only
three hours a day, Green was busy in the galley from early morning until long after supper at night.

Green was occasionally the victim of the almost merciless rib-
bing that all ships' cooks everywhere are subjected to, but he had
his jokes, too. Two or three times, when some crewman's birthday was to be celebrated, he produced a cake for the occasion.
One proved to be a blown-up toy balloon which he had carefully
frosted, and another was a block of wood, daintily covered with
icing.

Hudson, the navigator, was a peculiar sort. He meant well,
all right, but he was just a little dull. He owed his nickname—
Buddha—to a practical joke he had fallen for once while the ship
was at South Georgia. The men had convinced him that there was
to be a costume party ashore . . . and any man who had seen South
Georgia with his own eyes—its glaciers and rugged mountains,
the stink of whale entrails rotting in the harbor—and who could
believe it to be the scene of a costume party . . . but Hudson did.
They got him to remove most of his clothing and they dressed
him in a bedsheet. Then they tied the lid of a teapot on his head

with pieces of ribbon running under his chin. Thus attired, he was rowed to shore, shivering in the icy blasts that howled down off the mountains. A party was held at the home of the whaling factory manager. But when Hudson walked in, he was most assuredly the only one in costume.

In any practical joke such as this, the men knew that the one to look for was Leonard Hussey, the meteorologist. A slightly built little fellow in his early twenties, Hussey was universally liked for his unfailing good humor. He had a sharp, satiric tongue, but he could take a joke against himself without losing his good spirits. It was not always easy to get the best of Hussey in an exchange of wits, though. They liked him, too, because he played the zither banjo and was willing to strike up a tune whenever anybody wanted to sing. Hussey's name was corrupted into a variety of nicknames—Hussbert, Hussbird, and just plain Huss.

A great many of the men looked on McIlroy, one of the surgeons, as a man of the world. He was a handsome, aristocratic-looking individual, slightly older than most of the others, and they immensely enjoyed listening to his tales of past conquests. McIlroy could be bitingly sarcastic, but the others admired him for it. It seemed to go along with his cosmopolitan nature, and there was never any malice in what he said. They called him Mick.

George Marston, the expedition's artist, was a moody fellow, up one day and down the next. He was unique among them in that he worried outwardly about the future, whereas almost everybody else was confident that everything was going to be all right. But Marston, whenever he was feeling downcast, would brood over his wife and children at home. His attitude was not improved by Shackleton's obvious and increasing dislike for him. It was one of those inexplicable things. Perhaps Marston's uneasiness itself was at fault. Shackleton seemed to fear that this attitude would spread to other men. But, apart from his changeable nature and the fact that he was not overly eager to turn out for work, Marston was well liked by most.

Among the forecastle hands, the seamen and firemen, the only outstanding individual was John Vincent, a young, ambitious bully. He was quite short, but ruggedly built and much stronger than any of the other seamen. And he sought to use his superior strength to dominate his shipmates by intimidation. He insisted on being served first at mealtimes so that he could pick the best portion, and when grog was issued, he always managed to get more than his share. The other seamen not only disliked him personally, they had very little respect for his abilities aboard ship. Vincent had been in the Navy, but most of his experience at sea had been aboard trawlers in the North Sea. Unlike How, Bakewell, and McLeod, who had served for years aboard square riggers, Vincent had had no previous experience in sail. Nevertheless, he had his eye on the vacant post of boatswain, and he felt that the best way to get it was to demonstrate a capacity for tyranny. After a time the forecastle hands got fed up, and How, a soft-spoken, agreeable, and extremely competent little chap, went to Shackleton and complained. Shackleton immediately sent for Vincent. Though it is not known what Shackleton told him, Vincent's attitude was considerably less domineering after that.

It was remarkable that there were not more cases of friction among the men, especially after the Antarctic night set in. The gathering darkness and the unpredictable weather limited their activities to an ever-constricting area around the ship. There was very little to occupy them, and they were in closer contact with one another than ever. But instead of getting on each other's nerves, the entire party seemed to become more close-knit.

Early in the winter, George Marston and Frank Wild decided to give each other haircuts. Before they were through, they had shaved off all their hair with the ship's barber clippers. The next evening the fever had spread throughout the crew. Everyone, including Shackleton, had his hair trimmed down to the scalp.

After that, there were many pranks. The following evening, Wild appeared for supper with his face buried in the neck of his jersey, revealing only the top of his shaved head, on which Marston had painted what Greenstreet described as an "imbecilic looking Johnny."

And the next night "Wuzzles" Worsley was put on trial for "robbing a Presbyterian church of a trouser button out of the offertory bag and having turned the same to base and ignoble use." The proceedings were long and disorderly. Wild was the judge, James the prosecuting attorney, and Orde-Lees the defense attorney. Greenstreet and McIlroy gave testimony against the defendant, but when Worsley promised to buy the judge a drink after the trial, Wild charged the jury to find the defendant innocent. Nevertheless, Worsley was found guilty on the first ballot.

Besides these spontaneous affairs, there was a regular series of social occasions. Each Saturday night before the men turned in a ration of grog was issued to all hands, followed by the toast, "To our sweethearts and wives." Invariably a chorus of voices added, "May they never meet."

On Sunday evenings the men listened to music from the hand-crank phonograph for an hour or two as they lay in their bunks or wrote up their diaries. But the playing of the phonograph was limited because of a shortage of needles. Five thousand had been ordered in England, but Wild, in sending off the requisition, had failed to specify the word "gramophone." Only long after the ship had sailed did Orde-Lees, the storekeeper, discover they had five thousand extra sewing needles, and only a small package of the phonograph variety.

Then once each month all hands gathered in the Ritz and Frank Hurley, the photographer, delivered a "lantern chat"—a slide-illustrated lecture on the places he had visited: Australia,

New Zealand, the Mawson expedition. The favorite was one called "Peeps in Java," which featured waving palm trees and native maidens.

The Ritz on nights like these was a cozy place. It had been a cargo area just below the main deck and aft of the crew's quarters in the forecastle. Then the stores and men traded places. The supplies were moved to the wardroom area in the deckhouse, and the men took over the hold. The area was about 35 feet long and 25 feet wide, and McNeish had erected partitions to form individual sleeping cubicles for the officers and scientists. In the center was a long table with a paraffin-burning lamp overhead. Here they ate their meals, wrote their diaries, played cards, and read. In one corner was a coal-burning stove which kept the temperature inside quite comfortable. The *Endurance's* thick sides were excellent insulation.

Outside, however, the weather was getting steadily worse. Late in May the temperature dropped below zero, and stayed there. During the first half of June, the average reading was –17 degrees. But the scene from the deck of the *Endurance* was often fantastically beautiful. In clear weather, if the moon was out, it swept in bold, high circles through the starlit skies for days on end, casting a soft, pale light over the floes. At other times, there were breathtaking displays of the *aurora australis,* the Antarctic equivalent of the northern lights. Incredible sunbursts of green and blue and silver shot up from the horizon into the blue-black sky, shimmering, iridescent colors that glinted off the rock-hard ice below. But apart from the increasing cold, the weather remained remarkably stable and free from gales.

Toward the middle of June, at the blackest part of the winter, a chance boast by Frank Hurley that he had the fastest team resulted in a dog derby. Even at high noon when the race was run, it was so dark out that the spectators at this "Antarctic Sweepstakes" couldn't see the far end of the race course. Wild's team won, but

Hurley claimed that he was carrying more weight than Wild, and demanded a rematch. He later won when Shackleton, who was riding as passenger on Wild's sledge, slipped off going around a turn, and Wild was disqualified.

The following night, cagy Dr. McIlroy "brought to light" a pair of dice he happened to find among his things. He first shook with Greenstreet to see who would buy champagne when they got home. Greenstreet lost. By that time several men had gathered around the table in the Ritz, and in subsequent rolls of the dice, an entire evening's entertainment was wagered. Wild got stuck for buying the dinner, McIlroy himself lost the roll for the theater tickets, Hurley the after-theater supper, and parsimonious "Jock" Wordie, the geologist, was committed to pay for the taxis home.

They held a special celebration on Midwinter's Day, June 22. The Ritz was decked out with bunting and flags, and Hurley built a stage of sorts which was lighted by a row of acetylene gas footlights. Everyone gathered for the festivities at 8 P.M.

Shackleton, as chairman, introduced the participants. Orde-Lees, the storekeeper, was dressed as a Methodist minister, the "Rev. Bubbling-Love," and he exhorted his listeners against the wages of sin. James, as "Herr Professor von Schopenbaum," delivered a lengthy lecture on the "Calorie." Macklin recited a tropical verse he had written about "Captain Eno," the effervescent seafarer, who could have been no one but the effervescent Worsley.

Greenstreet described the evening in his diary: "I think I laughed most over Kerr who dressed up as a tramp and sang Spagoni the Toreador. He started several keys too high and notwithstanding the accompanist, Hussey, who was vainly whispering 'Lower! Lower!' and playing in a much lower key, he kept going until he lost the tune altogether. When he came to the word Spagoni he had forgotten the word so came out with Stuberski the Toreador and had completely forgotten the chorus, so simply saying, 'He shall die, he shall die, he shall die!' It was killing and we laughed until the tears ran down our cheeks. McIlroy dressed up as a Spanish girl and a very wicked looking one at that, with very low evening dress and slit skirt showing a bare leg above her stocking tops . . . gave the Danse Espagnol."

Marston sang, Wild recited "The Wreck of the Hesperus," Hudson was a half-caste girl, Greenstreet was a red-nosed drunk, and Rickenson was a London streetwalker.

The evening ended at midnight with a cold supper and a toast. Then everyone sang, "God Save the King."

And so the winter was half done.

CHAPTER 6

The men's thoughts began to turn to spring, the return of the sun and warmth when the *Endurance* would break out of her icy prison and they could make a new assault on Vahsel Bay.

Only once in the last part of June did they hear any sounds of pressure. That was on the twenty-eighth, and Worsley described it in his diary: "At times during the night a distant, rich, deep booming note is heard—changing at times to a long creaking groan which seems to carry a menacing tone. It starts up gradually but stops abruptly, and sounds best in the distance—the greater the distance, the better the sound."

But then on July 9, the barometer began to fall—very, very slowly. For five consecutive days, the reading slid downward: 29.79 . . . 29.61 . . . 29.48 . . . 29.39 . . . 29.25.

On the morning of July 14 the bottom fell out of the glass—28.88. An ominous gloom came on about noon. The wind backed to the southwest and began to blow, though not much at first. It wasn't until 7 P.M. that the snow began to fall.

By two o'clock the following morning the whole ship vibrated as the wind screamed through the rigging at 70 miles an hour. The snow was like a sandstorm blown up from the pole. Nothing could keep it out, though they lashed tarpaulins over the hatches trying to seal them off. By noon it was impossible to see much more than half the length of the ship. The temperature was 34 degrees below zero.

Shackleton ordered that no man venture farther than the dog kennels which were only a few feet from the ship. The men who fed the dogs had to crawl on their hands and knees to keep from being blown away. Within two minutes after leaving the ship the blinding, suffocating snow blocked their eyes and mouths.

On the *Endurance's* lee side, the force of the wind eroded the ice, leaving it grooved and channeled. On the windward side, snowdrifts 14 feet high built up, weighing probably 100 tons over-all. The floes alongside the ship bent downward under the weight of it, and the ship herself, with the load she was carrying, sank a foot.

On the following day the temperature dropped to −35 degrees, and the dogs were fed a half pound of lard each to help them ward off the cold. After breakfast Shackleton ordered all hands onto the ice to try to clear the floes on the port side of snow. The area around the kennels was becoming dangerously weighted down, and he feared it might buckle under, carrying the dogs with it.

All that night the blizzard raged; but on July 16 the snow began to thin out and by early morning there were patches of clear sky overhead. In the faint glow of light at noon, newly created pressure ridges could be seen in every direction. They looked like hedgerows separating different fields of ice. Against these, banks of snow had drifted, but otherwise the howling wind had blown the surface of the ice free from snow and polished it smooth.

Before the storm the pack had been almost one solid mass of ice, but now it was broken into pieces, and there was an area of open water to the north.

It was a situation that made pressure inevitable. The ice, now that it was twisted and broken up, provided ten million new surfaces to catch the wind. And each floe was capable of movement independent of the rest. The pack would move with the wind, and a kind of behemothic momentum would be set up through the ice. The resulting force is called pressure—and it began on July 21. Not against the ship herself, for she was in the center of a thick, tough floe. But there were sounds of ice working toward the south and southwest.

The noise continued all night and into the next morning. After lunch Worsley decided to have a look around. He put on his knitted helmet and watch coat, and climbed the ladder. Almost immediately he returned with the news that their floe had cracked. There was a rush to grab Burberrys and helmets and everyone dashed on deck. The crack was there, about 2 feet wide, running from the outer edge of the floe, where extreme pressure had jumbled one slab on top of another, to within about 40 yards of the *Endurance's* port quarter. The sledges were immediately brought on board and the sea watches set.

A breakup seemed imminent. They waited all that day and into the night and all the next day. No breakup occurred. The pressure could be heard all around, and occasionally they felt a heavy shock transmitted through the ice, but still the *Endurance* remained locked in the unbroken center of the floe. The crack on the port quarter froze over, and as the days wore on without any significant change in their situation, the sense of expectancy diminished. The sea watches were canceled and sledging practice was resumed on a limited scale.

Each time a party went out, they came upon pressure, and occasionally a demonstration of power the like of which they had never witnessed before. On July 26, Greenstreet went with Wild's team for a short run. Seeing some working ice, they paused to watch. As they stood looking, a solid, blue-green floe 9 feet thick was driven against a neighboring floe, and together they rose as easily as if they had been two pieces of cork.

When he got back to the ship, Greenstreet wrote in his diary: "Lucky for us if we don't get any pressure like that against the ship for I doubt whether any ship could stand a pressure that will force blocks like that up."

Among the other men, too, the feeling of security was rapidly disappearing. After supper that night there was a somber quiet in the Ritz. The whole party had been cheered by the sun's refracted image appearing over the horizon for one minute just after noon. It was the first time they had seen it in seventy-nine days. But it did not quite offset the general uneasiness.

McNeish, who was never one to dodge the issue, came straight to the point in his diary that night:

"That [the sun] means a lot to us now as we will have more daylight as we go along. We are looking for higher temperatures now but we don't want this floe to break up until there is some open water for it would mean the ship being crushed if we got adrift at present."

Six days later, at 10 A.M. on August 1, while the dog drivers were shoveling snow away from the kennels, there was a tremble, followed by a scraping, grinding sound and the *Endurance* rose suddenly upward, then heeled to port and dropped back into the water again, rolling slightly. The floe had broken and the ship was free.

Shackleton was on deck immediately, followed by the rest of the crew. Swiftly, he saw what was happening and he shouted to get the dogs on board. All hands dropped onto the shuddering floe alongside the ship and went among the dogs, wrenching their chains out of the ice and hurrying them up the gangway. The entire operation took only eight minutes.

It was just in time. As the gangway was being hoisted, the ship moved violently forward and sideways, propelled by the force of the ice driving in and under her. The stout old floe that had protected her so long became an attacker, battering her sides and churning the little dogloos to bits against her.

The worst of the pressure was toward the bow, and all hands watched in helpless anxiety as the floes below broke into fragments, reared up, and were overlapped by other fragments which smashed into the greenheart sheathing along the waterline.

It went on for fifteen agonizing minutes, and then, driven from astern once more, the *Endurance's* bow slowly climbed up onto a floe ahead. The men could feel her rise, and a spontaneous shout of relief went up. For the moment, she was safe.

The ice near the ship remained under intense pressure until shortly after noon, and then settled down. The *Endurance* remained perched atop the ice, with a 5-degree list to port. The boats were cleared for lowering and all hands were instructed to have their warmest clothing handy in case they should have to "get out and walk." But all remained quiet throughout the afternoon and into the evening.

Worsley, after recording the day's events, concluded the entry in his diary that evening: "If anything held the ship from rising to such pressure she would crush up like an empty eggshell. The behavior of the dogs was splendid. . . . They seemed to regard it as an entertainment we had got up for their benefit."

During the night the wind picked up from the southwest, and by morning it was blowing a gale. These winds, compressing the pack ahead of them, had been responsible for the pressure.

By morning, the chunks of ice around the ship had refrozen into a solid mass. Curiously, in the general breakup, one large section of the old floe had come through intact. But it had been driven in against the ship and tilted up at a 45-degree angle so that the well-worn sledge tracks in its surface were now running uphill.

Most of the men were put to the task of building new kennels on deck for the dogs. The job required several days' work, and amazingly, even before it was finished, the memory of what had happened was beginning to fade.

On August 4, just three days after the breakup, Shackleton came upon a group of men in the Ritz speculating confidently that the *Endurance* was equal to any pressure. He sat down at the table with them.

Shackleton said there once was a mouse who lived in a tavern. One night the mouse found a leaky barrel of beer, and he drank all he could hold. When the mouse had finished, he sat up, twirled his whiskers, and looked around arrogantly. "Now then," he said, "where's that damned cat?"

In spite of Shackleton's meaningful parable, the growing confidence among the men refused to be stifled. They knew now what pressure was like. They had seen the ship come through it, and she was none the worse for having done so. The returning sun also did much to raise their spirits. There was now actual daylight for about three hours every day, plus seven or eight hours of twilight. The men resumed their hockey games on the ice, and some spirited contests were held. When oversized Tom Crean harnessed up the puppies for their first attempts at sledging practice, his efforts stimulated great interest. Worsley observed: "Partly persuaded, mainly driven, they pursue a devious and uncertain course, even more erratic than the poor ship's, across the Weddell Sea."

Again, in an entry for August 15, Worsley reflected the general high spirits among them. In describing the intense rivalries among the dog team drivers, or "owners," Worsley related, with a characteristic touch of exaggeration:

" . . . some very tall bragging is indulged in by some in respect to their teams merits and performance. One team appears to suffer from heart disease, their owner evidently expecting the whole creation to hold their breath as they pass by. A vulgar person who often indulges in whoops and yells of 'Yoicks Tally Ho,' had the indescribable effrontery to let go his horrid war cry whilst riding on the imposing conveyance drawn by these dignified but nervous creatures, and was reproved by their indignant owner pointing out to the Vulgar Person into what terror his voice had thrown the beautiful but highly strung and delicate doggies. It is my painful duty to relate that this Awful Vulgar Person the very next day being out with an ordinary team gave vent to his fearsome bellow when passing the 'Heart Disease' Team. The result was disastrous, 2 of the poor creatures fainted and had to be brought round with hartshorn, etc., while the remainder went into hysterics until the Vulgar Person and his associates disappeared over the horizon."

The "Heart Disease" team belonged to Macklin, who believed in treating his dogs as gently as possible. The "Awful Vulgar Person" was Worsley himself.

Another factor contributing to the general cheerfulness of the party was their drift. Ever since the blizzard in July they had been blessed much of the time with strong southerly winds, and during that period they had covered a distance of more than 160 miles.

But just at midnight on August 29 a single heavy shock struck the ship. A moment later there was a sound like a distant clap of thunder. The men sat up in their bunks, waiting for something more to happen, but nothing did.

The next morning they saw a thin crack running out astern, but that was all. The rest of the day passed uneventfully. Then, about 6:30 P.M., just as the crew was finishing supper, the *Endurance* shuddered to the blow of a second shock. Several men jumped up from the table and rushed on deck. Again there was nothing, except that the crack astern had widened to a mere half inch.

The thirty-first was quiet until about ten o'clock in the evening. Then the *Endurance* began to creak and groan like a haunted house. The night watchman reported that the ice ahead and along the port side was on the move, but there was nothing the men could do so they turned in. But a series of loud snapping noises which reverberated throughout the ship kept them awake most of the night.

Those whose bunks were on the port side suffered the most. As they lay trying to sleep, they could hear the ice scraping and battering against the hull outside—less than 3 feet from their ears. The noise stopped just before dawn, but it was a tired, jittery group of men who sat down to breakfast that next morning.

The pressure began again late in the afternoon and continued into the evening. That night it was the worst it had been. Worsley described it in his diary:

"Just after midnight there was a series of loud and violent cracks, groans and bumps to the ship making her jump and shake fore and aft. Many dressed hastily and rushed on deck. Personally, I've got tired of alarms against which we can do absolutely nothing, so when the loudest crash came I listened to make sure that no ripping, tearing sound of smashing timbers was indicating an entrance of the ice into the hold, then turned over and went to sleep."

By the next afternoon, the pressure had ceased—and the *Endurance* had survived her second attack.

CHAPTER 7

The confidence of the men in their ship should have improved. As Greenstreet recorded in his diary on September 1: "She is stronger than we thought, and providing we don't get much heavier pressure . . . we should pull through all right."

But there was no real ring of confidence in Greenstreet's words. Who could say that there wouldn't be heavier pressure? It was not that they doubted the staunchness of the *Endurance,* but they were acutely aware that she had not been designed to encounter real pressure, much less the fearful pressures of the Weddell Sea, unquestionably the worst on earth.

Furthermore, the three-day attack on the ship had left them all tired and on edge. They had no idea what the future might bring. The novelty was past, and so too was their optimism. The pack was not yet through with them, and they knew it. But all they could do was to wait in helpless, frustrating uncertainty, living through the passage of each day as the drift of the ice carried them north in its own good time, and hoping every day that the *Endurance* would encounter nothing worse than what she had already endured.

Even Worsley, whose spirits rarely flagged, reflected the general anxiety in his diary:

"Many of the tabular bergs appear like huge warehouses and grain elevators, but more look like the creations of some brilliant architect when suffering from delirium, induced by gazing too long on this damned infernal stationary pack that seems . . . doomed to drift to and fro till the Crack of Doom splits and shivers it N., S., E. & W. into a thousand million fragments—and the smaller the better. No animal life observed—no land—no nothing!!!"

They felt most keenly the absence of seals, which would have provided both the pleasures of the chase and the opportunity to taste some fresh meat—a treat they had not had for five months.

Still there were occasional signs that the Antarctic spring was coming. The sun now shone for nearly ten hours every day, and on September 10, the temperature climbed to 1.9 degrees above zero—the highest reading for seven months. To the men it seemed like a heat wave; they could go aloft with bare heads and hands in reasonable comfort. A week later, Bobbie Clark's biological dredge brought up evidence that the amount of plankton in the water was increasing—a definite sign of the approach of spring.

In the Antarctic, plankton—tiny one-celled plants and animals—is the basis for all life. The smallest fishes subsist on it, and they in turn become the food of larger fish, which are eaten by squids and seals and penguins, who constitute the food for killer whales, sea leopards, and giant sperm whales. The cycle of life begins with plankton, and when it is present, the other creatures of the Antarctic are never far behind.

Five days after Clark's report, Jock Wordie sighted an emperor penguin and enticed it out of a patch of open water. It was speedily killed. The following day, a female seal was slain.

But in spite of these encouraging signs, an unmistakable air of apprehension was spreading. October 1 was getting close. Twice before, in August and September, the first of the month had been the signal for severe pressure, and the men had grown superstitious about it.

This time the fates miscalculated by one day. The pressure started on September 30, about three o'clock in the afternoon. Altogether it lasted only one terrifying hour.

The attacker this time, a floe off the port bow, bore in mercilessly beneath the foremast. The decks below shuddered and jumped, and the uprights buckled. Chippy McNeish was down in the Ritz. The giant beams over his head bent "like a piece of cane." Greenstreet, on deck, was unable to take his eyes off the foremast which looked as if it were "coming out of her with the tremendous jerks it gave."

Worsley was aft by the wheel, and when the pressure was past, he wrote in his diary: "She shows almost unconceivable strength . . . every moment it seems as though the floe must crush her like a nutshall. All hands are watching and standing by, but to our relief, just as it appears she can stand no more, the huge floe weighing possibly a million tons or more yields to our little ship by cracking across, ¼ of a mile, and so relieves the pressure. The behavior of our ship in the ice has been magnificent. Undoubtedly she is the finest little wooden vessel ever built. . . . "

When it was all over the crew went below to find that many of the decks were permanently buckled and all manner of articles had been shaken off the shelves. But the ship was still under them.

A little of the old optimism began to creep back. The *Endurance* might just make it. Three times the ship had come under attack from the ice, and always the pressure had been worse than the time before. But each time the *Endurance* had fought back and she had won. As the early days of October passed, the ice showed definite signs of opening. Temperatures, too, began to rise. On October 10, the thermometer climbed to 9.8 degrees above zero. The floe which had been jammed under the ship's starboard side since July broke free on October 14, and the *Endurance* lay in a small pool of open water—truly afloat for the first time since she was beset nine months before.

The officers and scientists could now move back into the wardroom in the deckhouse. The partitions in the Ritz were taken down and the area was reconverted into a hold for stores.

Shackleton decided on October 16 that the opening tendency of the pack justified getting up steam on the chance that they could force a way through. All hands were put to pumping up the boilers with water. This exhausting three-and-a-half hour job was hardly finished when a serious leak was discovered in one of the fittings—and the boilers had to be pumped out again so the engineers could make repairs. By the time the job was completed, it was too late to get under way. Early the next afternoon a lead of open water appeared ahead of the ship. There wasn't time to get up steam, so the men set all sails trying to force her into the crack. She wouldn't budge. October 18 dawned a misty, snowy morning. The lead ahead had disappeared, and the ice was a little closer. Throughout the day the ship felt little nips of pressure, but nothing serious. Then at 4:45 P.M., the floes on either side of the *Endurance* closed in against her, and kept on closing.

Every man on board stiffened, as if he himself had been touched. Several raced up the ladders onto deck. In the next instant, the deck seemed to slide away from beneath their feet as the ship rolled suddenly over to port. A second's pause—then everything movable let go with a rush—wood, kennels, ropes, sledges, stores, dogs, and men cascaded across the deck. James was caught under two boxes of winter clothing onto which a pile-up of dogs descended in whining, howling confusion. Clouds of steam rose from the galley and the wardroom where pots of water were upset onto the fires.

In the space of five seconds, the *Endurance* was heeled over 20 degrees to port—and she continued to fall off. Worsley rushed to the lee rail and watched as plank after plank disappeared under the ice. Greenstreet stood nearby, ready to jump.

The floe to starboard had got a grip on the bulge of her hull and was simply rolling her over. At 30 degrees to port she slowed, then stopped with her bulwarks resting on the ice and the lifeboats nearly touching. Said Worsley: "She seemed to say to the grinding, hungry pack, 'You may smash me but I'm damned if I'll go over another inch for you; I'll see you melting in Hell first.'"

The moment the *Endurance* came to rest, Shackleton ordered the fires extinguished; then everyone went systematically about the job of restoring order. They lashed down everything that was loose and nailed small strips of wood to the deck to give the dogs a foothold. About seven o'clock the work on deck was finished and the men went below—to behold a scene in which every hanging article looked as if it were caught in a high wind. Curtains, pictures, clothing, and cooking utensils all hung out from the starboard bulkhead.

Green managed to prepare a supper while the rest of the crew nailed more battens to the decks below. The meal was eaten with most of them sitting on the deck, one above another, holding their plates in their laps. "We look like we're sitting in a grandstand," James remarked.

About eight o'clock, the floes under the *Endurance* drew apart, and the ship quickly righted herself. The crew was set to chopping away the ice from around the rudder. They finished about 10 P.M. A ration of grog was issued, and then they began pumping up the boilers again. At one o'clock in the morning all hands except the watch turned in—bone tired.

October 19 was a day free from pressure, and there was very little activity of any sort. A killer whale surfaced in the lane of open water alongside the ship and cruised with graceful arrogance up and down for a time. The last barometer reading of the day was 28.96, the lowest since the disastrous blizzard in July.

Again on October 20 there was little change in the pack. Nevertheless, everything was made ready to get under way whenever an opening appeared. The engines were turned over slowly and found to be in good order. Regular four-hour sea watches were set. The twenty-first and the twenty-second similarly were days of watchful waiting; the only change in the pack was that it appeared to close slightly. The temperature dropped from 10 above zero to –14 degrees. Late on the twenty-second, the wind swung around 180 degrees from southwest to northeast. McNeish wrote in his diary that night: " . . . very quiet, but there looks as if there was going to be a bit of pressure."

CHAPTER 8

I t was slow to arrive. October 23 dragged by uneventfully, except that the pack was working somewhat under the influence of the northeast wind.

When, at 6:45 P.M. on October 24, the pressure did arrive, it wasted no time. There had been pressure in the past, but nothing like this. It moved through the pack like a sluggish shock wave, making the entire surface of the ice into a chaos of churning, tumbling destruction. Macklin watched it briefly, then turned away in disbelief. "The whole sensation," he recorded, "was of something colossal, of something in nature too big to grasp."

Effortlessly, the ice jostled and badgered the ship until she was pinned up against two floes, fore and aft on the starboard side, and kneed in the center on the other.

A heavy mass of ice ground across her stern, tearing the sternpost partly away from the starboard planking. Water poured in. McNeish was sent to check and reported back that it was rising rapidly in the foreward hold. Rickenson said the same of the engine room.

The small portable Downton pump was rigged and steam was raised to operate the engine-room bilge pumps. They were going by 8 P.M., but they failed to hold the water in check. All hands that could be spared were put on the primary hand pumps along-side the mainmast. But after several minutes of pumping, no water had come up. The intakes were obviously frozen.

Worsley took Hudson and Greenstreet with him down into the bunkers. Working in almost total darkness and icy cold, they dug and squirmed their way down to the keel through the wet, slimy coal into which the blubber from threescore seals had been dumped. The sounds of the tormented ship were deafeningly close. They poured bucket after bucket of boiling water into the frozen pipe. One of the men played the flame of a blowtorch on the stubborn fittings while the other two pounded to loosen the clogged intakes. Finally, after an hour's work, the pumps broke loose.

McNeish commenced to build a cofferdam 10 feet forward of the sternpost to seal off the after section of the ship and hold back the water. Between fifteen-minute spells at the pumps, some of the crew helped him calk the cofferdam with strips of torn blankets. Others went over the side with picks and ice-saws to cut lines of weakness in the attacking floes. But as soon as each trench was dug, the ice crumpled along it, then bore in again.

All night long they kept at it . . . fifteen minutes on the pumps, fifteen minutes off, then over the side or back to the engine room. Though they were lean and hard after a year's tough work on the ship and on the sledges, ten hours at the pumps and saws left even the strongest so exhausted they stumbled as they walked. At dawn, Shackleton ordered an hour's rest, and Green ladled out a bowl of porridge for each man. Then it was time to begin again. Toward midmorning, Shackleton sent the dog drivers over the side to ready their teams and sledges in case of an immediate abandonment. Worsley took a party of seamen and cleared the boats for lowering.

Most of them had stopped watching the pack in their struggle to save the ship. It had settled down some, but it was behaving strangely. Pressure ridges of a height never before seen rose be-tween the floes, and the compression was fantastic, as if the pack had been shoved up against some solid barrier over the horizon.

The men worked at the pumps and at building the cofferdam through the day and evening. About midnight, after twenty-eight hours of ceaseless work, McNeish finished his job, at least as well as it could be finished. But it only slowed the flow of water, and the pumps had to be kept going. Each spell was an agony of ef-fort, and when it was finished, the men staggered to their bunks or slumped into a corner. It took perhaps ten minutes for their exhausted muscles to loosen enough to let them sleep. Then just as they dozed off, they were prodded up for their next turn.

Toward evening, the pressure increased again. The floe along the port side ground against the ship, warping her along her en-tire length, and wringing animal-like screams from her as the ice sought to break her back. At 9 P.M., Shackleton instructed Worsley to lower the boats and to get all essential gear and provi-sions onto the floe to starboard, which seemed the least likely to break up.

Late in the evening, the men on deck saw a band of about ten emperor penguins; they waddled slowly up toward the ship, then stopped a short distance away. Emperors, singly or in pairs, were a common sight, but nobody had ever seen so large a group before. The penguins stood for a moment watching the tortured ship, then raised their heads and uttered a series of weird, mourn-ful, dirgelike cries. It was all the more eerie because none of the men—not even the Antarctic veterans among them—had ever before heard penguins voice anything except the most elemental, croaking sorts of noises.

The sailors stopped what they were doing, and old Tom McLeod turned to Macklin. "Do you hear that?" he asked. "We'll none of us get back to our homes again."

Macklin noticed Shackleton bite his lip.

About midnight the movement of the ice partly closed the wound in the stern, and the flow of water decreased. But still the hand pumps had to be manned to keep the water from gaining. They stayed at it all night, working with closed eyes, like dead men attached to some evil contrivance which would not let them rest.

It was no better at dawn, or at noon. About four o'clock the pressure reached new heights. The decks buckled and the beams broke; the stern was thrown upward 20 feet, and the rudder and sternpost were torn out of her. The water ran forward and froze, weighting her down in the bow, so that the ice climbed up her sides forward, inundating her under the sheer weight of it. Still they pumped. But at five o'clock they knew it was time to give up. She was done, and nobody needed to tell them.

Shackleton nodded to Wild, and Wild went forward along the quaking deck to see whether anybody was in the forecastle. He found How and Bakewell trying to sleep after a turn at the pumps. He put his head inside.

"She's going, boys," he said. "I think it's time to get off."

PART II

CHAPTER 1

May the Lord help you to do your duty & guide you
through all the dangers by land and sea.
May you see the Works of the Lord & all His Wonders
in the deep.

These words were written on the flyleaf of a Bible given to
the expedition by Queen Mother Alexandra of England.
Shackleton carried the Bible in his hand as he left the *Endurance*
and walked slowly across the ice toward the campsite.

The others hardly noticed his arrival. They were busy crawling
in and out of the tents, trying, numbly, to create some degree
of comfort with what energy remained in them. Some arranged
pieces of lumber to keep themselves off the snow-covered ice.
Others spread pieces of canvas as ground-covers. But there was
not enough flooring for everybody and several men had to lie directly on the bare snow. It made little difference. Sleep was all that
mattered. And they slept—most of them embracing their nearest
tentmates to keep from freezing.

Shackleton did not even try to sleep. He paced continually
around the floe. The pressure was still intense, and several times
the campsite sustained a violent shock. The dark outline of the

Endurance 200 yards away rose against the clear night sky. About 1 a.m., as Shackleton walked back and forth, there was a jolt; then a thin ribbonlike crack snaked across the floe among the tents. Almost immediately it began to widen. Shackleton hurried from tent to tent, waking the exhausted sleepers. It required an hour's tricky work in the dark to transfer the camp to the larger half of the floe.

Thereafter all was quiet in the camp, though just before dawn there was a loud report from the *Endurance.* Her bowsprit and jib boom had broken and dropped onto the ice. For the rest of the night, Shackleton could hear the ghostly rhythm of the chain from the martingale boom being slowly dragged back and forth by the movement of the ship.

When morning came, the weather was dull and overcast, but the temperature had climbed to 6 above zero. The men turned out stiff and cold from sleeping on the ice. It took a very long time for them to wake up. Shackleton did not press them, and after a time they turned to the job of sorting out equipment and stowing it securely on the sledges. It was a quiet time, and very few orders were given. Everyone understood his job and went about it without having to be told.

The plan, as they all knew, was to march toward Paulet Island, 346 miles to the northwest, where the stores left in 1902 should still be. The distance was farther than from New York City to Pittsburgh, Pennsylvania, and they would be dragging two of their three boats with them, since it was assumed that they would eventually run into open water.

McNeish and McLeod began mounting the whaler and one of the cutters onto sledges. The boats with their sledges would weigh more than a ton apiece, and nobody had any delusions that it would be easy to drag them over the chaotic surface of the ice, with its pressure ridges occasionally two stories high.

Nevertheless, there was a remarkable absence of discouragement. All the men were in a state of dazed fatigue, and nobody paused to reflect on the terrible consequences of losing their ship. Nor were they upset by the fact that they were now camped on a piece of ice perhaps 6 feet thick. It was a haven compared with the nightmare of labor and uncertainty of the last few days on the *Endurance.* It was quite enough to be alive—and they were merely doing what they had to do to stay that way.

There was even a trace of mild exhilaration in their attitude. At least, they had a clear-cut task ahead of them. The nine months of indecision, of speculation about what might happen, of aimless drifting with the pack were over. Now they simply had to get themselves out, however appallingly difficult that might be.

Periodically throughout the day, little groups of men made pilgrimages back to the derelict that had been their ship. But she was no longer a ship. She was not even afloat, really. She was a torn, twisted framework of wood. The ice, in its frenzy to wreck her, had driven through her sides and remained there, supporting the broken hull. She would remain on the surface only as long as the pressure lasted.

On one trip, a group of men ran the blue Union Jack up to the forward yardarm, the only rigging still standing. When the *Endurance* went, she would at least go with her colors flying.

The work of packing the sledges continued the next day, and in the afternoon Shackleton called all hands together into the center of the circle of tents. His face was grave. He explained it was imperative that all weight be reduced to the barest minimum. Each man, he said, would be allowed the clothes on his back, plus two pairs of mittens, six pairs of socks, two pairs of boots, a sleeping bag, a pound of tobacco—and two pounds of personal gear. Speaking with the utmost conviction, Shackleton pointed out that no article was of any value when weighed against their ultimate survival, and he exhorted them to be ruthless in ridding themselves of every unnecessary ounce, regardless of its value.

After he had spoken, he reached under his parka and took out a gold cigarette case and several gold sovereigns and threw them into the snow at his feet.

Then he opened the Bible Queen Alexandra had given them and ripped out the flyleaf and the page containing the Twenty-third Psalm. He also tore out the page from the Book of Job with this verse on it:

> Out of whose womb came the ice?
> And the hoary frost of Heaven, who hath gendered it?
> The waters are hid as with a stone.
> And the face of the deep is frozen.

Then he laid the Bible in the snow and walked away.

It was a dramatic gesture, but that was the way Shackleton wanted it. From studying the outcome of past expeditions, he believed that those that burdened themselves with equipment to meet every contingency had fared much worse than those that had sacrificed total preparedness for speed.

As the afternoon wore on, the number of nonessentials dumped in the snow grew steadily. It was an "extraordinary collection of stuff," James noted. Chronometers, axes, an ophthalmoscope, saws, telescopes, socks, lenses, jerseys, chisels, books, stationery—and a large number of pictures and personal keepsakes. For some men, the two-pound limit on personal gear was relaxed for special reasons. The two surgeons, of course, were permitted a small amount of medical supplies and instruments. The men with diaries were allowed to keep them. And Hussey actually was ordered to take his zither banjo along, even though it weighed 12 pounds. It was lashed in its case under the bow sheets of the whaler to keep it out of the weather.

The journey would begin the next day. On the eve of setting out, Shackleton wrote: "I pray God I can manage to get the whole party safe to civilization."

October 30 was gray and overcast with a bit of occasional wet snow. The temperature was an uncomfortably warm 15 degrees, which made the surface of the ice soft—far from ideal for sledging.

They spent the morning readying the last bit of stores. About eleven-thirty, Shackleton, with Wild, went out to prospect for a route. Before he left, Shackleton ordered the three youngest puppies killed, along with Sirius, an older puppy from an earlier litter, whose only fault was that he had never been broken to harness. McNeish's tomcat, which had mistakenly been named Mrs. Chippy before his sex was determined, also was to be destroyed. There was only food for those who could pull their weight.

Tom Crean, tough and practical as ever, took the younger puppies and Mrs. Chippy some distance from camp and shot them without a qualm, but it was Macklin's duty to destroy Sirius, and he could hardly face the task. Reluctantly he got a 12-gauge shotgun from Wild's tent; then he led Sirius off toward a distant pressure ridge. When he found a suitable spot he stopped and stood over the little dog. Sirius was an eager, friendly puppy, and he kept jumping up, wagging his tail and trying to lick Macklin's hand. Macklin kept pushing him away until finally he got up nerve enough to put the shotgun to Sirius' neck. He pulled the trigger, but his hand was shaking so he had to reload and fire a second time to finish the puppy off.

The journey was begun about 2 P.M. Shackleton, Wordie, Hussey, and Hudson went ahead with a sledge and an assortment of shovels and mountaineering pickaxes. They tried to guide the main party along a level route, but every few hundred yards it was necessary to cross a pressure ridge. Then they set to work, chopping away at it until they had carved out a miniature mountain pass for the boats. On particularly high ridges, they had to build a ramp of ice and snow up one side and down the other.

The teams came next, pulling sledges loaded with up to 900 pounds apiece. The boats, drawn by fifteen men harnessed in traces under Worsley's command, were last. It was killing toil. Because of their weight, the boats sank into the soft surface of the snow. To move them, the men in the traces had to strain forward, at times leaning nearly parallel with the ground, and the whole operation was more like plowing through the snow than sledging.

Shackleton wisely instructed the party to advance in short relays of about a quarter of a mile each. He was fearful that cracks would open up, and if the line of march were stretched out over a long distance the party might be divided. Their progress was slow and arduous, for all hands had to retrace their steps every thousand yards or so. By 5 P.M., after three hours on the trail, they were 1 mile from the ship in a direct line, though with detours they had traveled perhaps twice that far. Some of the dog teams, which had gone back time after time to bring up equipment, had probably covered more than 10 miles altogether.

Supper was at six o'clock, and the weary men immediately crawled into their sleeping bags. During the night it began to snow heavily, and by dawn there was a mushy 6-inch blanket. The temperature soared to 25 degrees, making the prospects for sledging extremely bad.

In the morning, Shackleton and Worsley found a fairly good route to the west, and the whole party set out at one o'clock. But it was torturously slow going in the deep snow, and most of the men were sweating profusely and beset by thirst within minutes.

Their major efforts were devoted to beating down a path in the snow for the boat sledges. Even so, the fifteen men on the boats felt as if they were hauling their burdens through mud. After a time, Wild and Hurley took their teams back to help. They hitched onto the cutter, and succeeded in getting it moving.

About 4 P.M., having covered only a scant three-quarters of a mile, the party arrived at a thick, level floe. Since there wasn't another suitable camping place within sight, Shackleton decided they would spend the night where they were. Almost as fast as the tents were pitched, they were soaked inside. It was impossible to crawl into them without bringing in quantities of wet, clinging snow.

Macklin commented: "I cannot help feeling sorry for Worsley at the mouth of our tent, for he gets the wet brought in by everybody."

Worsley, however, was far from distressed. He wrote in his diary that same night: "The rapidity with which one can completely change one's ideas . . . and accommodate ourselves to a state of barbarism is wonderful."

Shackleton was pleased by the general cheeriness of the men. "Many look on this as a spree," he recorded. "It is better so."

He also observed: "This floe really strong. Will sleep tonight."

The floe was indeed a giant, more than a half mile in diameter and made up of ice 10 feet thick, with 5 feet of snow on top of that. It was probably more than two years old, Worsley estimated.

Its sturdiness was very much on Shackleton's mind the following morning when he went out with Wild and Worsley to look for a route. They saw tumbled confusion to the west, "a sea of pressure," Shackleton declared, "impossible to advance." The boats and sledges would not last 10 miles over such a surface.

On the way back to camp, Shackleton came to a decision. When he arrived he called all hands together. He told the men that they had made less than a mile a day, and that the route ahead appeared to get progressively worse. Their advance, he said, hardly merited the effort it required. And since they were not likely to find a better place to camp, they would stay where they were until the drift of the ice should carry them closer to land.

There was a flicker of disappointment on several faces, but Shackleton allowed no time for regrets. He dispatched dog teams back to the original camp, a mile and three-quarters to the rear, to bring up all the food, clothing, and gear possible.

Wild, with six men, was sent back to the ship to salvage anything of value. When they reached the *Endurance* they discovered that in the past two days the ice had further mutilated her twisted hull. Her bow had been shoved deeper into the ice so that the entire forecastle was submerged and littered with bits of floes. Her rigging was an indescribable tangle of broken masts and snarled tackle which had to be cut away to make it safe to work. Later they hacked a hole in the galley roof and recovered a few cases of stores. But their biggest prize for the day, which required the combined efforts of several dog teams to get back to camp, was the third boat.

For supper that night, Shackleton ordered Green to put some lumps of blubber into the seal meat stew so that the party might get accustomed to eating it. Some of the men, when they saw the rubbery, cod-liver-oil–flavored chunks floating around in their "hoosh," meticulously removed every trace. But the majority were so hungry they were delighted to gobble down every mouthful, blubber included.

CHAPTER 2

They had been on the ice exactly one week. In seven short days they had gone from the well-ordered, even pleasant existence on board the *Endurance* to one of primitive discomfort, of unending wet and inescapable cold. A little more than a week before they had slept in their own warm bunks and eaten their meals in the cozy atmosphere around the mess table. Now they were crammed together in overcrowded tents, lying in reindeer or woolen sleeping bags on bare ice, or at best on odd pieces of hard lumber. At mealtimes, they sat in the snow, and each man ate out of an aluminum mug they called a pannican, into which everything was dumped at the same time. For utensils, each had a spoon, a knife—and his fingers.

They were castaways in one of the most savage regions of the world, drifting they knew not where, without a hope of rescue, subsisting only so long as Providence sent them food to eat.

And yet they had adjusted with surprisingly little trouble to their new life, and most of them were quite sincerely happy. The adaptability of the human creature is such that they actually had to remind themselves on occasion of their desperate circumstances. On November 4, Macklin wrote in his diary: "It has been

85

a lovely day, and it is hard to think we are in a frightfully precarious situation."

It was an observation typical of the entire party. There was not a hero among them, at least not in the fictional sense. Still not a single diary reflected anything beyond the matter-of-fact routine of each day's business.

There was only one major change in their general outlook—their attitude toward food. Worsley had this to say: "It is scandalous—all we seem to live for and think of now is food. I have never in my life taken half such a keen interest in food as I do now—and we are all alike. . . . We are ready to eat anything, especially cooked blubber which none of us would tackle before. Probably living totally in the open and having to rely on food instead of fire for body heat makes us think so much of food. . . . "

They were up at six the following morning, November 5, and nearly everyone returned to the ship. Several men attempted some personal salvage operations. Macklin went after a Bible his mother had given him. He crawled through a hole in the slanting deckhouse to reach the passageway leading to his old cabin. In the passageway he had to stand on a handrail above the ice and water, and inch his way down, crouching over. But his progress was halted at the water's edge, some 12 feet short of the cabin. He could see the door, down under the dark, icy water, but he couldn't reach it.

Greenstreet was luckier, and managed to get far enough into his cabin to secure a few books. How and Bakewell, whose quarters in the forecastle were hopelessly submerged, went treasure-hunting elsewhere. Carefully making their way along a passageway below, they passed the door of the compartment Hurley had used as a darkroom. Looking in, they saw the cases containing Hurley's photographic negatives. After hesitating a moment, the two seamen squeezed past the half-jammed door, stepped into the ankle-deep water, and grabbed the cases off the shelves. It was a real treasure, and they returned the negatives to Hurley that night.

As a whole, the salvage party worked with abandon, scarcely considering the usefulness of each item removed. And indeed there was very little from the ship that couldn't be used in one way or another. Wood could always serve as fuel for cooking; canvas was useful for ground covers and for patching tents; ropes could be made into sledge harnesses. The men removed the entire wheelhouse as a unit and returned it to camp to serve as a sort of portable storehouse. Lumber, spars, sails, and rigging followed.

They worked until nearly five o'clock, and then returned to camp, bringing one final load with them. As they trudged along beside the sledges, Hurley spotted a large Weddell seal about a thousand yards off to the right. He had no gun with which to kill it, so he took a piece of wood and approached the seal cautiously. When he was close enough, he stunned the animal with his club. Then he brained it with a mountaineer's pickaxe. Two other seals were killed in this fashion on the way back to camp.

But the amount of stores thus far salvaged from the ship was disappointingly small. Most of the provisions were below decks in what had been the Ritz. To get at them would require tearing the deck away, and it was more than a foot thick in places and nearly 3 feet underwater. But it was imperative that the stores be obtained, so the next day McNeish was put in charge, and after hours of work with ice chisels and various rigs of tackle the party wrenched and pried a hole through the deck.

Almost immediately, stores began to float up, beginning with a barrel of walnuts. Other supplies were grappled to the surface—a case of sugar, a boxful of baking soda. By the end of the day, nearly 3½ tons of flour, rice, sugar, barley, lentils, vegetables, and jam had been rescued and sledged back to camp. It was an extremely rewarding haul, and the whole party was jubilant. Green prepared them a treat of curried seal for supper in celebration. But after the first bite, most of the men could hardly swallow more. Green had put in easily three times too much curry. "I had to eat it to satisfy my hunger," Macklin later wrote in his diary, "but now my mouth is like a limekiln and I am almost parched with thirst."

Salvage work had to be suspended on the afternoon of November 6, when a southerly blizzard came up and drove the men into their tents. It was their first blizzard on the ice. The tents shook and rattled with the force of the gale, while the men huddled inside, cold and cramped. The only cheering thought was that the gale was driving them north—toward civilization, so infinitely far away.

Shackleton took the opportunity to meet with Wild, Worsley, and Hurley to evaluate their food situation. They now had some 4½ tons of stores, not counting the concentrated sledging ration which was to have been used by the six-man transcontinental party, and which Shackleton intended to save for emergencies. They reckoned their food supplies would last three months at full rations. And since they were sure to get increasing numbers of seals and penguins, they decided it was safe to go on full rations for the next two months.

This would carry them into January, the midpoint of the Antarctic summer. By that time, Shackleton was sure, they would know what fate lay in store for them. Then the ultimate decision would have to be made while there was still time to act before the onslaught of winter.

Everything depended on the drift of the pack. The ice might continue to go generally northwest, carrying them toward the Palmer Peninsula, possibly as far as the South Orkney Islands, some 500-odd miles to the north. Or the drift might be arrested for some reason, and they would remain more or less in the same spot. Finally, the pack might veer northeast or even east, carrying them away from land.

Whatever happened, January would mark the point of no return. If the drift was toward land, they should have enough open water by then to launch the boats and make for the most promising spot. It seemed reasonable, in theory at least. If the pack were to stop moving, that fact would be apparent by January. Then, rather than spend the winter camped on the ice, the party would abandon their boats except for a small punt the carpenter had built, and make a dash for the nearest land, using the punt to ferry across any open water they ran into. It would be a risky business, but better than wintering on the ice.

The third prospect was grim indeed. If the pack drifted northeast or east and if they were unable to launch the boats—they would have to spend the winter adrift on the floes, somehow surviving the polar night with its paralyzing cold and violent storms. If this were to happen, they would know by January. And there would still be time to lay in meat to see them through. But nobody even cared to think much about such a possibility.

CHAPTER 3

The presence of Frank Hurley at this high-level meeting about the food situation had special significance. He was invited, not because of his Antarctic experience—there were several others, such as Alf Cheetham or Tom Crean, who were much more knowledgeable—but because Shackleton did not want to antagonize him. The incident revealed one of Shackleton's basic traits.

Though he was virtually fearless in the physical sense, he suffered an almost pathological dread of losing control of the situation. In part, this attitude grew out of a consuming sense of responsibility. He felt he had gotten them into their situation, and it was his responsibility to get them out. As a consequence, he was intensely watchful for potential troublemakers who might nibble away at the unity of the group. Shackleton felt that if dissension arose, the party as a whole might not put forth that added ounce of energy which could mean, at a time of crisis, the difference between survival and defeat. Thus he was prepared to go to almost any length to keep the party close-knit and under his control.

Though Hurley was a skilled photographer and an excellent worker, he was also the sort of man who responded best to flattery, who frequently needed to be jollied along and made to feel important. Shackleton sensed this need—he may even have overestimated it—and he was afraid that unless he catered to it, Hurley might feel slighted and possibly spread discontent among the others.

And so Shackleton frequently sought Hurley's opinion, and he was careful to compliment him on his work. He also assigned Hurley to his own tent, which appealed to Hurley's snobbishness and also minimized his opportunities for gathering other latent malcontents around himself.

Several other tent assignments were made with an eye to avoiding trouble. Shackleton shared No. 1 tent with Hudson, the navigator, and James, the physicist, as well as Hurley. Although neither of these men was by any means a troublemaker, Shackleton seemed concerned that they might cause friction if they were in close contact with the others too long.

Hudson was just as he had always been, simple and a little irritating. His attempts at humor were often more foolish than funny because he lacked perception. He was a young dandy, a little impressed with his own good looks, but really not too sure of himself. As a result of this fundamental insecurity, he was quite self-centered and a poor listener. He could be counted on to interrupt any conversation to inject something about himself—even though what he said bore no relation to the subject being discussed. And his self-centeredness made it difficult for him to tell when his leg was being pulled, as was the case in the practical joke from which he got his nickname, Buddha. Strangely, he seemed to enjoy a joke on himself—at least it gave him the chance to occupy center stage. Shackleton was not at all fond of Hudson, but he preferred putting up with him to inflicting him on others.

As for James, he probably never should have gone with the expedition at all. He had had an academic background and a rather sheltered upbringing. He was a scholar and an extremely capable and dedicated scientist, but in practical matters he was very unhandy and a little unwilling. The adventurous side of the expedition, which was its chief appeal for most of the other men, interested James very little. In personality, he was roughly the antithesis of Shackleton. For James's own sake, as much as for any other reason, Shackleton took him into his own tent.

The assignment of McNeish to No. 2 tent under Wild's care was also a calculated move. As a ship's carpenter, McNeish was a master craftsman. Nobody ever saw him use a ruler. He simply studied a job briefly, then set to work sawing the proper pieces—and they always fitted exactly.

But McNeish, though physically a giant of a man, and proportionately strong, was fifty-six years old—more than twice the average age of the other expedition members—and he was troubled with piles. He was homesick, too, almost from the day the expedition sailed. In fact, nobody really understood why he came at all. Whatever the reason, McNeish tended to be querulous. And because of his long experience as a mariner, he fancied himself something of a "sea lawyer," well versed in the rights of seamen. All things considered, Shackleton felt McNeish could bear some watching, and he instructed Wild accordingly.

But even dour old McNeish was happy during the blizzard which blew up out of the southeast on November 6. Though it kept the men in their tents, and living conditions were miserable, they were certain it was giving them a considerable shove to the north. "We all hope it lasts for a month," McNeish wrote.

It did last for forty-eight hours, and when the weather cleared, Worsley obtained a sight which showed they had been blown 16 miles northwest—a highly satisfactory run.

That afternoon, Shackleton went back to the ship with a small party and three of the dog teams to continue salvage operations. But the *Endurance* had sunk another 18 inches, and was just about level with the surface of the ice. Further salvage would be impossible. Just before leaving, the party fired a signal bomb as a salute in farewell to the *Endurance*.

The men began the next day to build a lookout tower out of the odds and ends of spars and planking they had brought back from the ship. And McNeish went to work on a better sledge for the whaler, using some of the tremendously strong greenheart sheathing that had once protected the sides of the *Endurance* from the ice.

The days now were considerably longer than the nights, with the sun setting about 9 P.M., and rising again near three o'clock in the morning. In the evenings there was plenty of light for reading or playing cards. Frequently Hussey took his banjo around to the galley tent where the flicker of flame in the blubber stove warmed his fingers enough to play, and there was always a good turnout of singers. The seven men under Worsley's charge in No. 5 tent instituted the practice of reading aloud each night. Clark was first, and he chose a volume inappropriately titled *Science from an Easy Chair*. Clark and his seven listeners lay snuggling together for warmth, arranged in a circle around the tent with their feet thrust under a pile of sleeping bags to generate a little collective heat. When it came Greenstreet's turn, he elected to read Sir Walter Scott's *Marmion*. And Macklin allowed as how "I must confess I find his reading an excellent soporific."

Underlying the optimism and good spirits of the party was a deep-seated confidence that their situation was only temporary. Things were certain to improve before very long. Summer was coming. They were positive that the drift of the pack, which had been at a creeping pace, would pick up speed. Even if it didn't, the summer weather would loosen the ice, and they could take to the boats.

On November 12, four days after the end of the blizzard, the wind swung around to the north, and suddenly summer seemed to arrive. The thermometer rose to a record 35 degrees, and several of the men stripped to the waist to indulge in the luxury of a wash in the snow.

Otherwise, the heat wave made living conditions increasingly miserable. During the daytime it was almost stiflingly hot in the tents—Shackleton once recorded a temperature of 82 degrees in his. Worsley insisted that he could actually see the snow turning into water. The surface of the floe became a quagmire of melted snow and rotting ice. Walking was treacherous because the porous ice would unexpectedly give way, letting a man plunge into a water-filled ice pocket up to his knees or even his waist. Sledging heavy seals back to camp was worst of all. The drivers were usually wet through when they returned.

But life had its compensations. Orde-Lees, the expedition's tight-fisted storekeeper, known to the men variously as the "Colonel," the "Old Lady," the "Belly Burglar," the "Man of Action," and a host of other derogatory nicknames, decided on November 12 to move out of No. 5 tent for a while.

Worsley, with sarcastic relish, described the reaction in his diary: "Sounds of bitter sobs and lamentations are heard this evening from No. 5 tent at the loss of their dearly beloved 'Colonel' who has removed himself for a season to sleep in his store in the old wheelhouse. He indulgently yields to our earnest entreaties to continue to dine with us and comforts us with the assurance that he will return promptly to our Humble but Happy Home immediately we prepare to get on the march."

Of all the expedition members, Orde-Lees was undoubtedly the strangest. And probably the strongest, too. Before joining the expedition, he had been physical education director of His Majesty's Royal Marines, and he could easily have whipped any of the other twenty-seven men. Yet for all the abuse his crewmates heaped on him, Orde-Lees was never provoked into a fight. He would usually reply in a hurt tone of voice, "Now, really, you shouldn't say things like that."

Still he was anything but a coward. In fact he was almost fool-hardy in the risks he took. Out seal hunting, he would dash across leads of open water, leaping from one chunk of ice to the next while killer whales cruised around. Once during the darkest part of the winter when the *Endurance* had been beset, he found a bicycle in the hold of the ship and went out for a ride across the frozen floes. He was gone two hours in the perilous cold, and a searching party had to go out to find him. When he was brought back to the ship, Shackleton ordered him thereafter never to leave unless he was accompanied by another man, and instructed Worsley to see that he obeyed.

Orde-Lees had an enigmatic, childlike personality. He was fundamentally lazy, except for a few activities such as skiing, which gave him pleasure. But he was not ashamed of his laziness, and he made no effort to disguise it. Even in the most desperate circumstances, when other men were on the point of collapse from fatigue, he seemed to openly shirk his duty. It was perhaps only his guilelessness about it that made him tolerable to the others.

As a storekeeper, however, he was excellent, at least under their meager circumstances. He suffered from a morbid fear of starving to death, so he was as miserly as possible with their stores. Several times Shackleton reprimanded him for issuing insufficient food.

He continually antagonized his tentmates. Frequently, when it was his turn to bring the pot of hoosh from the galley to the tent, he would get distracted along the way, so that the food was cold when it arrived. No amount of pleading, curses, or threats could get him to improve. He saved everything, and his collection of clutter occupied much more space than he was entitled to.

With Shackleton, however, he was obsequious—an attitude which Shackleton detested. Shackleton, like almost everybody else, disliked Orde-Lees intensely and even told him so once. Characteristically, Orde-Lees dutifully recorded the incident in his diary, writing it in the third person as if he had been an onlooker during the conversation.

For all his undesirable traits, however, Orde-Lees appeared to be incapable of malice. Most of the men wrote him off as a fool, so that when he was most infuriating, he was also rather ludicrous.

Shackleton, who had been busily studying possible escape routes, announced on November 13 that he had formed a plan.

Their drift thus far appeared to be carrying them directly toward Snow Hill Island, about 275 miles to the northwest. It lay off the coast of the Palmer Peninsula and was probably connected to the peninsula by ice. If the pack opened enough to let them launch the boats in time, they might land there. They would then be in a position to travel overland about 150 miles to the west coast of the Palmer Peninsula, eventually arriving at Wilhelmina Bay, a frequent summertime stopping place for whalers. Once contact had been established with the whalers, their rescue would seem assured.

Shackleton planned to have a small party of four men make the overland journey across the 5,000-foot glaciers of the Palmer Peninsula, while the rest of the party waited at Snow Hill for rescue.

There was no assurance that the plan could be put into effect; but even the remotest possibility had to be considered and exploited to the fullest. Hurley went to work filing down screws and fixing them as cleats into four pairs of boots for the men who might have to climb the glaciers. Shackleton himself pored over every available chart of the region, figuring out the best route.

That night, as if to underscore the precariousness of their situation, a noise like distant, muffled thunder rumbled through the pack. A new wave of pressure had begun, and 3,500 yards away they could see the ice once again attacking the ship. About 9 P.M. they heard the sound of a splintering crack, and looking over they saw her foremast come crashing down, carrying the blue ensign with it.

CHAPTER 4

Though their floe remained undamaged throughout the pressure, Shackleton, who did not want a false sense of security to develop among the men, issued an Emergency Stations Bill on November 15. Unlikely as escape was, every man was assigned a specific duty in case the party should suddenly have to strike camp. If their route was to be over the ice, the sledge drivers would harness their teams with all possible speed while the other men gathered stores and equipment, struck the tents, and then stood by the sledges. Or if, as they hoped, they could escape by water, they were to ready the boats.

But it was impossible to prevent a certain amount of complacency as the men became increasingly accustomed to the well-established day-in, day-out routine of camp life. The line of pale-green tents seemed now almost as familiar as the ship had been. Two of the tents were the conventional sort, with a bamboo pole in the center. The others—the "hoop" tents designed by Marston for the expedition—operated on the same principle as the sunshade on a baby carriage, and they could be set up or struck in a matter of seconds. Their ability to weather storms, however, was not equal to that of the center-pole variety.

Each day in camp began at 6:30 A.M., when the night watchman drew off a tablespoon of gasoline from a drum in the galley and poured it into a small iron saucer in the bottom of the stove. He then lighted the gasoline and it, in turn, ignited strips of blubber draped on grates above the saucer. Hurley had fashioned the stove from an old oil drum and a cast-iron ash chute taken from the ship.

The stove sat in the center of the galley, which was itself little more than a makeshift windbreak, constructed of spars driven into the ice, over which pieces of sail had been stretched and lashed in place. The galley also served as the library, and the few books that had been salvaged from the *Endurance* were kept there in plywood packing cases. In addition, a chronometer hung on one post, a mirror on another.

As soon as the stove was burning, the night watchman awakened Green to begin breakfast. By seven o'clock, the men had begun to emerge from their tents to relieve themselves off behind some nearby hummocks. Many carried frayed toothbrushes, and on their way back they paused to clean their teeth with snow. The heavy sleepers who were not up by 7:45 were awakened by the night watchman, who went among the tents shouting, "Lash up and stow." The men rolled up their sleeping bags and sat down on them to wait for breakfast—sometimes seal steak, sometimes canned fish, sometimes porridge or pemmican, and tea.

After breakfast, the men went about their customary chores. Green spent the morning making "bannocks." These were lumps of fried flour, frequently mixed with dog pemmican or lentils or anything that would give them some flavor. And there was always ice to be melted into water.

Old Chippy McNeish, usually assisted by McLeod, How, and Bakewell, spent these days raising the sides of the whaler and one of the cutters to make them as seaworthy as possible. However, they were hampered by a shortage both of tools and of materials.

Only a saw, a hammer, a chisel, and an adze had been salvaged. And McNeish had obtained his few nails by pulling them one by one out of the superstructure of the *Endurance.*

Hurley, too, was busy preparing for the boat journey. He was not only an excellent photographer but a skilled tinsmith as well, and he was now at work fashioning a primitive boat pump from a tubelike portion of the ship's compass binnacle.

The rest of the party spent their time hunting. Most of the men went out in pairs to look for seals while the dog drivers exercised their teams around the floe. Often while they were exercising the dogs, the drivers would see one of the hunting parties in the distance waving a small flag—the signal that a seal had been sighted. One of the teams would then go to bring in the carcass.

Killing the seal was usually a bloody business. Wild had brought from the ship a revolver, a 12-gauge shotgun, and .33-caliber rifle, but ammunition was limited. As a result, the men killed the seals by hand whenever possible. This involved approaching the animal cautiously, then stunning it across the nose with a ski or a broken oar and cutting its jugular vein so that it bled to death. Sometimes the blood was collected in a vessel to be fed to the dogs, but most often it was allowed to run out into the snow. Another technique was to brain the seal with a pickaxe. But the two surgeons discouraged this practice, for it often left the brains inedible and they were prized as food because they were believed to be high in vitamin content.

In the beginning a few of the men, particularly little Louis Rickenson, the chief engineer, were squeamish about this seemingly cold-blooded method of hunting. But not for long. The will to survive soon dispelled any hesitancy to obtain food by any means.

After lunch, which usually consisted of a bannock or two per man, with some jam and tea, the men went to work strengthening sledge harnesses, repacking equipment, or helping with the boats. The dogs were fed at 5 P.M., amidst a terrific amount of barking, and supper for the men was at five-thirty—most often seal hoosh, a bannock, and a mug of hot watered cocoa.

In the evenings, activities varied somewhat from tent to tent. There was the reading aloud in Worsley's tent. In No. 1, Shackleton's four-man tent, invariably there was a game of poker patience or bridge. The seamen and firemen in No. 4 tent also played cards or sat around "yarning." The subject of sex was rarely brought up—not because of any post-Victorian prudishness, but simply because the topic was almost completely alien to the conditions of cold, wet, and hunger which occupied everyone's thoughts almost continually. Whenever women were discussed, it was in a nostalgic, sentimental way—of a longing to see a wife, a mother, or a sweetheart at home.

The official lights-out—a figure of speech since there was daylight now nearly sixteen hours a day—was at 8:30 P.M. A good many men turned in earlier, after removing their trousers and jerseys and possibly putting on a pair of dry socks. Nobody ever took off his underwear. Some men stayed up after the official curfew, though they had to talk in subdued voices. In the cold, crisp air any noise carried an unusually long distance.

By 10 P.M. everything was quiet in the camp except for the lone night watchman, patrolling among the tents and keeping an eye on the galley chronometer which told him when his one-hour tour of duty was over.

During these three weeks since the *Endurance* had been abandoned, perhaps the most striking change in the party was their appearance. Some men had always worn beards, and they were now just a little shaggier than before. But faces that had previously been clean-shaven were now covered with a scrubby, half-inch growth of whiskers.

And everybody's face grew filthy from the blubber smoke. It infiltrated everywhere, clung tenaciously to whatever it touched, and responded poorly to snow and the small amount of soap that could be spared for washing.

There were two schools of thought on the matter of cleanliness. Though any over-all bathing was out of the question, some men scrubbed their faces in snow whenever the weather permitted. Others purposely let the dirt accumulate on the theory that it would toughen their skin against frostbite.

Similarly, the camp was divided on the matter of eating into the savers and the nonsavers. Worsley headed the nonsavers, who gobbled down anything they could get whenever they could get it. Orde-Lees, with his all-consuming fear of starving to death, was the leading advocate of the savers' school of thought. He rarely ate his entire ration at any meal. Instead, he stored a little piece of cheese or a bit of bannock somewhere in his clothing to be eaten later or saved for the leaner days he was sure would come. He could and often did produce from his pocket a lump of food that had been issued a week, two weeks, three weeks before.

But there was no shortage of food these days. Obliging animals even presented themselves in camp. On November 18 a woebegone little seal scarcely a month old wandered in amongst the tents. He had apparently lost his mother to a killer whale, and though he was so small that he was almost worthless as food, the men reluctantly killed him anyhow, since he obviously could not survive alone. On the nineteenth pandemonium among the dogs announced the presence of a seal in camp—this time a big bull crabeater. After several such appearances, Worsley advanced the theory that whenever seals sighted the camp, they mistook it for land or a rookery and headed straight toward it.

Early on the morning of November 21, a salvage party went back to the ship. They noticed that the floes which had driven into the sides of the ship were moving slightly. They returned to camp and were unharnessing and feeding the dogs, when Shackleton came out to watch. He was standing close to Hurley's sledge. It was 4:50 P.M. Out of the corner of his eye he noticed the ship move. He turned quickly and saw her stack disappear behind a hummock.

"She's going, boys!" he shouted, and dashed up the lookout tower. A moment later all hands were out of the tents and scrambling to gain a vantage point. They watched in silence. Away across the pack, the stern of the *Endurance* rose 20 feet into the air and hung there for a moment with her motionless propeller and her smashed rudder held aloft. Then slowly, silently, she disappeared beneath the ice, leaving only a small gap of black, open water to mark where she had been. Within sixty seconds, even that was gone as the ice closed up again. It had all happened in ten minutes.

Shackleton that night noted simply in his diary that the *Endurance* was gone, and added: "I cannot write about it."

And so they were alone. Now, in every direction, there was nothing to be seen but the endless ice. Their position was 68°38½′ South, 52°28′ West—a place where no man had ever been before, nor could they conceive that any man would ever want to be again.

CHAPTER 5

The final loss of the *Endurance* was a shock in that it severed what had seemed their last tie with civilization. It was a finality. The ship had been a symbol, a tangible, physical symbol that linked them with the outside world. She had brought them nearly halfway around the globe, or, as Worsley put it, " . . . carried us so far and so well and then put forth the bravest fight that ever a ship had fought before yielding to the remorseless pack." Now she was gone.

But the reaction was largely a sentimental one, as after the passing of an old friend who had been on the verge of death for a long time. They had been expecting her to go for weeks. When she had been abandoned twenty-five days before, it had seemed that she would sink at any moment. Indeed, it was remarkable that she had stayed on the surface so long.

The next morning, Worsley obtained an encouraging sight indicating that in spite of four days of northerly winds, they had not been blown back. The pack appeared to be under the influence of a favorable current from the south. Hussey, however, had detected a disturbing change in the behavior of the ice. It no longer showed much tendency to open up under the influence of winds from the north. Furthermore, these winds—which in the past had been comparatively warm after blowing across the open seas—were now almost as cold as the winds from the Pole. There could be only one conclusion: quantities of ice—not open water—extended for a great distance to the north.

Still the men showed an astonishing optimism. The task of raising the whaler's sides was almost complete and everyone was impressed with the job McNeish had done. The shortage of tools and lack of materials seemed not to have handicapped him in the least. To calk the planks he had added, he had been forced to resort to cotton lamp wick and the oil colors from Marston's artist's box.

That night, the first after the sinking of the *Endurance*, Shackleton sanctioned a special treat, the serving of fish paste and biscuits for supper. Everyone was delighted.

"Really, this sort of life has its attractions," Macklin wrote. "I read somewhere that all a man needs to be happy is a full stomach and warmth, and I begin to think it is nearly true. No worries, no trains, no letters to answer, no collars to wear—but I wonder which of us would not jump at the chance to change it all tomorrow!"

Macklin's good humor continued into the next day when he and Greenstreet were out seal-hunting. They were suddenly taken with the idea of going for a ride along one of the small leads of open water. But they knew that Shackleton, who could not abide unnecessary risks, would be furious if he saw them, so they went some distance away behind a number of pressure ridges. They found a stable little floe and climbed on board, poling along with ski poles.

They were doing beautifully when they spied Shackleton a short distance away, riding on Wild's sledge. Shackleton caught sight of them at the same time.

"We both felt," said Greenstreet, "like guilty schoolboys caught robbing an orchard, and immediately paddled for the bank and landed and went on with our seal hunt, finally meeting him as he returned to camp. Instead of the long harangue as we expected he only gave us an awful look and passed on."

Shackleton's aversion to tempting fate was well known. This attitude had earned for him the nickname "Old Cautious" or "Cautious Jack." But nobody ever called him that to his face. He was addressed simply as "Boss"—by officers, scientists, and seamen alike. It was really more a title than a nickname. It had a pleasant ring of familiarity about it, but at the same time "Boss" had the connotation of absolute authority. It was therefore particularly apt, and exactly fitted Shackleton's outlook and behavior. He wanted to appear familiar with the men. He even worked at it, insisting on having exactly the same treatment, food, and clothing. He went out of his way to demonstrate his willingness to do the menial chores, such as taking his turn as "Peggy" to get the mealtime pot of hoosh from the galley to his tent. And he occasionally became furious when he discovered that the cook had given him preferential treatment because he was the "Boss."

But it was inescapable. He was the Boss. There was always a barrier, an aloofness, which kept him apart. It was not a calculated thing; he was simply emotionally incapable of forgetting—even for an instant—his position and the responsibility it entailed. The others might rest, or find escape by the device of living for the moment. But for Shackleton there was little rest and no escape. The responsibility was entirely his, and a man could not be in his presence without feeling this.

His aloofness, however, was mental—rarely physical. He was very much in evidence, taking part in all the men's activities. Shackleton, in fact, was one of the early arrivals when word got around on November 26 that somebody in No. 5 tent had unearthed a fresh deck of playing cards. Along with McIlroy, he spent hours teaching them how to play bridge.

The two instructors could hardly have found more enthusiastic students. Within forty-eight hours, the popularity of the game reached epidemic proportions. On the twenty-eighth, Greenstreet noted that "from each tent may be heard, '1 club, 2 hearts, 2 no-trump, double 2 no-trump' etc." Those who didn't join in found themselves almost ostracized. On one occasion Rickenson and Macklin were driven out of their tent by the crowd that assembled there to play and to kibitz.

At the same time, preparations were being completed for the "journey to the west." The boats were now as ready as McNeish could make them. Nothing remained except to name them, and Shackleton did so. He decided the honor should go to the expedition's principal backers. Accordingly, the whaler was christened the *James Caird*; the No. 1 cutter became the *Dudley Docker*, and the second cutter, the *Stancomb Wills*. George Marston, the artist, got busy with what remained of his paints and lettered the proper name on each boat.

Shackleton also adopted Worsley's suggestion that they call the floe on which they were established "Ocean Camp." He then issued the individual boat assignments. He himself would be in charge of the *James Caird*, with Frank Wild as his mate. Worsley would captain the *Dudley Docker*, with Greenstreet second-in-command, and "Buddha" Hudson was put in charge of the *Stancomb Wills*, with Tom Crean as mate.

And so November was drawing to a close. They had been on the ice just a month. And for all the trials and discomforts, these weeks of primitive living had been peculiarly enriching. The men had been forced to develop a degree of self-reliance greater than they had ever imagined possible. After spending four hours sewing an elaborate patch on the seat of his only pair of trousers, Macklin wrote one day, "What an ingrate I have been for such jobs when done for me at home." Greenstreet felt much the same way after he had devoted several days to scraping and curing a piece of sealskin to resole his boots. He paused in the midst of his task to write in his diary: "One of the finest days we have ever had . . . a pleasure to be alive."

In some ways they had come to know themselves better. In this lonely world of ice and emptiness, they had achieved at least a limited kind of contentment. They had been tested and found not wanting.

They thought of home, naturally, but there was no burning desire to be in civilization for its own sake. Worsley recorded: "Waking on a fine morning I feel a great longing for the smell of dewy wet grass and flowers of a Spring morning in New Zealand or England. One has very few other longings for civilization— good bread and butter, Munich beer, Coromandel rock oysters, apple pie and Devonshire cream are pleasant reminiscences rather than longings."

The fact that the entire party had been kept occupied contributed much to their feeling of well-being. But toward the close of November, they simply began to run out of things to do. The boats were completed and ready to go. A test launching had been held, and they had been found entirely satisfactory. The stores for the trip had been repacked and consolidated. Charts of the area had been studied, and probable winds and currents had been plotted. Hurley had finished the boat pump and gone on to make a small portable blubber stove for the journey.

They had completed their part of the bargain. Now all that remained was for the ice to open.

But it didn't open. One day wore on into the next, and the pack remained substantially the same. Nor was their drift particularly satisfactory. During this period the winds had been southerly but never very strong, so the pack continued to move north at the same sluggish pace, about 2 miles a day.

Frequently, even the recreation of exercising the teams was denied them. Often the ice would loosen somewhat, leaving their floe an island with up to 20 feet of open water around it. At such times, all they could do was run the dogs around the perimeter. Worsley wrote: "Men and dogs exercise around the floe. The complete distance is about 1½ statute miles, but to do it more than once proves damnably monotonous to the dogs as much as to ourselves."

Time, indeed, was beginning to weigh a little heavily. Each day blurred anonymously into the one before. Though they invariably tried to see the good side of things, they were unable to fight off a growing sense of disappointment. Macklin wrote on December 1:

"We have done a degree [of latitude—60 miles] in less than a month. This is not as good as it might be, but we are gradually getting north, and so far everything is hopeful."

And on December 7, McNeish rationalized: "We have drifted back a bit, but I think it will be for our good as it will give the ice between us & the Land a chance to get out & us a chance in."

Since abandoning the *Endurance*, they had covered 80 miles in a straight line almost due north. But their drift had described a slight arc, which was now curving definitely to the east, away from land. Not enough to cause real worry, but enough to stir concern.

Shackleton had suffered a bad attack of sciatica which had kept him confined to his tent and more or less out of touch with things. But, toward the middle of the month his condition improved and he became aware of the growing restiveness among the men. The situation was not improved on December 17. Just after they had drifted across the 67th parallel of latitude, the wind hauled around to the northeast. The next day's observation showed that they had been blown back across it.

An air of tension, of patience pushed too far, settled on the camp that night, and conversation was scant. Many of the men went to sleep right after supper. McNeish let go some of his

Sir Ernest Shackleton
—"Never the lowered
banner, never the last
endeavour."(Royal
Geographic Society)

Captain Frank Worsley (*left*), Frank Wild (*right*), second in command
(Royal Geographic Society)

The crew of the *Endurance* taken on the bow shortly after leaving Buenos Aires. Stowaway Perce Blackboro is missing from this shot—possibly he was still hiding in the ship's hold at the time (Royal Geographic Society)

Endurance frozen in the ice (Royal Geographic Society)

(*Top*) Dr. Leonard Hussey and Frank Hurley playing chess on board the *Endurance* (Royal Geographic Society). (*Bottom*) James Wordie, Alfred Cheetham, and Alexander Macklin (left to right) washing the galley floor of the *Endurance*. Crew members shared all duties, including a bi-weekly scrub of the Ritz floor (Royal Geographic Society)

"The Spectre Ship"—Photographer Frank Hurley took several nighttime photos of the *Endurance* by "flash light," blowing up charges of flash powder in shielded receptacles. Timing was crucial, and this shot alone required at least 20 flashes (Royal Geographic Society)

Taking the dogs down the gangway of the *Endurance* for their daily exercise
(Royal Geographic Society)

The *Endurance* in full sail, stuck fast in the ice of the Weddell Sea, January 25, 1915 (Royal Geographic Society)

The Night Watchmen, gathered around the stove in the wardroom (or Ritz) of the *Endurance* (Royal Geographic Society)

One of the many toasts to "Sweethearts and Wives" that occurred every Saturday evening—with or without a ship or rum (Scott Polar Research Institute)

(*Top*) Playing soccer on the ice; there were enough crew members for full eleven-a-side teams, plus a referee (Royal Geographic Society). (*Bottom*) Participants pose in their costumes after the three-hour "smoking concert" on Midwinter's Day, 1915 (Scott Polar Research Institute)

(*Above*) Igloo dog kennels on the ice, also known as Dogloos. (*Left*) Frank Wild with his dogs (Royal Geographic Society)

The crew of the *Endurance* poses in front of their trapped ship
(Royal Geographic Society)

Frank Worsley looks back at the *Endurance*. Worsley often accompanied photographer Frank Hurley on his rounds, and was used as a prop in several photographs (Royal Geographic Society)

Tom Crean with his pups Roger, Toby, Nell, and Nelson (Royal Geographic Society)

Perce Blackboro, stowaway, with Mrs. Chippy (Scott Polar Research Institute)

Thomas Orde-Lees, motor expert and storekeeper (Scott Polar Research Institute)

pent-up frustration in his diary, choosing as his target the profanity of his tentmates:

"One would imagine he is in Ratcliff Highway [a nineteenth-century red-light district on the London waterfront] or some other den by the language that is being used. I have been shipmates with all sorts of men both in sail and steam, but never nothing like some of our party—as the most filthy language is used as terms of endearment, and, worse of all, is tolerated."

Shackleton was concerned. Of all their enemies—the cold, the ice, the sea—he feared none more than demoralization. On December 19, he wrote in his diary: "Am thinking of starting off for the west."

The need for action was settled in his mind the next day, and he announced his plan that afternoon. He said that on the following morning, he would go with Wild, Hurley, and Crean's teams to survey the country to the west.

The reaction was immediate. Greenstreet wrote: "The Boss seems keen to try to strike to westward, as we don't make headway as we are. That will mean travelling light and taking only two boats at the most and leaving a lot of provisions behind. As far as I have seen the going will be awful, everything being in a state of softness far worse than when we left the ship, and in my opinion it would be a measure to be taken only as a last resort and I sincerely hope he will give up the idea directly. There have been great arguments about the matter in our tent. . . . "

Indeed there were. Worsley felt much the same way: "My idea is to stay here—unless the drift should become large to the East. . . . The advantages of waiting a little longer are that the drift will convey us part of our journey without any exertion on our part, that probably we should be able to keep 3 boats, and that in the meantime leads may open in the pack."

But a great many others defended Shackleton's decision warmly. As Macklin put it: " . . . personally I think that we ought to push west as hard as we can. We know that there is land 200 miles west, therefore the pack edge should be somewhere about 150–180 miles off in that direction. . . . At our present rate of drift it would take us to the end of March to reach the latitude of Paulet Island, and even then we cannot be certain of breaking out. Consequently my view is, 'Make as hard and as far as possible to the west.' The drift will take us north, and the resulting direction will be NW, the direction in which we want to go. . . . Anyway we will see what they think of things tomorrow."

CHAPTER 6

The inspection party set out at 9 A.M., and the four men were back at three o'clock, having gone a distance of some 6 miles. Shackleton called all hands together at five o'clock and informed them that "we could make progress to the west." He said they would leave about thirty-six hours later, very early on the morning of December 23, and they would travel mostly at night when temperatures would be lower and the ice surface firmer.

Furthermore, he said, since they would be on the trail over Christmas, they would observe the holiday before leaving and all hands could eat everything they wanted for supper and the next day. A great deal of food would have to be left behind anyway.

This last announcement was enough to win over all but the stanchest holdouts against the plan. The Christmas "gorgie" began immediately and lasted almost all the next day, with every man eating all he could hold—"and everybody finishing up feeling full as a tick," Greenstreet remarked.

The men were called at three-thirty the following morning, and they started an hour later. All hands were put on the sledge supporting the *James Caird*, and succeeded in getting it across the open water surrounding their floe. They pushed her until they reached a high pressure ridge; then half the party went to work hacking a way through it, while the others returned for the *Dudley Docker.* The *Stancomb Wills* was to be left behind.

By about 7 A.M., they had relayed the boats more than a mile to the west, and all hands went back to camp to eat breakfast. At nine o'clock, the teams were harnessed and set off toward the boats, pulling all the stores and equipment the sledges could carry. At 1 P.M., the tents were pitched at the new campsite and everybody turned in.

It was dismally wet. The tent floorings the men had devised at Ocean Camp had been left behind. Now they had only canvas ground covers or pieces of sail from the *Endurance,* which offered almost no resistance to the water covering the ice. After a time, Macklin and Worsley gave up trying to sleep in their tent and spread their soaked sleeping bags in the bottom of the *Dudley Docker.* It made a very uncomfortable surface for sleeping, but at least it was relatively dry.

Shackleton summoned Worsley at seven o'clock that evening. He handed him a corked pickle bottle containing a note, and instructed Worsley to return to Ocean Camp with Greenstreet's team and leave it there.

In essence the note said that the *Endurance* had been crushed and abandoned at 69°5′ South, 51°35′ West, and that the members of the Imperial Trans-Antarctic Expedition were then at 67°9′ South, 52°25′ West, and proceeding to the west across the ice in the hope of reaching land. The message concluded: "All well." It was dated December 23, 1915, and signed, "Ernest Shackleton." Worsley placed the bottle with its message in the stern of the *Stancomb Wills* back at Ocean Camp.

The note was very simply a message to posterity, explaining to those who might come after what had happened to Shackleton and his men in 1915. Shackleton had purposely refrained from leaving the note until after the party had left Ocean Camp for fear that the men might find it and interpret it as a sign that their leader was not sure they would survive.

Worsley returned to camp in time for breakfast, and they resumed the journey at 8 P.M. But toward eleven o'clock, after they had made nearly a mile and a half, their way was blocked by a number of large cracks and bits of broken ice. The party pitched the tents at midnight and turned in. Most of the men were soaked through—from the water in which they lay, and from their own sweat. And none of them had a change of clothes except for socks and mittens, so they were forced to crawl into their sleeping bags wearing their soggy garments.

Shackleton went out with a three-man party early the following morning but could find no safe route for the boats. A long, dismal day was spent waiting to see what the ice might do. Just after supper they saw the ice begin to close, but it was not until 3 A.M. the next morning that they were able to get on the trail again.

The pitiful little line of march straggled across the floes in the pale half-light, with Shackleton in the lead, prospecting for the best route. Behind him were the seven sledges pulled by the dogs, keeping a healthy distance apart to avoid a fight between two teams. Next came a small sledge loaded with the blubber stove and cooking gear. It was pulled by Green and Orde-Lees, whose faces from being so close to the stove each day were black with blubber soot. At the rear of the column seventeen men under Worsley's command dragged the boats.

Even at 3 A.M., the coldest time of the day, the surface of the ice was treacherous. A crust had frozen over the rotting, saturated floes, and on top of this there was a layer of snow. The surface had a deceptively sturdy appearance, and at each step, it would seem capable of supporting a man. But just as he shifted his entire weight to that foot, he would burst through the crust with a jarring shock into the numbing water underneath. It was usually knee-deep, sometimes more.

Most of the men wore heavy Burberry-Durox boots—ankle-high leather boots with gaberdine uppers reaching to the knee—designed for marching on hard ice. But as the party struggled over the slushy floes, those boots continually filled with water. In the soaked state, each weighed about 7 pounds. It was an exhausting exertion at every step to lift one foot and then the other out of 2-foot holes full of snowy slush.

Of all the party, the worst off were the men pulling the boats. The shock they suffered at every step was greatly increased by their burden. They could take only about 200 to 300 yards of such punishment at a time. So they would abandon that boat and walk slowly back for the second, trying to catch their breath along the way. Frequently, they would find that the sledge runners under the second boat had frozen into the ice. There was nothing to do but slip into the traces, and then, with Worsley counting, "One, two, three . . . go!" they would make three or four violent, concerted lunges until the runners broke free.

At eight o'clock, after five hours on the trail, Shackleton signaled for a halt. They had covered a miserable half mile. After an hour's rest, they struggled on until noon. The tents were pitched and supper was issued: cold seal steak and tea—nothing more.

On this same night exactly one year before, after a festive dinner on board the *Endurance*, Greenstreet had written in his diary: "Here endeth another Christmas Day. I wonder how and under what circumstances our next one will be spent." That night he failed even to mention what day it was. And Shackleton recorded briefly all that really needed to be said: "Curious Christmas. Thoughts of home."

The men were up at midnight, and resumed the march at 1 A.M. But at five o'clock, after four hours of all-out effort, the column stopped before a line of high pressure ridges and broad leads of water. While the rest of the party waited, Shackleton went out with Wild to look for a more passable route. The two men returned at eight-thirty with news that a half-mile beyond the area of pressure ridges was a floe 2½ miles in diameter, from which they had seen more level floes to the NNW. But they decided to wait until night before pressing on.

Most of the men turned in about noon and slept fitfully in the wet until they were called at 8 P.M. After breakfast, all hands went out along the route that Shackleton and Wild had found. They set to work breaking through the pressure ridges and building a sort of causeway 7 to 8 feet wide at the summit for the boats.

This done, the dog drivers harnessed their teams while Worsley's seventeen boat haulers slipped into their traces, and everyone set off behind Shackleton. At 1:30 A.M., they reached the edge of the big floe discovered the day before. The party camped there long enough to have some tea and a lump of bannock, and then started out again about two o'clock.

Within an hour they had reached the opposite side of the floe, where they encountered another area of high pressure ridges. Never had the going been worse, especially for the men pulling the boats. After two hours of struggling they had covered less than a thousand yards.

McNeish suddenly turned on Worsley and refused to go on. Worsley gave him a direct order to resume his position guiding the rear of the sledge. McNeish refused.

He argued that legally he was under no obligation to follow orders since the ship had gone down, and therefore the articles he had signed to serve on board her had been terminated, and he was free to obey or not, as he chose. It was the "sea lawyer" in him coming out.

Almost from the start of the journey, the old carpenter had been growing increasingly disgruntled. And as the days passed, the strain of the work, coupled with the personal discomfort, had slowly eaten away at what was never an optimistic outlook. For the past two days he had been complaining openly. Now he simply refused to continue.

It was a situation far beyond Worsley's limited abilities as a leader. Had he been a less excitable individual, he might have been able to cope with McNeish. But Worsley himself was almost at the breaking point. He was tired to the marrow of his bones, and he was disgruntled, too. Each day on the march had intensified his feeling that their journey was useless.

So instead of reacting decisively in the face of McNeish's stubbornness, Worsley impulsively notified Shackleton. This served only to aggravate McNeish's resentment.

Shackleton hurried back from the head of the column and took McNeish aside and told him "very strongly" what his duty was. McNeish's contention that the loss of the *Endurance* absolved him of all obligation to obey orders would have been true under ordinary circumstances. The articles signed by the crew are usually terminated automatically if the ship sinks—and their pay stops at the same time. However, a special clause had been inserted in the articles signed by those who sailed aboard the *Endurance*, "to perform any duty on board, in the boats, or on the shore as directed by the master and owner"—Shackleton. They were now, by Shackleton's definition, "on shore."

Quite apart from the legality of it, McNeish's position was absurd. He couldn't continue as a member of the party without doing his share of the work. And if he were to strike out on his own—even assuming Shackleton would permit such a thing—he would be dead in a week. McNeish's one-man mutiny was simply an unreasoning, exhausted protest, called up by an aging and aching body that demanded rest. Even after Shackleton's talk, he remained obstinate. After a time, Shackleton walked away to let the carpenter come to his senses by himself.

At 6 A.M., when they set out again to find a good campsite, McNeish was in his assigned position at the stern of the boat sledge. But the incident had worried Shackleton. In case others might feel similarly, Shackleton mustered all hands before they turned in and read aloud the articles they had signed.

The men slept until eight that night, and they were on the trail an hour later. Though the condition of the ice seemed to get progressively worse, by five-twenty the next morning, after only a one-hour stop for hoosh at 1 A.M., they had covered a gratifying 2½ miles. But Shackleton was uneasy about the condition of the ice, and after camp had been pitched, he went with Hurley's team to survey what lay ahead. The two men reached a fragment of a berg and climbed it. The view from the top justified Shackleton's fears. He could see 2 miles ahead, and the ice was truly impassable—criss-crossed by leads of open water and the jumbled remains of broken pressure ridges. Moreover, it was dangerously thin. The two men returned to camp about seven o'clock and Shackleton reluctantly announced that they could not go any farther. Most of the men received the news with dismay. Not that they hadn't expected it, but to hear Shackleton himself say that they had been beaten sounded almost unnatural—and a little frightening.

None of them, however, could possibly have felt their defeat so intensely as Shackleton, to whom the thought of quitting was abhorrent. He wrote in his diary that night, with characteristically peculiar punctuation: "Turned in but could not sleep. Thought the whole matter over & decided to retreat to more secure ice: it is the only safe thing to do. . . . Am anxious: For so big a party & 2 boats in bad conditions we could do nothing: I do not like retreating but prudence demands this course: Everyone working well except the carpenter: I shall never forget him in this time of strain & stress."

The retreat began at seven that night. They made their way back about a quarter mile to a fairly solid floe, and pitched camp. All hands were called early the next morning. Most of the men were sent out to hunt seals while Shackleton and Hurley prospected for a route to the northeast, and Worsley went with McIlroy's team to look for a way to the south. Neither party found a route that was safe.

Shackleton had noticed some breaking up of the ice around them. As soon as he returned to camp, he ordered the recall flag hoisted at once to summon the seal hunting parties. Then once more the party retreated, this time about a half mile to a very flat, heavy floe. Even here they were not safe. A snow-filled crack was discovered in the ice the following morning, so they shifted camp about 150 yards toward the center of the floe in search of fairly stable ice. But there wasn't any to be found.

Worsley described the situation: "All the floes in the neighborhood appear to be saturated by the sea to the very surface, so much that on cutting 1 inch below the surface of a 6 or 7 feet thick floe, water almost at once flows into the hole."

But what disturbed them most was that they were trapped where they were. Greenstreet explained that "it looks as if we can get no further and we can't get back to Ocean Camp either as the floes have disintegrated considerably since we passed [over] them."

The following day was December 31. McNeish wrote: "Hogmany [the Scottish feast of New Year's] & a bitter one too, being adrift on the ice instead of enjoying the pleasures of life like most people. But as the saying is, there must be some fools in this world."

James recorded: "New Year's Eve, the second in the pack & in much the same latitude. Few people are having a stranger one. . . . "

Macklin noted: "The last day of 1915 . . . tomorrow 1916 begins: I wonder what it will bring forth for us. This time last year we prophesied that just now we would be well across the Continent."

Finally, Shackleton wrote: "The last day of the old year: May the new one bring us good fortune, a safe deliverance from this anxious time & all good things to those we love so far away."

PART III

CHAPTER I

Worsley named the place "Mark Time Camp," but it didn't seem an especially appropriate name. It implied that they had halted only temporarily, and would soon be on the move again. But nobody really believed they would.

After five days of exhausting struggle, they were suddenly idle. Now there was almost nothing to do, except to think. And there was altogether too much time for that.

Many of them, it seemed, finally grasped for the first time just how desperate things really were. More correctly, they became aware of their own inadequacy, of how utterly powerless they were. Until the march from Ocean Camp they had nurtured in the backs of their minds the attitude Shackleton strove so unceasingly to imbue them with, a basic faith in themselves—that they could, if need be, pit their strength and their determination against any obstacle—and somehow overcome it.

But then came the march, a journey which was to carry them nearly 200 miles. Yet after only five days and 9 small miles in a straight line to the northwest, they had been stopped completely, and even forced to retreat. A gale could easily have carried them that far in twenty-four hours. So now they sat in Mark Time Camp, disillusioned and humbly aware how truly pygmy they were to overcome the forces they faced, regardless of how much strength and determination they put forth. The realization was not so much humiliating as frightening.

Their ultimate goal was still to get themselves out, but now it was an empty phrase. They wouldn't get themselves out. Only if the pack chose, they might be permitted to escape, but for the present they were powerless; there was no goal, not even the smallest achievable objective to aim for. They were faced with total uncertainty. Their position was if anything worse than it had been. They had abandoned a goodly quantity of stores, along with one of their boats. And while the floe they were camped on was adequate, it was no match for the giant back at Ocean Camp.

"It is beginning to be an anxious time for us," Macklin wrote on New Year's Day, "for so far there is not much sign of any opening of the floe, and the broken mushy stuff is quite un-navigable for our boats. If we cannot get away very soon our position will be a very serious one, for if it comes to travelling in the autumn to Paulet by sledge, where will we get food for the dogs and food for ourselves, supposing the depot at Paulet fails us? The seals will have disappeared for the winter, and we may have to undergo some of the trials of Greely."*

Many of them made a sincere effort to be cheerful, but without much success. There was little to be cheerful about. The temperature remained just about at the freezing point, so that during the day the surface of the floes became a bog. They had to trudge about through knee-deep slush, and a man would often plunge up to his waist into an unsuspected hole. Their clothes were thus continually soaked, and their only comfort was crawling into

---

*The American explorer Adolphous Greely spent the years 1881–1884 in the Arctic. Seventeen of his twenty-four men died of starvation when their relief ship failed to reach them.

the comparatively bearable dampness of their sleeping bags each night.

The food situation was also far from reassuring. There remained only fifty days' full trail provisions at 2 pounds per man—and the time when they would have looked upon such a supply as ample to see them out of the pack was long since past. They could hope to supplement their stores with seals and penguins, but there was disappointingly little game available—nowhere near as much as they had expected for this time of year. But on January 1, it seemed that the New Year might have brought with it a change of luck. Five crabeater seals and an emperor penguin were killed and brought into camp.

Returning from a hunting trip, Orde-Lees, traveling on skis across the rotting surface of the ice, had just about reached camp when an evil, knoblike head burst out of the water just in front of him. He turned and fled, pushing as hard as he could with his ski poles and shouting for Wild to bring his rifle.

The animal—a sea leopard—sprang out of the water and came after him, bounding across the ice with the peculiar rocking-horse gait of a seal on land. The beast looked like a small dinosaur, with a long, serpentine neck.

After a half-dozen leaps, the sea leopard had almost caught up with Orde-Lees when it unaccountably wheeled and plunged again into the water. By then, Orde-Lees had nearly reached the opposite side of the floe; he was about to cross to safe ice when the sea leopard's head exploded out of the water directly ahead of him. The animal had tracked his shadow across the ice. It made a savage lunge for Orde-Lees with its mouth open, revealing an enormous array of sawlike teeth. Orde-Lees' shouts for help rose to screams and he turned and raced away from his attacker.

The animal leaped out of the water again in pursuit just as Wild arrived with his rifle. The sea leopard spotted Wild, and turned to attack him. Wild dropped to one knee and fired again and again at the onrushing beast. It was less than 30 feet away when it finally dropped.

Two dog teams were required to bring the carcass into camp. It measured 12 feet long, and they estimated its weight at about 1,100 pounds. It was a predatory species of seal, and resembled a leopard only in its spotted coat—and its disposition. When it was butchered, balls of hair 2 and 3 inches in diameter were found in its stomach—the remains of crabeater seals it had eaten. The sea leopard's jawbone, which measured nearly 9 inches across, was given to Orde-Lees as a souvenir of his encounter.

In his diary that night, Worsley observed: "A man on foot in soft, deep snow and unarmed would not have a chance against such an animal as they almost bound along with a rearing, undulating motion at least five miles an hour. They attack without provocation, looking on man as a penguin or seal."

The hunting parties continued to operate the next day, though the warm, muggy weather kept the surface of the ice soggy. Four crabeater seals were secured and returned to camp. While they were being butchered, Orde-Lees came back from a trip on skis and announced that he had found and killed three more. But Shackleton contended that the party already had a month's supply, and ordered that the slain seals be left where they were.

Several men found Shackleton's attitude difficult to understand. Greenstreet wrote that he considered it "rather foolish . . . as things have not turned out at all as he had estimated up to the present, and it is far the best to be prepared for the possible chance of having to winter here."

Greenstreet was right. Like most of the others, he considered the laying in of all possible meat the prudent thing to do, as any ordinary individual might. But Shackleton was not an ordinary individual. He was a man who believed completely in his own invincibility, and to whom defeat was a reflection of personal inadequacy. What might have been an act of reasonable caution to the average person was to Shackleton a detestable admission that failure was a possibility.

This indomitable self-confidence of Shackleton's took the form of optimism. And it worked in two ways: it set men's souls on fire; as Macklin said, just to be in his presence was an experience. It was what made Shackleton so great a leader.

But at the same time, the basic egotism that gave rise to his enormous self-reliance occasionally blinded him to realities. He tacitly expected those around him to reflect his own extreme optimism, and he could be almost petulant if they failed to do so. Such an attitude, he felt, cast doubt on him and his ability to lead them to safety.

Thus it was that the simple suggestion of bringing in three seals could be, to Shackleton's mind, an act of disloyalty. At another time he might have overlooked the incident. But just now he was hypersensitive. Almost everything he had undertaken— the expedition, saving the *Endurance*, and two attempted marches to safety—had failed miserably. In addition, the lives of twenty-seven other men were in his hands. "I am rather tired," he wrote one day. "I suppose it is the strain." Then later, "I long for some rest, free from thought."

Matters did not improve during the next several days. The weather continued to deteriorate, which seemed hardly possible. Daytime temperatures climbed as high as 37 degrees, with long periods of wet snow falling, mixed with rain, "a regular Scotch mist," Worsley called it. There was little for them to do but lie in their tents, trying to sleep, playing cards—or simply thinking about how hungry they were.

"A skua gull appeared," wrote Macklin. "He settled down on our refuse pit—entrails of seals, etc.—and gorged himself to his hearts content—lucky gull."

James, in Shackleton's tent, "did some physics trying to recall some of my theory work," but soon tired of it. The occupants of

Wild's tent had to shift their sleeping bags because the heat from their bodies was melting the snow, robbing them of this last bit of comfort offered by a dry place to sleep. Even Hussey's banjo lost its appeal for some. McNeish complained: "Hussey is at present tormenting [us] with his six known tunes on his banjo."

Shackleton recorded on January 9: "I am growing anxious now with all this party." And well he might have been. For almost a month, there had been no wind stronger than a breeze, and even this had been mostly from the north. And during the past week they had killed only two seals. They thus remained almost motionless, while their supply of meat dwindled alarmingly. Shackleton's contention that it would last a month proved grossly exaggerated. After only ten days at Mark Time Camp, the strain was beginning to tell. Greenstreet wrote: "The monotony of life here is getting on our nerves. Nothing to do, nowhere to walk, no change in surroundings, food or anything. God send us open water soon or we shall go balmy."

Then on January 13, a rumor spread that Shackleton was considering killing the dogs to ease the drain on the food supplies. Among the men, reactions ranged from simple resignation to outraged shock. Stormy debates on the value of the dogs against the food they consumed broke out in each tent that night. But the fundamental, underlying factor in these discussions was that, for many men, the dogs were more than so many pounds of pulling power on the trail; there was a deep emotional attachment involved. It was the basic human need to love something, the desire to express tenderness in this barren place. Though the dogs were vicious, surly beasts with one another, their devotion and loyalty toward the men was above question. And the men responded with an affection greatly surpassing anything they would have felt under ordinary circumstances.

At the thought of losing Grus, a puppy born a year before on the *Endurance*, Macklin reflected: "He is a fine little dog, hardworking and of a good disposition. Also I have had him, fed him and trained him since he was born. I remember taking him out when he was a puppy in my pocket, only his nose peeping out and getting covered with frost. I used to take him on the sledge when I was driving the team, and in those early days he used to take an active interest in the doings of the dogs."

Under the best circumstances it would have been upsetting news. Under their present circumstances it was amplified in the minds of some men almost to a catastrophe. In their bitterness, a few, like Greenstreet, were inclined to fix the blame on Shackleton—with some justification: " . . . the present shortage of food," Greenstreet wrote, "is due simply and solely from the Boss refusing to get seals when they were to be had and even refusing to let Orde-Lees to go out to look for them. . . . His sublime optimism all the way thro being to my mind absolute foolishness. Everything right away thro was going to turn out all right and no notice was taken of things possibly turning out otherwise and here we are."

Shackleton made no mention of killing the dogs the next morning. Instead he ordered the men to shift camp because their floe was melting at a dangerous rate. The soot from the blubber stove had been tracked all over the surface of the ice, and it was holding the heat of the sun. The men began at noon to construct a roadway of blocks of ice and snow to bridge the gap to a floe about 150 yards to the southeast. The move was completed early in the afternoon. They named their new location "Patience Camp."

Then, in a quiet, level voice, Shackleton ordered Wild to shoot his own team along with McIlroy's, Marston's, and Crean's.

There was no protest, no argument. The four drivers obediently harnessed their teams and drove the dogs about a quarter of a mile away from the camp. The drivers then returned alone, except for McIlroy; he and Macklin were to assist Wild.

Each dog in turn was taken off his trace and led behind a row of large ice hummocks. There Wild sat the animal in the snow, took the muzzle in his left hand, and placed his revolver close to its head. Death was instantaneous.

After each dog had been killed Macklin and McIlroy dragged its body a short distance away, then returned to the waiting teams for the next animal. None of the dogs seemed to sense what was happening, and each went unsuspectingly around the ice hummock to his death with his tail wagging. When the job was done, the three men piled snow on top of the heap of dog bodies and walked slowly back to camp.

Shackleton decided to spare Greenstreet's team of year-old puppies "for the present," and he also granted a one-day reprieve to Hurley's and Macklin's teams so that they might be used to make a trip back to Ocean Camp for some of the food that had been left there.

The two sledges were made ready, and Hurley and Macklin started off at six-thirty that evening. It was an exhausting journey, lasting almost ten hours because they had to travel mostly over deep, soft snow and broken ice, and the dogs sank down to their bellies.

As Macklin wrote later: "The going was so bad that they could not pull my weight, and I had to get off and flounder along beside the sledges. The dogs too kept falling back, and as soon as one dog collapsed or let his weight come on to the trace the whole line stopped. On these occasions they all lay down, and only violent abuse and vigorous treatment had any effect in raising them. Several pressure ridges had to be broken with pick and shovel. Finally with all the dogs dead beat we crawled into Ocean Camp about 4 A.M."

They found the place almost under water. To get into the galley where the stores were they had to lay down a bridge of planks. However, they managed to collect two loads of about 500 pounds apiece, consisting of canned vegetables, tapioca, dog pemmican, and jam. They prepared themselves a good meal of canned stew, fed the dogs, and started back at 6:30 A.M.

The return journey was comparatively easy because they had their own tracks to follow. The dogs pulled magnificently, though old Bos'n, Macklin's leader, was so exhausted he repeatedly vomited and staggered badly. The two sledges reached Patience Camp at one in the afternoon, and the dogs "dropped in the snow," Macklin recorded, "some of them not even rousing themselves to take their food."

Lying in his sleeping bag that night, Macklin wearily recorded the events of the journey in his diary. In a tired hand he concluded the entry: "My dogs will be shot tomorrow."

CHAPTER 2

Two tents away, old Chippy McNeish was also writing his diary. It had been a discouraging day of muggy, dead-calm weather and the carpenter was tired. Since early morning he had been busy coating the seams of the boats with seal blood to keep the calking in once they were in the water. "No wind of any kind," he wrote. "We are still in hope of a sw breeze to relieve us before the winter sets in."

The next morning, three seals were sighted, and Macklin was sent out with Tom Crean to fetch them. When they returned, Shackleton told Macklin that since the party now had a fair supply of meat, his dogs would not be killed quite yet. Hurley's team though, including the leader, Shakespeare, the biggest of all the dogs, was shot. Wild, as usual, was executioner, and he took the dogs over to a distant floe to kill them. Macklin later found one of the dogs still alive, and immediately took out his knife and stabbed the animal to death.

About 3 P.M., the wind gently eased around to the southwest, and a chill came into the air. Throughout the night the temperature crept downward, and all the next day the southwest breeze held steady. That night Shackleton wrote, almost timorously, "This may be the turn in our fortune." By now the wind was not taken lightly. "It is spoken of with reverence," Hurley observed, "and wood must be touched when commenting thereon."

Somebody, it appeared, had touched the proper piece of wood. The wind came on the next day, a whole gale out of the southwest, with driving snow filling the air and the tents quaking with its violence. They huddled in their sleeping bags, dismally uncomfortable but radiantly happy. "Fifty miles an hour," McNeish recorded blissfully, "but it is welcome & as much more—as long as the tents stand." It howled on into January 19 unabated. Shackleton, the man of unbridled optimism, confined himself to guarded phrases lest he somehow hex this glorious wind. "We ought to be making North some now," he said with the utmost restraint.

On the twentieth, as the gale continued, a very few of them began to tire of the wet from the wind-driven snow filtering into the tents. "We are never satisfied," Hurley wrote, "as we are looking forward to a fine day. Our gear in the tents is becoming very wet and the opportunity of drying same will be hailed."

But most of them cheerfully endured the dreadful conditions, happy in the knowledge that they must be making good progress to the north.

"One hardly likes to guess what our distance may be," Shackleton wrote, more boldly, "but tonight is the fourth of this blow and there are no signs of it abating so we ought to have made a good distance to the North. Lees & Worsley are the only pessimistic ones in the camp but this strong wind even made Lees suggest larger steaks on the strength of our distance."

The next day the gale roared on, with a few gusts to 70 miles an hour. But twice during the morning the sun broke through the clouds. Worsley was ready with his sextant, and James stood by with his theodolite to catch the angle of the sun. They took their sights, worked out the calculations, and announced the result.

"Wonderful, amazing splendid," Shackleton wrote. "Lat. 65°43′ South—73 miles North drift. The most cheerful good fortune for a year for us: We cannot be much more than 170 miles from Paulet. Everyone greeted the news with cheers. The wind still continues. We may get another 10 miles out of it. Thank God. Drifting still all wet in the tents but no matter. Had bannock to celebrate North of the circle." The Antarctic Circle now lay nearly a full degree of latitude behind them.

The gale eased down the following day, and the sun shone brightly. All hands emerged from their tents, glad to be alive. They took oars from the boats and drove them into the ice, rigged lines between them, and hung up sleeping bags, blankets, boots, and floor cloths. "One would have thought it our washing day," McNeish reported cheerfully.

Later in the day, Worsley got another sight which put their position at 65°32½′ South, 52°4′ West—11 miles north in twenty-four hours. It brought the total run since the beginning of the gale to 84 miles—in six days. Furthermore, the drift to the east, away from land, amounted to only a paltry 15 miles.

By evening the gale had blown itself out and the wind shifted to the north. But nobody minded. A northerly wind was just what they needed to open up the pack so that they could take to the boats. The wind continued into the next day without loosening the pack perceptibly. They waited.

The following day Worsley climbed to the top of a 60-foot berg a short distance to the southeast. He returned with the news that the floe on which Ocean Camp had stood had apparently been blown closer during the gale and was now only about 5 miles away. Through the glasses, he had seen the old wheelhouse storeroom and the third boat, the *Stancomb Wills*. What about open water? Worsley shook his head. None, he said, except a small patch far to the south.

Still the opening would come—it was bound to. A heavy mist rolled in on January 25, and to McNeish it was a "proper sea fog," indicating the presence of the ice-free ocean nearby. Shackleton, too, thought it must be a sea fog. But the opening still did not come, and the Boss felt his patience growing thin. On the twenty-sixth, after a day of unrelieved monotony, he took his diary and wrote across the space provided for that day:

Waiting
Waiting
Waiting.

But by the time a week had passed, most of the men were abandoning their hopes. They could see almost no change in the pack. If anything it was tighter than before, packed together by the force of the winds, perhaps driven against some unknown land to the north or northwest. The sense of immediacy gradually diminished, and the atmosphere in camp settled once more into reluctant resignation.

Fortunately, the men were kept fairly well occupied. At their new position, game was abundant, and all hands were busy hunting seals and sledging them into camp. By January 30, eight days after the gale ended, they had laid in a stock of eleven seals. Shackleton decided to send Macklin's and Greenstreet's teams on another trip to Ocean Camp. Since Greenstreet, who had been suffering an attack of rheumatism for about two weeks, could not make the trip, his team was assigned to Crean. The two men were instructed to bring back anything of value they could find.

This time sledging conditions were considerably better and the trip took less than ten hours. The teams returned with some odds and ends of stores, including a quantity of canned herring, 60 pounds of boullion cubes, and a large amount of tobacco. They also obtained a good number of books, among them several volumes of the *Encyclopaedia Britannica,* which were especially welcome. Even McNeish, a devout Presbyterian, allowed as how he would enjoy a change from his Bible, which he had repeatedly reread from cover to cover.

For the next two days, Shackleton carefully observed the movements of the pack, and then he decided that a party of eighteen under Wild should start out early the next morning to bring up the *Stancomb Wills*. The news came as a great relief. For some time many of the men, particularly the seamen, had had strong misgivings about the advisability of trying to crowd the entire party into two boats.

"I am very glad," Worsley wrote. "If it comes to boats we shall be far safer in three; with only two it would be a practical impossibility to bring 28 men alive through a boat voyage of any length."

The sledging party was awakened at 1 A.M. the next morning, and after a good heavy breakfast they started off, dragging an empty boat sledge with them. It was an easy journey with so many men, and they arrived two hours and ten minutes later. Wild appointed Hurley cook, with James as his "mate and general hoosh stirrer." They put together a meal of anything they could find, and it wound up a mixture of dog pemmican, baked beans, and canned cauliflower and beets, cooked together in an empty gasoline can. Macklin pronounced it "very good," and James remarked with satisfaction that it was a "great success."

The party started back for Patience Camp at 6:30 A.M., and while the going was considerably heavier, they made good progress. They were within a mile of their goal by noon. Shackleton and Hussey went out to meet them with a pot of hot tea—"the most welcome tea I ever had," James reported. The *Stancomb Wills* was safe in camp by one o'clock.

Shackleton immediately asked Macklin if he felt too tired to go back again to Ocean Camp, this time with his team, to bring up a further load of supplies. Macklin agreed, and set off at

3 P.M., with Worsley and Crean, who had taken over the puppy team. Less than 2 miles from Ocean Camp, they were stopped by large leads of open water. Worsley tried desperately to talk the sledge men into pressing on. He ran up and down along the edges of the floes, pointing out possible ways to get across which were really "quite impossible," Macklin said. "I was sorry for him, but it would have been foolish to have continued under the circumstances."

Worsley wrote in his diary that night how disappointed he was that they had been forced to turn back, but added: "I was very pleased that the Pack had kept solid long enough to bring our third boat across."

He also noted: "I think many of our stomachs are rebelling against the excessive meat diet. I expect we will soon get used to it, but I think it would be better for us if we cooked some blubber with it. A good many of us suffer from, to put it mildly, flatulence, & what might almost be described as squeaky gut." Actually it was not a humorous matter. As a result of their short rations, almost all of the men were constipated, which complicated what was already a very disagreeable chore. The usual procedure, whenever a man felt the need, was to go off behind a nearby pressure ridge—more for protection against the weather than for privacy—and get the job done as quickly as possible. Since one of the items they had been forced to do without since abandoning the *Endurance* was toilet paper, they had to substitute the only disposable material at hand—ice. Thus, almost all of them were badly chafed, and unfortunately treatment was impossible since all the ointments and most of the medicines were now at the bottom of the Weddell Sea.

In cold weather they were also greatly troubled with their eyes watering. The tears ran down a man's nose and formed an icicle on the end, which sooner or later had to be broken off. And no matter how carefully it was done, a little patch of skin invariably came off with it, leaving a chronically unhealed sore on the end of his nose.

The trip to Ocean Camp to bring up the *Stancomb Wills* changed the attitude of many men. Until then some vestige of anticipation that the pack might open had remained. But they had observed during the 12-mile round-trip journey to Ocean Camp that the ice was tighter than ever. The days of wishful thinking were over; there was nothing to do but sit down and wait.

Day after day after day dragged by in a gray, monotonous haze. The temperatures were high and the winds were light. Most of the men would have liked to sleep the time away, but there was a limit to the number of hours a man could spend inside his sleeping bag. Every available time-killing pastime was exploited to the fullest and often much beyond. On February 6, James wrote: "Hurley & Boss play religiously a set of six games of poker patience every afternoon. I think each rather regards it a duty but it certainly passes away an hour. The worst thing is having to kill time. It seems such a waste, yet there is nothing else to do."

Each day became so much like the one before that any unusual occurrence, however small, generated enormous interest.

"We got quite homesick tonight," James wrote on the eighth, "at the smell of a piece of burning twig which we found [in some old seaweed]. Any new smell or a smell bringing old associations appeals to us in a wonderful way. Probably we smell a little ourselves & would be very noticeable to strangers since it is nearly four months since we had a bath. . . . "

"Just now," he continued, "we regard the panels of our tent most earnestly to see which bellies out under the influence of the wind . . . I long for a place where the direction of the wind does not matter a Tinker's cuss."

"We also suffer from '*Amenomania*'" [literally—wind-madness], he wrote later. "This disease may be exhibited in two forms: Either one is morbidly anxious about the wind direction and gibbers continually about it, or else a sort of lunacy is produced by listening to the other *Amenomaniacs*. The second form is more trying to hear. I have had both."

Only one topic other than the wind was sure to spark a discussion—food. Early in February they had gone for almost two weeks without getting a seal, and while their meat supply was not yet too small, their stock of blubber for cooking was alarmingly low—only about enough for ten more days. On February 9, Shackleton wrote: "No seals. Must reduce blubber consumption . . . oh for a touch of dry land under our feet."

The following day, a party of men were set to digging into the snow-covered refuse heap to recover all possible blubber from the bones there. Seal flippers were cut up, and the decapitated heads of seals were skinned and scraped of every trace of blubber they would yield. But the amount obtained was insignificant, so Shackleton reduced their ration to one warm beverage a day—a serving of hot powdered milk at breakfast. The last of their cheese was served out the next day, and each man received a 1-inch cube. McNeish commented: "I smoked myself sick through trying to stifle the hunger this afternoon."

They had looked forward to Shackleton's birthday on February 15, when a good meal had been promised them, "But owing to lack," Macklin wrote, "we cannot have it. We are going to have a bannock made with flour and dog pemmican, and are looking forward to it."

Then on the morning of February 17, as the blubber situation was becoming really desperate, somebody saw a flock of little Adélie penguins—about twenty altogether—sunning themselves a short distance from camp. A score of men seized any weapons that were handy—axe handles, picks, lengths of broken oars— and crept cautiously along almost on their hands and knees. They stealthily surrounded the flock, cutting off their escape into the water. When everybody was in position, the men rushed forward, clubbing furiously at the squawking, skittering Adélies. They secured seventeen penguins in all. Other little bands were sighted during the morning, and parties of men were sent out to get them. Before a dense fog rolled in early in the afternoon, they had a total of sixty-nine penguins. Later in the day, as they sat in their fog-shrouded tents, the men could hear Adélies in every direction, calling and quarreling in their raucous voices. "Had the weather been clear," Worsley wrote, "we probably would have seen hundreds."

Despite the welcome addition to their larder, supper that night was frugal, consisting, McNeish noted, of "stewed penguin heart, liver, eyes, tongues, toes & God knows what else, with a cup of water" to wash it down. "I don't think any of us will have nightmares from over-eating."

After supper, a northeast gale came up, with heavy snow falling. It continued the next day, forcing the men to remain inside their tents. But all the while the croaking of Adélies continued. The weather finally cleared on February 20, and as soon as it was light, the men emerged from their tents—and it seemed almost as if it were in the midst of an Adélie rookery. Thousands of penguins dotted the pack in every direction, strutting around the floes, frolicking in the water, and making a frightful racket. The penguins must have been migrating north, and Patience Camp fortunately lay in the path of their trek.

All hands were put to the slaughter, bringing in every penguin that could be reached. By nightfall, they had killed, skinned, gutted, and cut up 300 Adélies. The following morning the men saw that the migration had moved on as suddenly as it had arrived. But though only about 200 penguins were observed during the day, the men managed to kill about fifty. For several days afterwards, small bands of stragglers continued to appear, and by February 24 the party had secured a total of nearly 600. The Adélie, however, is a small and not very meaty bird, so that the amount of food obtained was not nearly so impressive as might be supposed. Futhermore there is very little blubber on an Adélie.

Nevertheless, the sudden appearance of the Adélies had removed, for the moment, the most serious threat they faced—starvation. And with starvation no longer an immediate danger, their thoughts inevitably turned once more to their ultimate escape.

Greenstreet observed: "The food now is pretty well all meat. Seal steaks, stewed seal, penguin steaks, stewed penguin, penguin liver, the latter being very good indeed. The cocoa has been finished for some time and the tea is very nearly done and soon our only beverage will be [powdered] milk. Flour also is very nearly finished and is now used only with dog pemmican in the making of bannocks, which are damn fine. Our distance from Paulet I. is now 94 miles which means we have completed ¾ of the distance we had to do when we got on the floe. I wonder if we shall ever get there."

Macklin noted: "We have just been a third of a year on the floe, drifting as Nature has willed. I wonder when we shall see home again."

And James, ever the scientist, put it into laboratory terms: "We make all kinds of theories based sometimes on what we see about us of ice conditions, but more of this based on nothing at all. Can't help thinking of 'Theory of Relativity.' Anyhow we have only an horizon of a few miles & the Weddell Sea is roughly 200,000 sq. miles [actually it is closer to 900,000 square miles]. A bug on a single molecule of oxygen in a gale of wind would have about the same chance of predicting where he was likely to finish up."

CHAPTER 3

It had been slightly more than a month since the end of the southerly gale. They had covered 68 miles, for an average daily drift of a little more than 2 miles. The over-all direction was northwest, but the day-by-day drift was an erratic, pattern-less movement, sometimes northwest, sometimes due west, even south, and, for a time, straight north. But they were definitely approaching the end of the Palmer Peninsula.

Worsley spent long, cold hours every day atop a small berg fragment looking anxiously to the west, hoping to sight land. On February 26, he saw "what may be Mount Haddington thrown up by refraction, 20 miles beyond its ordinary limits."

They wanted to believe it, but few of them did, least of all McNeish. "The skipper says he has seen it," he wrote, "but we know him to be a liar." Worsley was guilty of a bit of wishful thinking. Mount Haddington on James Ross Island lay more than 110 miles west of their position.

The year 1916 happened to be a leap year, and Shackleton seized the feeble excuse offered by February 29 to boost the men's morale. They celebrated a "Bachelor's Feast" with a very sparing "gorgie." "For the first time for many days," said Greenstreet, "I have finished a meal without wanting to start all over again."

And so they drifted into March. On the fifth, Greenstreet wrote: "Day passes day with very little or nothing to relieve the monotony. We take constitutionals round and round the floe but no one can go further as we are to all intents and purposes on an island. There is practically nothing fresh to read and nothing to talk about, all topics being absolutely exhausted. . . . I never know what day of the week it is except when it is Sunday as we have Adélie liver and bacon for lunch and is the great meal of the week and soon I shall not be able to know Sunday as our bacon will soon be finished. The pack around looks very much as it did four or five months ago and with the low temperature we have been getting at night, i.e., zero and below, the open patches of water get covered with young ice which is neither fit to go over nor would allow the passage of the boats. My opinion is that the chances of getting to Paulet Is. now are about 1 in 10. . . . "

Indeed, the chances of reaching Paulet Island did appear more remote each day. It now lay exactly 91 miles away. But it was off to the WNW, and their drift had steadied onto a course almost true north. Unless there was a radical change in the northerly movement of the pack, it seemed that they would simply pass Paulet Island by. And there was nothing they could do about it, except to wait helplessly.

Shackleton was just as hard put to find ways to pass the time as everyone else. His tentmate, James, noticed on March 6 that "the boss has just discovered a new use for blubber and is industriously cleaning the backs of our cards with it. These playing cards have got so dirty that some are almost unrecognizable. The blubber, however, cleans it all off again. Truly, the seal is a useful beast."

Worst of all were the days of bad weather. There was nothing then to do but stay inside the tents. And to avoid tracking snow inside the men restricted exits and entries to those "who must answer nature's call." March 7 was such a day, with a strong southwest breeze blowing and heavy snow falling. Macklin described conditions in No. 5 tent: " . . . there are eight of us living in it, packed like sardines. . . . Clark has an almost intolerable sniff—he sniffs the whole day long and almost drives one mad when one has to remain inside with him. Lees and Worsley do nothing but argue and chatter about trivial matters, and the rest of us can do nothing to escape from it. Lees at night snores abominably, and also Clark and Blackboro, but not so badly . . . at times like this, with Clark sniff-sniffing into my ear, my only relief is to take up my diary and write. . . . "

Then, on March 9, they felt the swell—the undeniable, unmistakable rise and fall of the ocean. There was no wishful thinking this time. It was there for all to see, and feel, and hear.

They noticed it first early in the morning as a strange, rhythmic creaking in the pack. The men gathered outside their tents and looked, and they could see it. The loose chunks of ice around the floe drew apart and closed again, 4 to 6 inches at a time. The large floes rose almost imperceptibly—not more than an inch—then ever so slowly, fell again.

The men stood in excited little groups, pointing out to one another what was perfectly obvious to everyone—a gentle, lazy movement across the entire surface of the pack. Some pessimist suggested that it could be a tidal seiche or rise, caused by a local atmospheric condition. But Worsley took his chronometer out to the edge of the floe and timed the interval between swells—eighteen seconds, much too short to be a tidal seiche. There was no doubt—it was the swell from the open sea.

But how far away was it? That was the question. "How far," James pondered, "can the swell make itself felt through the dense pack. Our experience suggests not far, but of course we never examined the ice with the minuteness approaching that which we employ now. . . . "

Long, speculative discussions were held all day as Worsley crouched by the edge of the floe and continued to time the infinitely slow rise and fall of the ice. By evening everyone was satisfied that the open ocean lay, at most, 30 miles away. Shackleton alone seemed to sense in the swell a new and far more grave threat than almost any they had faced. He wrote that night: "Trust will not increase until leads form."

He knew there could be no escape if the swells were to increase while the pack remained closed. The action of the sea would then crack and break the floes, ultimately grinding the ice to bits on which they could not camp, and through which they could not sail.

Before he turned in, Shackleton took one final look around the camp to satisfy himself that the tents and boats were not so close together that their combined weight might in itself crack the floe. A further advantage of this precaution was that, while their equipment was spread out over a large area, they were not likely to lose a sizable amount of gear into a crack.

The men crawled out of their tents the next morning expecting to see that the swell had increased. Instead, there wasn't the slightest suggestion of movement in the pack, and the ice was as close as ever. A disappointment amounting to grief swept through most of the party. The first real sign of the open sea, the tantalizing promise of escape for which they had waited so long, had been dangled in front of them briefly—then snatched away.

That afternoon Shackleton ordered a drill to see how quickly the boats could be removed from their sledges and loaded with stores in case of an emergency. The men did what they had to do, but the raw edge of their tempers was beginning to show and there were a number of savage exchanges. Nor were matters improved when the stores were placed in the boats, and everybody could see for himself just how pitifully small their supplies really were. Certainly overloading was not going to be one of their problems. After the drill, the men returned moodily to their tents, hardly speaking to one another.

"Nothing to do, see or say," James recorded. "We find our-selves getting more taciturn daily."

Until the appearance of the swell, many of the men had strug-gled for months not to let hope creep into their minds. For the most part, they had convinced themselves not only that the party would have to winter on the floes—but even that such a fate would be quite endurable.

But then came the swell—the physical proof that there really was something outside this limitless prison of ice. And all the defenses they had so carefully constructed to prevent hope from entering their minds collapsed. Macklin, who had consistently struggled to remain hard-headedly pessimistic, found it impossi-ble to hold out any longer. He let himself go on March 13, say-ing, "I am absolutely obsessed with the idea of escaping . . . We have been over 4 months on the floe—a time of absolute and ut-ter inutility to anyone. There is absolutely nothing to do but kill time as best one may. Even at home, with theatres and all sorts of amusements, changes of scene and people, four months idleness would be tedious: One can then imagine how much worse it is for us. One looks forward to meals, not for what one will get, but as definite breaks in the day. All around us we have day after day the same unbroken whiteness, unrelieved by anything at all."

A sense of mounting desperation began to infect them. James wrote on the following day: "Something decisive must occur soon & what ever it may be will be preferable to continued inactiv-ity. This is our fifth month since our ship wreck. When we left we were going to be ashore in a month! 'Man proposes————'* applies here with a vengence."

Even the southerly gale that blew up that afternoon, did lit-tle to raise their spirits. They all found it increasingly difficult to

---

*For some reason, James omitted the last portion of the quotation: "Man proposes, God disposes."

endure the hardships such a gale brought with it—even though they knew, as Worsley put it, that "we are probably hurtling to the NORTH at the incredible speed of 1 mile an hour!"

The squalls in the gale, Worsley continued, "tear and haul at our flimsy tent as though they would burst it to tatters. It rattles, flaps and trembles incessantly. . . . So thin is the material that the smoke from our pipes and cigarettes eddies, swirls and sways about with every gust of the wind outside."

Each hour of the night, one man left to take up his watch and another returned, crawling into the tent and then trying to brush off the snow in the pitch blackness before making his way to his sleeping bag. Invariably, the returning watchman awakened most of the other men. How could one sleep, said Worsley, through such things as "snow on your face, feet on your tummy, the low pitched thunder of the wind, the drumming of the tent or the raucous bellow of the Colonel's snore?"

That night, as the gale howled across the pack, pushing them north, James observed darkly: "Paulet Island probably already to the South of us."

CHAPTER 4

To make matters worse, the problem of food—especially blubber for cooking—was again approaching the critical point. It was three weeks since they had killed a seal, and the meager store of blubber from the Adélies was almost gone. Their stock of provisions from the ship was also nearly exhausted. On March 16, the last of their flour was used up. It was made into dog pemmican bannocks, and several men nipped and nibbled at their 1-ounce portions for more than an hour.

Inevitably the old resentments against Shackleton's refusal to get in all possible game when it was available cropped up. Even Macklin, who had refrained from all criticism of Shackleton's policy in the past, felt so strongly that he devised a code so he could comment on the subject in his diary without fearing that his thoughts would be read by others.

On the seventeenth, he wrote in code: "I think the Boss was a bit improvident in not getting in all the food possible whilst the going was good. It was worth the risk." Then on the eighteenth: "Lees tackled the Boss a few days ago about getting in all food possible [from Ocean Camp] in the event of having to winter on the floe. Boss rather snapped at him saying 'It will do some of these people good to go hungry, their bloody appetites are too big!'"

As the days went by their rations had to be steadily decreased. The tea and coffee now were finished, and because of the shortage of blubber for fuel to melt ice into water, they were allowed only one ration of "very diluted" powdered milk a day. It was served at breakfast, along with five ounces of seal steak. Lunch was cold, a quarter can of frozen broth and one canned biscuit. Supper consisted of a serving of seal or penguin hoosh.

Most of the men felt the shortage of food almost as physical pain. The compulsive craving of their bodies for more fuel to burn to ward off the cold caused a gnawing, ceaseless hunger. And the weather was becoming increasingly bitter, with nighttime temperatures frequently dropping as low as 10 below. Thus, when their need for calories was greatest, they were forced to get along on less than ever. Many men found that a few hours after eating they had to crawl into their sleeping bags to keep from shivering until the next meal put some warmth back into them.

There were some intrepid attempts to make jokes about cannibalism. "Greenstreet and I," wrote Worsley, "amuse ourselves at Marston's expense. Marston is the plumpest man in the Camp and we become very solicitous about his welfare and condition, making a great show of generosity by offering him old penguin bones that we have gnawed till there is nothing left. We implore him not to get thin and even go so far as to select chops, etc., off him and quarrel about who shall have the tenderest part. Finally he gets so disgusted with us that whenever he sees us approaching he turns and walks away."

It was a poor attempt at humor, because there was an element of pertinence in the subject matter. And Worsley himself, apart from these painful efforts to be funny, had grown silent and morose.

By March 22, the food situation was so critical that Shackleton told Macklin that his dogs would have to be shot the next day so that the party might eat the food set aside for the dogs. Macklin reacted indifferently: "I must confess that I cannot see that they will be of much more use to us. Ocean Camp has apparently disappeared. We have now only 10 more days blubber fuel—it is to be hoped that we can get more seals, or we shall be in a bad way indeed."

The morning of March 23 dawned cold, with a patchy fog lying across the pack. Shackleton was up early to take a constitutional. He walked to the edge of the floe, and when the fog cleared for a moment he saw a black object far in the distance to the southwest. He watched it for a few minutes, then hurried back to his tent and roused Hurley. The two men returned to the edge of the floe and peered for several minutes through the intermittent bands of fog.

It was there, all right—and it was land.

Shackleton immediately ran back to camp, going from tent to tent shouting, "Land in sight! Land in sight!" The reaction was strange. Some men bounded out of their tents to see for themselves, but others—cold and discouraged and tired of mistaking distant bergs for land—refused to stir from their sleeping bags, at least until the sighting had been confirmed.

But this was not a distant berg or a mirage. It was one of the tiny Danger Islets, identifiable, according to the *British Antarctic Sailing Directions,* by its tabletop bluffs rising steeply out of the water. It lay exactly 42 miles away; only 20 miles beyond it lay what had been their destination, Paulet Island.

The men stood looking at the land for a short time, until the thickening fog cut off their view. Early in the afternoon, however, the weather cleared beautifully, revealing in the distance beyond the Danger Islets, the black base of a range of mountains, their peaks hidden in low-lying clouds. Worsley identified the tallest of the peaks as Mount Percy on Joinville Island off the very tip of the Palmer Peninsula.

The island lay just 57 miles very nearly due west of them—almost exactly at right angles to the direction of their drift. "If the ice opens we could land in a day," wrote Hurley.

But there wasn't a man among them who believed that the pack would open. Quite the contrary. There were fully seventy bergs in sight, many of them aground, and they seemed for the moment to be preventing the pack from either opening or drifting much to the north. If the boats had been launched, they would probably have been crushed within minutes. Furthermore, sledging across the ice was unthinkable. The pack was now a dense mass of broken bits of floes a thousand times more treacherous than three months before when they had struggled for five days and covered 9 miles from Ocean Camp.

Consequently, the sight of land was but another reminder of their helplessness. Greenstreet's attitude was rather typically cynical: "It is nice to think there is something else besides snow and ice in the world, but I fail to see any cause for excitement as it puts us no nearer getting out. What I would far rather see would be a crowd of seals coming up so that we might get food and fuel."

Yet frustrating as it was, the sight of land was welcome, as James noted, if for no other reason than "it is nearly 16 months since we last saw any black rock." Macklin especially benefited since, in the excitement, Shackleton apparently forgot his decision to have Macklin's team killed.

"Please God" wrote Shackleton that night, "we will soon get ashore." But there was precious little land left on which to get ashore. They had drifted to the absolute tip of the Palmer Peninsula, and reaching land there now seemed all but impossible.

Thus, between them and the open seas and Cape Horn rollers of the dreaded Drake Passage—the most storm-torn ocean on the globe—all that remained were two lonely, sentinel-like outposts of the Antarctic Continent—Clarence and Elephant Islands, about 120 miles to the north. Beyond these, there was nothing.

March 24 was a bright, sunshiny day, and the peaks of Joinville Island were clearly visible. James, looking across the dense, impassable pack, could not help but remark: "It is quite maddening to think that one little rift 20 feet wide or so would lead us out in a couple of days & all the time everything keeps as close as ever making a move of any sort an impossibility. We are all very silent and absorbed in the tent & don't get much conversation. There is an air of expectancy about, which causes much preoccupation."

The air of expectancy was heightened late in the day when two cracks developed in their floe, only about 90 feet from the boats. Fortunately they did not open.

Just after dawn the following morning, a sudden violent gale sprang up from the southwest. But it lasted only until midafternoon, and then the wind died off quickly and the weather cleared. The sunset was stormy looking, with fiery shreds of clouds passing across the face of the sun. Joinville Island once more came into view astern, though it was distant and indistinct.

The biting cold brought by the southerly gale continued into the night, and they all suffered bitterly. Their bodies seemed to lack even enough heat to warm their sleeping bags.

Less than a week's supply of blubber remained, so on March 26 the 5-ounce ration of seal steaks at breakfast was cut out. In its place the men were usually given a half-pound cake of cold dog pemmican and a half-ration of powdered milk; on very cold days, a few lumps of sugar were added. Lunch was one biscuit and three lumps of sugar, and supper, the only so-called hot meal of the day, consisted of seal or penguin hoosh, "cooked for the minimum possible time." No water was issued at any time. If a man wanted a drink, he packed snow into a small can, usually a tobacco tin, and held it against his body to melt, or slept with it in his sleeping bag. But a full tobacco tin of snow yielded only a tablespoonful or two of water.

Word reached Shackleton on the twenty-sixth that several men had taken bits of blubber and penguin meat from the general store and were trying to eat it—frozen and raw. Shackleton immediately ordered that their remaining supply of stores be placed directly outside his tent.

In addition, Macklin was told to pick out anything fit for human consumption from the stock of waste meat used to feed the dogs. Macklin sorted it out, setting aside everything "except that which was too stinking to contemplate eating." It was a repulsive collection of odd bits of flesh, Macklin noted, "and unfortunately, if we do not get more seals we will have to eat it raw."

It appeared, too, that the dogs would have to be eaten soon. They had been spared thus far because there was still a bare chance of making one last trip to Ocean Camp for the stores there. After that was done, or if it became evident that it could not be done, the dogs were to be shot and eaten.

"I would have no hesitation in eating dog cooked," wrote Macklin, "but I do not look forward to eating it raw."

For days, several men had strongly urged Shackleton to risk this one desperate dash back to Ocean Camp, now barely visible about 7 miles away. A 600- or 700-pound store of dog pemmican and about 60 pounds of flour still remained there. But Shackleton, though he was gravely concerned about the state of their supplies, could not bring himself to send the dog drivers across ice which was so obviously treacherous. Almost continually there were sounds of pressure, apparently caused by the ice being jammed against the curving arm of the Palmer Peninsula. The noise echoed through the ice and movement could be seen in almost every direction. "I hope our old packet isn't going to break up," Greenstreet commented, "as there isn't another decent floe anywhere to be seen."

The numerous bergs in the vicinity were also hastening the general disintegration of the ice. With their deep draft, the bergs seemed to be affected by erratic tidal currents. Periodically, one would cease to travel peacefully along with the rest of the pack and would suddenly veer off on its own, grinding through the ice and effortlessly shouldering aside anything in its path, leaving a wake of broken and upended floes. And there was no predicting what course these drunken juggernauts would take.

On March 27, Worsley noted that one huge berg unaccountably drew away to the northeast, "and a berg from the north came charging down towards our floe 5 miles in 4 hours but luckily passed just clear to the east."

The trip to Ocean Camp seemed to be growing less feasible by the hour, and Shackleton knew that it was now or never. Reluctantly he told Macklin that night to be ready for a possible start early the next morning. Macklin had already turned in, but he was so delighted at the news that he got up and worked for some time readying the harness and getting his sledge into shape. But at dawn the ice was very much on the move and a heavy mist had rolled in. Shackleton came to No. 5 tent just at breakfast time to inform Macklin that he had decided against the trip. It was a crushing disappointment, coming as it did on the heels of a miserable night of wet, misty weather, during which nobody had slept much.

Shackleton had hardly left when Macklin turned on Clark for some feeble reason, and the two men were almost immediately shouting at one another. The tension spread to Orde-Lees and Worsley and triggered a blasphemous exchange between them. In the midst of it, Greenstreet upset his powdered milk. He whirled on Clark, cursing him for causing the accident because Clark had called his attention for a moment. Clark tried to protest, but Greenstreet shouted him down.

Then Greenstreet paused to get his breath, and in that instant his anger was spent and he suddenly fell silent. Everyone else in the tent became quiet, too, and looked at Greenstreet, shaggy-haired, bearded, and filthy with blubber soot, holding his empty mug in his hand and looking helplessly down into the snow that had thirstily soaked up his precious milk. The loss was so tragic he seemed almost on the point of weeping.

Without speaking, Clark reached out and poured some of his milk into Greenstreet's mug. Then Worsley, then Macklin, and Rickenson and Kerr, Orde-Lees, and finally Blackboro. They finished in silence.

Just after breakfast, two seals were sighted and hunting parties were urgently organized. The first group secured the closer of the two, and the others were within a short distance of their quarry when Shackleton, feeling that the ice was too dangerous, summoned them back to camp.

On the way back, Orde-Lees collapsed from hunger. As usual, he had eaten only half his breakfast ration—an eighth of a pound of cold dog pemmican and a lump and a half of sugar—intending to save the rest for later. After several minutes' rest, however, he was able to regain his feet and make his way back to camp.

Later in the day, the misty weather turned into pure rain, with the temperature rising to 33 degrees. Most of the men crawled into their sleeping bags and stayed there while the rain continued—that night and all the next day. Macklin described it: "A stream of water collected and, running under my bag, soaked it completely through, the bottom being absolutely sodden, and mitts, socks and other gear got thoroughly soaked too. . . . Even as I sit and write this the water is drip-drip-dripping from the tent roof and every available receptacle—empty tins, etc.,—are in use to prevent our bags getting wetter. We are only partially successful, for the drips are coming in through four times as many places as we have receptacles for. I have spread my Burberrys over my bag, and when a pool has collected in them big enough I carefully lift and pour it into the snow at one side. It is pretty tedious having thus to keep a constant vigilance. . . . I pray God to send us dry weather soon, for this is misery. I have never seen such depression of spirits as there is in the tent today."

Later in the afternoon, the rain changed to snow, and by five o'clock it had ceased altogether. James was night watchman that evening from nine to ten, and as he was walking around the floe, he thought he detected a movement in the ice. Looking closely, he saw a "very distinct swell" slowly lifting the floe. He reported his discovery to Shackleton who gave orders that the watchman should be especially alert.

At five-twenty the next morning the floe split.

CHAPTER 5

L ittle Alf Cheetham was on watch, and he dashed among the tents.

"Crack!" he shouted. "Crack! Lash up and stow!"

Within seconds, all hands had tumbled out of their tents. They saw two cracks, one running the length of the floe and another extending at right angles to the first. In addition, the whole pack was rising to a very marked swell.

They ran to the *James Caird* and wrenched the frozen runners of her sledge free of the ice, then manhandled her to the center of the floe. By then the crack down the center had widened out to 20 feet in some places, and could be seen slowly working back and forth under the influence of the swell. Their store of meat was on the other side. Several men jumped across where the crack was not so wide and pitched the meat over the seam of open water.

By 6:45, everything was safely across and work was halted for breakfast. The men were standing around waiting for their ration when the floe cracked again, this time directly under the *James Caird,* 100 feet from the tents. No order was needed. The men dashed to the boat and quickly brought her up closer to the tent area. Finally, they were able to eat breakfast—the usual lump of dog pemmican, six pieces of sugar, and a half-mug of milk.

Breakfast was hardly finished when through the mists, a strange shape appeared, moving deliberately across a nearby section of their old floe. Wild ran to get his rifle from his tent, then he dropped to one knee and shot. The animal bucked, and slowly sank down onto the ice. Several men hurried to where it lay—a sea leopard nearly 11 feet long.

With one bullet, it seemed, Wild had changed the whole complexion of their lives. There at their feet lay nearly 1,000 pounds of meat—and at least two weeks' supply of blubber. Shackleton announced that they would feast on the sea leopard's liver for lunch.

In high good spirits, the party sent out the dogs to return the trophy to camp. When it was butchered, they found in its stomach nearly fifty undigested fish, which were carefully set aside to be eaten the next day. It was nine o'clock by the time the job was finished.

Shackleton then summoned Macklin and told him the time had come to shoot his dogs. Macklin made no protest, for there was really no longer any reason to spare them. The possibility of reaching Ocean Camp was more remote than ever in view of the new breakup, and now that they had the sea leopard, the need for risking such a trip was past.

Accompanied by Wild, Macklin drove his team across the narrow neck of a crack to where the galley formerly had stood. On the way, they passed what had been the meat dump. Songster, a wily old dog, grabbed up a discarded penguin head, and Bos'n got hold of a bone. They were both allowed to keep them.

Macklin was almost sick as he unharnessed one dog at a time and took it around the protective mound of ice. Wild, as before, sat each dog down in the snow, placed the muzzle of the revolver almost against its head, and pulled the trigger. Songster died with the penguin head in his mouth, and Bos'n died gripping his bone. When all the dogs had been killed, Macklin skinned and gutted the carcasses, preparing them for eating. Crean's team of puppies was also killed and butchered.

Back at camp, there was almost a holiday atmosphere in anticipation of the first hot lunch in more than two weeks. The suggestion was made that they sample the dog meat, and Shackleton agreed. Crean cut small steaks from his dog, Nelson, and Macklin did the same with Grus.

When the meat had been fried, Crean hurried around to distribute it. He went first to Shackleton's tent, poking his weathered, Irish face through the flap. "I've just brought a bit of Nelson for you to try," he said puckishly.

The meat of the dogs was universally acclaimed. "Their flesh tastes a treat," McNeish remarked. "It is a big treat to us after being so long on seal meat." James found it "surprisingly good and tasty." Worsley said that the piece of Grus he ate "has a better flavor than the sea leopard." And Hurley went so far as to say it was "exquisitely tender and flavorous, especially Nelson, which equalled veal."

Throughout the morning the swell had continued and even increased slightly, so at lunch Shackleton announced that they would immediately go on a "watch and watch" system, four hours on and four hours off. Shackleton would take charge of one watch, and Wild the other. Thus half the party would be on duty at all times, fully dressed, with their gear lashed and ready to move at a moment's notice. Two of the men on watch would be required to walk the floe continuously, looking for cracks or any other threatened emergency. The others would be permitted to stand by in their tents.

During the day, there were more and more signs of an imminent opening. Cape pigeons and terns could be seen overhead, and Worsley sighted a magnificent giant petrel, snow white except for two bands of black across its wings—a definite sign of open water. Clark spied a jellyfish in the crack between two floes, and stated flatly that such creatures were found only in the vicinity of ice-free seas. These, plus a black water sky to the northwest, the presence of the swell, and a high temperature of 34 degrees, led Worsley to remark: "It certainly looks promising." But then he added: "Hope tells a flattering tale."

Toward 3 P.M., the weather turned showery, and by eight o'clock when Wild's watch took over, it was raining steadily. Wild and McIlroy moved into No. 5 tent for the period of the watch, and in spite of the miserably crowded, wet conditions, there was a cozy atmosphere. Everyone delighted in listening to some new stories instead of the oft-repeated tales from the same wearisome tentmates.

Soon after the arrival of the newcomers, the men were permitted the luxury of a match. "Are you ready?" Wild asked as the smokers waited with their pipes and cigarettes. Then the precious match was struck, casting its glare on the circle of bearded faces. Individual tapers of tarry rope yarn were lighted from the match; then everyone settled back, puffing contentedly.

Wild launched into a series of stories about his past escapades involving ladies, and McIlroy lived up to his reputation as the most cosmopolitan member of the expedition by explaining to an attentive audience his recipe for mixing several cocktails, including one guaranteed aphrodisiac called "The Bosom Caresser." Otherwise the night passed uneventfully. By dawn the rain had ceased and the wind had shifted to the south, blowing cold and dry. The swell gradually subsided.

In spite of all the encouraging signs, the pack showed little change throughout the day and into the next morning. In the afternoon a very dark water sky appeared from the southwest, stretching all the way around to the northeast, but in view of the southerly wind, a sudden opening seemed unlikely, so Shackleton deemed it safe to cancel the sea watches. But one-man patrols were continued, day and night.

That evening, just at eight o'clock as Macklin was relieving Orde-Lees on watch outside, the floe unexpectedly rose to a swell and cracked, hardly 2 feet from Wild's tent. Macklin and Orde-Lees both spread the alarm.

But everybody had turned in, confident that there would be no breakup, and the emergency caught them almost totally unprepared. There was a great scramble to get dressed in the pitch black tents, with everyone trying to find the right clothes and attempting to get into boots that had frozen in the 20-degree cold. Even after the men were out of their tents, there was confusion about exactly what was the trouble and where the danger was. They groped their way around in the dark, bumping into one another and stumbling into unseen holes in the ice. But order was finally restored. The boats were moved closer to the tents, and the stock of meat, which again had been cut off by a crack, was pitched across in the darkness.

Shackleton ordered sea watches resumed, and that the off-duty men turn in "all standing"—fully dressed, including mittens and helmets.

It was hard to sleep. Throughout the night the floe lifted very noticeably to the heavy swell, perhaps a foot or more, and the repeated shocks as it bumped against other floes were disconcerting. They all knew that the floe was now so small that should it crack again, something—or somebody—would almost inevitably fall through and probably be crushed.

But when morning came the southerly wind dropped, and during the forenoon the swell disappeared. At noon, for the first time in six days, Worsley obtained a sight. It put their position at 62°33′ South, 53°37′ West. They had drifted an astonishing 28 miles north in six days, and this in spite of five days of adverse northerly winds. The pack was obviously under the influence of a northerly current.

It was April 3, McLeod's forty-ninth birthday. The party had just toasted his health at lunch when a sea leopard's head appeared at the edge of the floe. McLeod, who was a small but stocky man, went over and stood flapping his arms to imitate a penguin. The sea leopard apparently was convinced, for he sprang out of the water at McLeod, who turned and dashed for safety. The sea leopard humped forward once or twice, then stopped, apparently to take stock of the other strange creatures on the floe. The delay was fatal. Wild had reached into his tent for his rifle. He took deliberate aim and fired, and another thousand pounds of meat was added to the larder.

Thus, the store of provisions was growing steadily. As it did, and their rations were increased, the morale of the whole party improved accordingly. The gloomy, morose grumblings of a few days before, when they had faced the prospects of eating putrid seal meat raw, vanished, and occasionally their attention even turned to matters outside the sphere of simple survival. The afternoon of McLeod's birthday, Worsley and Rickenson launched into a long, noisy argument on the seemingly remote subject of the relative cleanliness of New Zealand versus English dairy farms.

Though everyone was fully aware that their situation was becoming more critical by the hour, it was much easier to face danger on a reasonably full stomach.

Their floe, which had once measured a mile in diameter, was now less than 200 yards across. Most of the time it was surrounded by open water, and it was constantly menaced by swells and collisions with other floes. Clarence Island lay 68 miles due north of them, and though they appeared to be making toward it, they were concerned with the gradual westerly set of their drift which threatened to increase. If it did, they would be swept out to sea through Loper Channel, the 80-mile-wide gulf between Elephant Island and King George Island.

"It would be hard," wrote McNeish, "after drifting into those straits & then be blown out to sea." And James noted: "A great air of expectancy everywhere. We are on the verge of something, there is no doubt. If all goes well we may be on land very soon. Our chief need is an opening in the ice. Our chief danger being carried beyond these islands in close pack. Our mark, Clarence and Elephant Islands. . . . "

It was impossible to obtain a sight the following day, which was damp and misty with an unpleasantly heavy swell running. However, on April 5, Worsley obtained a position—and it showed that they were headed straight for the open sea.

CHAPTER 6

Somehow in two days, their drift had veered to the west and carried them the incredible distance of 21 miles in forty-eight hours, in spite of headwinds.

The whole party was stunned by the news. In the space of a minute, the entire pattern of their thinking had to be changed. The goal had been Clarence Island or Elephant Island—but no more. These were now out of the question. "This proves the existence of a strong current to the west," Hurley said, "and places Elephant Is. beyond a hope of landing."

Abruptly, their attention was refocused on King George Island to the west. "We now hope for E. or N.E. winds to take us well west before we get too far north," wrote James. "It is most remarkable how the outlook can change from a very favorable to a most unfavorable one in a couple of days. . . . Conversation now either entirely fails or is purely concerned with winds and drifts."

There were many who doubted that even strong easterly winds would drive the pack far enough to the west before they drifted out to sea, where the ice would unquestionably be dissipated, leaving them at best adrift in the boats, exposed to the fury of the storms in the Drake Passage. "God forbid we should get that," wrote Greenstreet, "for I doubt if we would survive."

That night as they lay in their sleeping bags they knew the pack was on the move by the ominous sounds of pressure all around. The next day was overcast so that they were unable to obtain a position. But during the night of April 6, the sky cleared, and it was still fairly bright at daybreak. Away in the distance, almost due north, an enormous berg was sighted. But as the sun rose higher, they saw that the upper limits of the berg were shrouded in clouds. No berg was that high—it was an island. But which island?

From their estimated drift to the northwest, many men thought it was Elephant Island; others argued that it had to be Clarence. What puzzled them most was that they could see one and not the other, since the two should have been almost equidistant. The Clarence Island faction finally won out on the grounds that the 5,600-foot peaks there were fully 2,000 feet higher than any on Elephant Island, and would therefore be visible for a much greater distance.

By breakfast time the clouds had thickened, obscuring the land from sight. But at noon Worsley obtained a sight which removed all doubt that what they had sighted was Clarence Island, 52 miles away. Even more important, the position showed that the westerly set of their drift had been arrested, and that they had gone 8 miles very nearly due north in the past two days. An enormous wave of relief passed through the party.

" . . . the upshot," wrote James, "is that Elephant and Clarence Group is still the objective and as our present wind is s.w. prospects are a little brighter for the time. The ice got a little closer during the night and the pack is simply swarming with life. We hear and see whales blowing all around absolutely continuously at times. A particularly ugly killer poked his head up and had a look around by our floe. Penguins are croaking . . . and occasionally a shoal of them swim through a pool with a peculiar leaping movement like great fleas hopping along the water surface, and looking fine in the brilliant sunlight. About twenty seals were visible . . . this morning at one time. Crowds of snow petrels are on the wing, with occasional giant petrels and skua gulls."

Still, the damnable pack would not open. "Pray God we may find a landing here," wrote Macklin, "and so be off this drifting uncontrollable pack, taking us we know not where, and in spite of any efforts we may attempt to make. . . . But we are in the hands of a Higher Power, and puny mortals that we are, can do nothing to help ourselves against these colossal forces of nature. If we fail to make a landing, and it is quite likely, I think it might be a good plan to make an effort to get on a berg. Indeed many of us have talked and wished for this for many weeks now, but of course there are other more weighty opinions."

Those opinions belonged to Ernest Shackleton. He was dead set against moving onto a berg unless it became unavoidable. He knew that bergs, though they looked substantial, could become off balance because of one portion melting faster than another and might suddenly and unpredictably upend.

Throughout the night, the hoarse croaking of the penguins, punctuated by the explosive sound of schools of whales blowing, created almost a din. When dawn finally came the weather was clear and bright, with a moderate westerly wind blowing. Once again the men could see Clarence Island, and to the left of it, very faintly, the chain of peaks on Elephant Island. Worsley counted ten of them.

But the bearing of Clarence Island had altered considerably since the previous evening. It was now almost due north, indicating that they had gone to the east. Worsley's sight at noon confirmed the fact. During the past twenty-four hours they had scarcely gone north at all—2 miles at most. Instead they had covered 16 miles to the east.

It was almost unbelievable. The pack had done a complete about-face. Two days before they had been shocked to learn that they were drifting west; now they were confronted with the fact that they were traveling rapidly to the east—away from all land. "If the wind doesn't change round to the east," Greenstreet said, "we shall miss the island altogether."

There was also a dangerously heavy swell running from the northwest, rolling through the pack like low, moving hills of water which lifted their floe almost 3 feet at times. Orde-Lees actually became seasick.

The easterly movement of the pack could be seen against the slower moving bergs. The ice now had been reduced to such small pieces that it flowed around any obstacle in its path like syrup.

That evening about 6:45, McNeish was writing his diary. "There has been a large swell since yesterday," he recorded. "But it is doing us no harm now [since] our floe is broken up so small. It rises and falls with. . . . " He never finished the sentence.

There was a heavy thump, and the floe split under the *James Caird*. Worsley was on watch, and he shouted for help. All hands dashed from their tents and seized the *James Caird* just as the crack began to widen. The other two boats, which were on the separated portion of the floe, were hurried across. When it was over, the floe was a triangle of ice whose sides measured roughly 100 by 120 by 90 yards.

Not long after midnight, the wind shifted from the west to the southeast and dropped considerably. Almost at once great pools of open water appeared as the floes drew apart. But it didn't last. By daybreak the ice had closed again, though the sky to the north grew black as ink. The swell increased and the men had to brace themselves slightly as they made their way about.

Again at breakfast time, the ice mysteriously moved apart again. Small floes became isolated patches of white floating on the dark, cold surface of the water. But even as the entire party anxiously watched, the pack closed once more. The swell rose higher on all sides and their floe began to take a serious pounding.

Toward midmorning, for the third time, lanes and pools of open water unaccountably spread through the pack and widened.

At ten-thirty, Shackleton's booming brogue rang out: "Strike the tents and clear the boats!"

The men jumped to their tasks. In minutes the tents were struck, and the sleeping bags gathered and stowed in the bows of the boats. Then one at a time the boats were pushed on their sledges to the edge of the floe.

Crack!

Again the floe had split in two, this time exactly through the spot where Shackleton's tent had stood some minutes before. The two halves drew rapidly apart, separating the *Stancomb Wills* and a large amount of provisions from the rest of the party. Almost everyone leaped over the widening breach and shoved the cutter and the stores across.

Then they waited . . . torn between the overpowering desire to launch the boats regardless of the risk, and the certain knowledge that once they did so, there could be no turning back. Small as it was, theirs was the only decent floe in sight. If they abandoned it, and the pack closed up before they reached another campsite, there would be no escape.

Throughout the activity, Green had gone methodically about his duties. Now he was ready with some oily seal soup and a serving of hot powdered milk. Each man took his portion and ate it standing up, intently watching the pack all the while. It was twelve-thirty, and the pools of water were very slightly larger. The men looked at Shackleton.

For the moment the pack was open—but how long would it remain open? And yet, how long could they stay where they were? The immense floe that had once been Patience Camp was now an irregular rectangle of ice hardly 50 yards across. How long would it be before it was broken and ground to bits beneath their feet?

At twelve-forty, Shackleton gave the order in a quiet voice.

"Launch the boats."

The floe came alive with activity. Green ran to his stove and put out the fire. Other men took pieces of canvas and tied up small piles of meat and blubber. The rest of the party hurried to the boats.

The *Dudley Docker* was removed from its sledge and eased into the water. Then with all hands passing stores, she was loaded with cases of rations, a bag of meat, the blubber stove, and No. 5's rattly old hoop tent. An empty sledge was lowered into the water and tied onto her stern. Next the *Stancomb Wills* was rapidly launched and loaded, and finally the *James Caird*.

It was one-thirty in the afternoon when the crews scrambled on board each boat; they put out every available oar and pulled with all their strength for the open water.

Even as they drew away from Patience Camp, the ice began to close.

PART IV

CHAPTER 1

The first few minutes were crucial—and they were maddening. The oarsmen did their best to pull together, but they were clumsy and out of practice, and hampered by their own anxiety. The encircling ice fouled the oars, and collisions were unavoidable. Men crouched in the bows of each boat and tried to pole off the bigger pieces of ice, but a great many outweighed the boats themselves.

The raised sides of the *James Caird* and the *Dudley Docker* were an added hindrance. They made the seats too low for proper rowing, and though cases of stores were placed under the four oarsmen in each boat, it was still an awkward business.

The sledge astern of the *Dudley Docker* continually got hung up on bits of ice, and after a few minutes Worsley angrily cut it loose.

And yet, to their surprise and almost in spite of themselves and the jealous hands that tried to hold them back, they were making headway. With each boat-length the ice seemed looser. It was difficult to tell whether the pack was opening or whether they were escaping from the ice surrounding Patience Camp. In either case, for the moment, luck was on their side.

The overcast sky seemed almost alive with birds—Cape pigeons, terns, fulmars, and Antarctic, silver-gray and snow petrels by the thousands. The birds were so thick their droppings spattered on the boats and forced the rowers to keep their heads lowered. Whales, too, seemed everywhere. They surfaced on all sides, sometimes frighteningly close—especially the killers.

The *James Caird* was in the lead with Shackleton at the tiller. So far as the ice permitted he set a course for the northwest. Next came Worsley steering the *Dudley Docker*, then Hudson in the *Stancomb Wills*. The sound of their voices chanting, "stroke . . . stroke . . . stroke . . . " mingled with the cries of the birds overhead and the surge of the swell through the pack. With each stroke, the oarsmen fell more into the rhythm of their task.

In fifteen minutes, Patience Camp was lost in the confusion of ice astern. But Patience Camp no longer mattered. That soot-blackened floe which had been their prison for nearly four months—whose every feature they knew so well, as convicts know each crevice of their cells; which they had come to despise, but whose preservation they had prayed for so often—belonged now to the past. They were in the boats . . . actually in the boats, and that was all that mattered. They thought neither of Patience Camp nor of an hour hence. There was only the present, and that meant row . . . get away . . . escape.

Within thirty minutes they had entered an area of very open pack, and by two-thirty they were easily a mile away from Patience Camp. They could not have found it again even if they had wanted. Their course carried them close to a high, flat-topped berg which was taking a terrific pounding from the northwest swell. The seas broke against its ice-blue sides, flinging spray 60 feet into the air.

Just as they drew abeam of it, they became aware of a deep, hoarse noise that was rapidly getting louder. Looking to starboard, they saw a lavalike flow of churning, tumbling ice at least

2 feet high and as wide as a small river bearing down on them out of the ESE. It was a tide rip, a phenomenon of current thrown up from the ocean floor which had caught a mass of ice and was propelling it forward at about 3 knots.

For a moment they stared in disbelief. Then Shackleton swung the bow of the *James Caird* to port and shouted for the other two boats to follow. The oarsmen dug in their feet and pulled with all their strength away from the onrushing ice. Even so, it was gaining on them. The rowers were facing astern, looking straight at the ice, almost at eye level as it drove toward them. Those men who were not rowing urged the oarsmen on, counting cadence for them, and stamping their feet at the same time. The *Dudley Docker* was the most cumbersome boat to row, and twice she was almost overtaken, but she just managed to keep clear.

After fifteen minutes, as the strength of the men at the oars began to fail them, the tide rip showed signs of flattening out. Five minutes later it seemed to lose its strength, and before long it had disappeared as mysteriously as it had arisen. Fresh men took over the oars from the weary rowers, and Shackleton brought the *James Caird* back onto a northwest course. The wind gradually swung around to the southeast so that it was blowing from astern, and it greatly aided their progress.

The position when the boats were launched was 61° 56′ South, 53° 56′ West, near the eastern reaches of what is called Bransfield Strait. Bransfield Strait is about 200 miles long and 60 miles wide, lying between the Palmer Peninsula and the South Shetland Islands. It connects the hazardous Drake Passage with the waters of the Weddell Sea—and it is a treacherous place. It was named in honor of Edward Bransfield, who, in 1820, took a small brig named the *Williams* into the waters which now bear his name. According to the British, Bransfield was thus the first man ever to set eyes on the Antarctic Continent.

In the ninety-six years between the time of Bransfield's discovery and that afternoon of April 9, 1916, when Shackleton's men threaded their boats through the ice, precious little had been learned about conditions in these unfrequented waters. Even today, the U.S. Navy Department's *Sailing Directions for Antarctica*, in describing conditions in Bransfield Strait, begins with an apologetic explanation that there is a "paucity" of information about the area. "It is believed," the *Sailing Directions* continue, that strong, erratic currents are to be found, sometimes reaching a velocity of 6 knots. These currents are affected only slightly by the wind, so that often a condition known to sailors as a "cross sea" is set up—when the wind is blowing in one direction, and the current moving in another. At such times, angry hunks of water—3, 6, 10 feet high—are heaved upwards, much as when breakers are thrown back from a bulkhead and collide with incoming waves. A cross sea is a perilous thing to a small boat.

Furthermore, the weather in Bransfield Strait is reliably inhospitable. Some reports say the sky is clear only 10 per cent of the time. Snows are heavy and gales are common, beginning in the middle of February and becoming more frequent and more violent as the Antarctic winter draws closer.

The boats in which the party set sail upon this forbidding sea were sturdy enough, but no open boat was really equal to the voyage they faced. The *Dudley Docker* and the *Stancomb Wills* were cutters—heavy, square-sterned boats of solid oak. Their Norwegian builders called them "bottlenose killerboats," or *dreperbåts*, because they were originally designed for hunting bottlenose whales. In the bow of each was a stout post to which the harpoon line was intended to be fastened. They were 21 feet 9 inches long, with a 6-foot-2-inch beam, and they had three seats, or thwarts, plus a small decking in the bow and in the stern. They also mounted stubby masts to which a sail could be secured; but they were primarily pulling boats, designed for row-ing, not sailing. The only real difference between the two was that McNeish had added planks to the *Dudley Docker*, which raised her sides about 8 inches.

The *James Caird* was a double-ended whaleboat, 22 feet 6 inches long and 6 feet 3 inches wide. She had been built in England to Worsley's specifications of Baltic pine planking over a framework of American elm and English oak. Though she was somewhat larger than the other two, she was a lighter, springier boat because of the materials of which she was built. McNeish had raised her sides about 15 inches, so that even fully loaded she rose a little more than 2 feet out of the water. The *Caird* was thus by far the most seaworthy of the three.

In terms of weight, the boats were not overloaded. The *Wills* carried eight men, the *Docker* nine and the *Caird* eleven; in less stormy waters, with less bulky gear, each might have accommo-dated at least twice that number. As matters stood, the boats were uncomfortably crowded. The hoop tents and the rolled-up sleep-ing bags took up a disproportionate amount of room. There were also cases of stores and a considerable amount of personal gear—all of which left scarcely enough space for the men themselves.

Throughout the afternoon, as they held to a northwesterly course, the three boats made excellent progress. There were belts of ice that were fairly thick, but none so dense as to block their way. Shortly after five o'clock the light began to fail. Shackleton called to the other boats to stay close by until a suitable camping place was found. They rowed until about five-thirty when they came to a flat, heavy floe some 200 yards across, which Shackleton decided was sturdy enough to camp on. Nearly a half-dozen approaches were made in the surging swell before the boats were safely hauled onto the ice. It was six-fifteen by the time the landing was

completed. Green set up his blubber stove while the remainder of
the party pitched the tents, except for No. 5, which was so flimsy
that Shackleton granted permission for its occupants to sleep in
the boats.

Supper consisted of a quarter-pound of dog pemmican and
two biscuits apiece. It was finished by eight o'clock, and all hands
except the watch turned in. It had been a tiring but exciting
day. By Worsley's estimate, they had made a good 7 miles to the
northwest. Though the distance itself was not impressive, the fact
that they had finally taken to the boats was the fulfillment of a
dream. After five and a half months on the ice, they were underway at last, "doing some good for oneself," as Macklin put it.
They dropped off to sleep almost immediately.

"Crack-oh!" The watchman's cry rang out within minutes after
the last man had turned in. The weary men stumbled out of their
tents, some of them without even bothering to dress. But it was
a false alarm; there was no crack, and the men crawled back into
their sleeping bags.

Toward eleven o'clock, Shackleton became strangely uneasy,
so he dressed and went outside. He noticed that the swell had
increased and their floe had swung around so that it was meeting
the seas head on. He had stood watching for only a few moments,
when there was a deep-throated thud and the floe split beneath
his feet—and directly under No. 4 tent in which the eight forecastle hands were sleeping.

Almost instantly the two pieces of the floe drew apart, the tent
collapsed and there was a splash. The crewmen scrambled out
from under the limp canvas.

"Somebody's missing," one man shouted. Shackleton rushed
forward and began to tear the tent away. In the dark he could
hear muffled, gasping noises coming from below. When he finally
got the tent out of the way, he saw a shapeless form wriggling in

the water—a man in his sleeping bag. Shackleton reached down for the bag and with one tremendous heave, he pulled it out of the water. A moment later, the two halves of the broken floe came together with a violent shock.

The man in the sleeping bag turned out to be Ernie Holness, one of the firemen. He was soaked through but he was alive, and there was no time to worry about him then because the crack was opening once more, this time very rapidly, cutting off the occupants of Shackleton's tent and the men who had been sleeping in the *Caird* from the rest of the party. A line was pitched across and the two little groups of men, pulling toward one another, managed to bring the halves together once more. The *Caird* was hurriedly shoved across and then the men leaped to the larger floe. Shackleton waited until the others were safe, but by the time it was his turn, the pieces had drifted apart again. He took hold of the rope and tried to bring his chunk closer; but with only one man pulling it was useless. Within ninety seconds he had disappeared into the darkness.

For what seemed a very long interval, no one spoke; then from the darkness they heard Shackleton's voice. "Launch a boat," he called.

Wild had just given the order. The *Wills* was slid into the water, and a half-dozen volunteers scrambled on board. They put out their oars and rowed toward Shackleton's voice. Finally they saw his outline in the darkness, and they pulled up alongside his floe. He jumped into the *Wills*, and they returned to the campsite.

Sleep now was out of the question. Shackleton ordered the blubber stove lighted. Then he turned his attention to Holness who was shivering uncontrollably in his soaked clothes. But there weren't any dry garments to give him because their only clothes were the ones they were wearing. To prevent Holness from freezing, Shackleton ordered that he be kept moving until his own clothes dried. For the rest of the night, the men took turns walking up and down with him. His companions could hear the crackling of his frozen garments, and the tinkle of the ice crystals that fell from him. Though he made no complaint about his clothes, Holness grumbled for hours over the fact that he had lost his tobacco in the water.

CHAPTER 2

At 5 A.M., the first hint of a brightening sky marked the ending of the night. It was April 10.

The weather at daybreak was hardly encouraging—overcast and hazy, with a strong easterly wind driving intermittent snow squalls across the icy water. Neither Clarence nor Elephant Island was visible, and Worsley could only estimate that they lay generally to the north, between 30 and 40 miles away. The easterly wind had blown new masses of ice around their floe, so that once again they seemed trapped.

But there were signs of an opening, and after breakfast everything was made ready for a quick start. Shackleton decided to lighten the boats by abandoning some ice tools and several cases of dried vegetables. Shortly before eight o'clock, the pack began to loosen, and at eight-ten Shackleton gave the order to launch the boats.

The sea was broken by a nasty chop which made the boats lurch heavily, and rowing extremely difficult. But before long the ice began to open up, and within an hour or so they found themselves in a vast expanse of ice-free water, so broad they could hardly see the pack to either side. It was a welcome sight after more than a year of looking at nothing but ice. Shackleton had the word passed to hoist sail.

The *Caird* was fitted with two masts for a main and a mizzen-sail, plus a small jib in the bow. The *Docker* carried a single lug sail, and the *Wills* mounted only a very small mainsail and jib. The boats were thus hardly fit sailing companions—and this fact immediately became apparent when the sails were set. The *Caird* caught the wind and heeled to port, drawing steadily ahead of the other two boats. Though the *Docker* was somewhat faster than the *Wills*, the difference was slight, and neither boat could sail into the wind. There was nothing for the *Caird* to do but to hang back so as not to outdistance the others.

Toward midmorning the boats came to a boundary of pack ice stretching in a long, closely packed line, apparently following the current. The floes here were old and stately veterans that had survived years of pressure and had emerged at last from the Weddell Sea to melt on the fringes of Antarctica. Their edges, instead of being fresh and sharp where they had been newly broken, were worn and eroded by the water. For more than an hour, the three boats proceeded west along the edge of this line of ancient floes, and then, shortly after eleven o'clock, a passage was discovered and the men rowed through.

They realized immediately that they must be in the open ocean. Ironically, here was the moment they had dreamed of ever since the days at Ocean Camp—but the reality was vastly different from the dream. As soon as the boats emerged from the protective barrier of the pack, they were struck by the full force of the wind, and a high, breaking sea was running down from the northeast. Freezing spray burst over them as they tried to beat their way to the NNE under sail. Time after time, icy blasts whipped them across the face, and the penetrating wind seemed all the colder because of their lack of sleep. In the *Docker*, Orde-Lees and Kerr slumped down onto the pile of sleeping bags, miserably seasick.

Yet the men complained very little. They knew that some-where through the mists, probably not more than two dozen miles to the north, there was land, and they were actually making for it, and getting closer all the time. When it came time for lunch, Shackleton permitted a hearty ration of biscuits, cold sledging ra-tion, dog pemmican, and six lumps of sugar.

Early in the afternoon, however, the wind increased consid-erably, and the boats began to take on water at a dangerous rate. For more than an hour, Shackleton kept to a northeasterly course, hoping that the boats would somehow prove equal to the seas. But toward two o'clock, he realized that it was foolhardy to press on, and ordered them back behind the protective line of the pack.

The boats came about and sped southward before the follow-ing wind. Within minutes they had reached the edge of the pack, and they proceeded westward, looking for a floe to which they might make fast. The largest single piece of ice they could find was what Worsley described as a "floe-berg," a thick mass of dark blue pressure ice about 35 yards square, which rose in some places to a height of 15 feet above the water. It was floating alone, iso-lated from the rest of the line of pack, and it had obviously been adrift for a long time. The seas had eaten around its waterline, leaving an overhanging girdle of rotten ice.

The perils of the sleepless night before were still altogether too vivid in Shackleton's memory to risk again. The party would have to spend the night in the boats. They pulled up alongside the floe-berg, and drove oars into the ice. Then they made the bow lines of the boats fast to the oars, and the boats lay off to wait for darkness.

Within minutes, however, the wind freshened out of the northeast, and the sea picked up. The boats began to bump heavily against one another, and they threatened to uproot the oars which held them to the floe. In addition, the wind swirled across the surface of the berg, catching snow from its surface and hurling it straight into their faces. After about a half hour of this misery, Shackleton had no choice. If the men were to sleep—and they had to sleep—there was no alternative to camping on the ice. Reluctantly he gave the order.

The boats were maneuvered alongside the floe-berg and about half the party scrambled onto the ice. The stores and equipment were quickly passed up. Then came the ordeal with the boats. The rotten overhang around the edge of the floe-berg was steep and treacherous, rising an almost perpendicular 5 feet out of the water. Thus the boats had to be hauled almost straight up while the men pulled from a safe distance back from the edge.

The *Wills* was first, and she was raised without incident. The *Docker* was not so easy. She was halfway up when the ice gave way and Bill Stevenson, one of the firemen, plunged into the numbing water. A half-dozen hands pulled him to safety. The *Caird* was last, and again the overhang broke. Shackleton, Wild, and Hurley were just able to grab hold of the boat before they fell in. It was three-thirty before the boats were safe, and by then the men were very nearly exhausted. They had hardly slept for thirty-six hours. Their hands, unaccustomed to rowing, were blistered and a little frostbitten. Their clothes were soaked from the spray in the boats, and when they unrolled their sleeping bags they found them wet through.

But all that mattered then was sleep. After a supper of cold dog pemmican, milk, and two lumps of sugar, they wriggled, fully dressed, into their sleeping bags. A few men, before they closed their eyes, put forth one last bit of effort to record the day's events briefly in their diaries. Worsley wrote: "By my reckoning we make today [northwest] 10 miles, and the current should run us well to the West before this strong Easterly breeze." And Hurley recorded the one thought that was uppermost in all their minds: " . . . pray God [this floe] will remain entire throughout the night."

By some minor miracle it did, but long before dawn they became aware that something was seriously wrong. At sunrise, they
awakened to a terrifying spectacle of nature.

During the night, the wind had risen almost to gale force,
and from somewhere to the northeast, great quantities of pack
had drifted down on them. Now it extended unbroken to the
horizon in every direction. Berg fragments and shattered floes in
ten-thousand different shapes obliterated the surface of the water.
And out of the northwest, rollers 30 feet high, stretching from
horizon to horizon, swept down through the pack in long, implacable lines a half mile apart. At their summits the floe-berg was
lifted to what seemed like dizzying heights, then dropped into
valleys from which the horizon was obscured. The air was filled
with a dull, muddled roar—the low shriek of the wind, and the
seas breaking hoarsely amongst the pack, along with the incessant
booming grind of the ice.

Because of its size, their berg was drifting more slowly than
the rest of the pack which bore down upon it and pounded it on
every side, while the surge of the swell was undermining it by eating away at the waterline. Periodically, decayed chunks dropped
away from one side or another, and others were torn loose by floe
fragments hurled against the berg by the seas. At each impact, the
berg shuddered sickeningly.

This was precisely the situation Shackleton had feared since
the first appearance of the swell at Patience Camp. The berg was
crumbling beneath them, and might split or upend at any moment. And yet to launch the boats would have been idiocy. They
would have been splintered to bits in ninety seconds.

The whole scene had a kind of horrifying fascination. The
men stood by, tense and altogether aware that in the next instant
they might be flung into the sea to be crushed or drowned, or to
flounder in the icy water until the spark of life was chilled from

their bodies. And yet the grandeur of the spectacle before them was undeniable.

Watching it, many of them sought to put their feeling into words, but they could find no words that were adequate. The lines in Tennyson's *Morte d'Arthur* kept running through Macklin's head: " . . . I never saw, nor shall see, here or elsewhere, till I die, not though I live three lives of mortal men, so great a miracle. . . . "

Shackleton climbed to a knoll a dozen feet high at one end of the berg, from which he could see the limitless expanse of ice. Here and there, far away, a black line or a small dark patch revealed a lead or a pool of open water. The party's only hope was that one of these openings would drift down and surround the berg, making possible their escape. But time and time again, a lead would approach to within a short distance, then veer to one side or another or vanish altogether as the ice closed up. Hour after hour they waited—eight, nine, ten o'clock. Since dawn the boats had been ready, and the stores and equipment lay close by for immediate loading.

The men stood looking up at Shackleton atop the little knoll. From beneath, the defiant line of his chin was accentuated, but the tired circles around his eyes told of the strain he was under. Occasionally he would call to them to stand by. A chance was coming. The men would rush to the boats and wait, but after a time Shackleton would look down and shake his head. The chance was gone.

While they waited, the berg was being systematically destroyed, piece by piece. Late in the morning, a huge sea burst against it, and a 20-foot section slipped into the water, leaving a half-submerged shelf of ice behind. This ice shelf was awash, and it greatly increased the strain on the berg by keeping it from rolling naturally with the swell. There was a good chance that the berg would split through horizontally, and that the whole top would be sheered off.

Noon came. The berg was smaller, but the ice was just as close. If anything, the swell was higher. Some sledging ration was issued and the men ate standing in little groups, talking quietly. By one o'clock, a sickening thought had begun to spread through the party. What if darkness came and the ice was still tight? With the beating it was taking, the berg could not possibly last until the next morning. They would be pitched into the sea during the night.

The men made feeble jokes about it, tried to resign themselves, or simply tried not to think about it. Greenstreet took his diary and attempted to write: " . . . a very anxious time as our floe was rocking and rolling heavily being. . . . " The diary ended there in midsentence. It was no good; he couldn't keep his mind on it.

Shortly before two o'clock, when only about three hours of daylight remained, a somber quiet came over the party. Lead after lead had drifted past, too far away to do them any good. They were watching Shackleton as he followed still another lead approaching from the north, but no one thought it would really be their chance.

There was an excited shout. A pool was opening in the opposite direction. They turned and stared. What they saw was almost beyond belief. The ice was mysteriously drawing away, as if under the influence of some invisible force. As they looked, eddies and swirls riffled the surface of the water. A freak current had apparently risen from the depths of the sea and been deflected against the deep underside of the berg. They jumped up and down, pointing and gesturing wildly toward the pool of inky water that was widening out from the berg.

"Launch the boats," Shackleton cried as he raced down from his perch. "Chuck in the stores any old way." Anxious hands seized the boats and hurried them to the edge of the berg. The surface of the sea was 5 feet beneath them, so the men almost pitched the boats off the ice into the water. Crewmen dropped into them and the stores were hurried on board. There was a bad moment when the ice shelf rose up and threatened to capsize the *Docker,* but she was hurriedly shoved out of danger, and in five minutes the boats were away.

They pulled to the center of the pool, and from there they could see still another pool beyond a narrow neck of brash ice. They pushed through the ice, and then the pack, in its inexplicable way, began to dissipate, leaving an ample margin of open water around them.

Until now, the destination had been either Clarence or Elephant Island—whichever the party happened to strike. These were the most logical choices, the closest bits of land. At the time the boats were launched from Patience Camp, Clarence Island lay just 39 miles almost due north. By sailing northwest, they had reduced that distance to about 25 miles NNE, Worsley estimated. However, it had been two days since the last observation, and during that time the strong winds out of the northeast had probably blown the party a considerable distance to the west. Furthermore, the greatest quantities of open water now extended to the southwest—toward King George Island, 80-odd miles away. Shackleton made the decision on the spot: they would abandon the effort to reach Clarence or Elephant Island and take advantage of the following wind to make for King George Island.

It was a much more desirable destination anyhow. Both Clarence and Elephant Islands were remote, and so far as Shackleton knew, had never been visited. But from King George Island, a series of island-to-island voyages, the longest of which was 19 miles, would carry the party ultimately to Deception Island, some hundred miles beyond. Here the remains of a volcano's cone made an excellent harbor, and the place was a frequent port of call for whalers.

Too, there was thought to be a cache of food at Deception Island for the use of castaways. But most important, there was a small, rude chapel there, built by the whalers. Even if no ships stopped at the island, Shackleton was sure they could tear down the church and use its lumber to build a boat large enough to accommodate all of them.

They held to a southwest course throughout the afternoon. About three-thirty, Shackleton signaled from the *Caird* to hoist sail, and almost immediately, the inequalities in the three boats became apparent once more. The *Caird* clove neatly through the water, followed by the *Docker,* but the *Wills* limped along astern, dropping farther back all the while. After a time, Shackleton brought the *Caird* up under the lee of some ice and shouted to Worsley to go back after the *Wills*. It took almost an hour for the *Docker* to beat her way to windward, take the *Wills* in tow, and return to the *Caird.*

By the time the three boats were joined up once more, darkness was rapidly approaching, and Shackleton was afraid of a collision with the ice. The boats took in their sails and proceeded under oars. In the last glimmer of light, they found a floe and drew alongside it. But there was to be no camping this night—nor ever again, so far as Shackleton was concerned. They had learned their lesson twice over, and they were through with the ice for good. The only man to debark now was Green, who carried his blubber stove and supplies onto the floe. He brewed up some seal hoosh and warmed some milk. The men ate sitting in the boats.

When they had finished, they cast off. The boats were made fast, one behind the other, with the *Docker* in the lead. Then the party began to row, very slowly, toward the southwest. They took spells at the oars, two men pulling at a time. Others hunched in the bows of the boats as lookouts, watching for the edge of the pack so that the boats might stay behind its protective line, and keeping an eye out for bergs or large floes that might catch and crush the boats. It had begun to snow—large, wet flakes that clung and melted. The snow doubled the discomfort of the lookouts, straining their eyes into the wind to watch for ice drifting down out of the darkness.

The period at the oars was kept short so that each man had a turn as often as possible. It was the only way to keep warm. Those who were not rowing or on lookout did what they could to keep their blood moving. But sleep was out of the question, for there was nowhere to lie down. The bottom of each boat was so packed with stores that there was scarcely room for the men's feet. Sleeping bags and tents took up most of the space in the bows, and the two thwarts on which the oarsmen sat had to be kept free. That left only a small space midships for the off-duty men to sit in a tight little group, huddled together for warmth.

Throughout the night, the sudden eruption of water nearby and a sound like a steam valve popping under pressure told of whales blowing close at hand. They became the primary worry during that long, black night. Whales had been seen on hundreds of occasions tossing aside vast chunks of floes as they surfaced to breathe. And the ability of a whale to discriminate between the underside of a floe and the white bottoms of the boats was open to serious question.

About 3 A.M., the entire party was suddenly electrified by an almost hysterical shout from Hudson. "A light! A light!" He was pointing to the northwest. Every man sat upright, staring off in the direction Hudson indicated. The excitement lasted for only one cruel moment—until they were alert enough to realize the absurdity of it. Then they settled down again, cursing Hudson for his stupidity and for having raised their hopes. Hudson insisted that he had seen it, and for several minutes he sat disconsolately mumbling to himself because nobody would believe him.

Toward five o'clock, the sky began to brighten. Before long the dawn of April 12 broke in radiant splendor along the horizon.

The sun started its climb into a cloudless sky, and the mere sight of it seemed to change the whole shape of things. They rowed alongside a large floe, and Green again jumped ashore to prepare some seal hoosh and hot milk. After breakfast they cast off and set sail to the southwest under perfect conditions—wide stretches of open water protected by a line of pack on which hundreds of seals lay sleeping.

About ten-thirty, Worsley took out his sextant. Then, bracing himself against the mast of the *Docker,* he carefully took his sight—the first since leaving Patience Camp. At noon he repeated the procedure, as the boats lay to awaiting the result. Every face was turned toward Worsley as he sat in the bottom of the *Docker* working out his figures. They watched to see his expression when the two lines of position were plotted for a fix. It took him much longer than usual, and gradually a puzzled look came over his face. He checked his calculations over, and the expression of puzzlement gave way to one of worry. Once more he ran through his computations; then he slowly raised his head. Shackleton had brought the *Caird* alongside the *Docker*, and Worsley showed him the position—62°15′ South, 53°7′ West.

They were 124 miles nearly due east of King George Island and 61 miles southeast of Clarence Island—22 miles farther from land than when they had launched the boats from Patience Camp three days before!

CHAPTER 3

They continually sailed west, with strong easterly winds driving them along—and yet they had actually been going in the opposite direction. They were 20 miles east of where they started and 50 miles east of where they had thought they were.

The news was so heartbreaking some men refused to believe it. It couldn't be. Worsley had made a mistake. But no. He obtained a third sight early in the afternoon which showed that Joinville Island, which had dropped from sight two weeks before, now was only 80 miles away.

Some unknown and undetectable easterly current had caught them—a current of such tremendous strength that it had driven them backward into the teeth of a gale.

To reach King George Island would mean sailing directly into that current, so for the third time, Shackleton announced that the destination had been changed. This time it became Hope Bay, about 130 miles away at the tip of the Palmer Peninsula, beyond Joinville Island. The boats were set on a southerly course, and the men sat in almost absolute silence, tired through and discouraged, their hopes for an early landing completely shattered.

Late in the afternoon, the wind increased from the NNW, and the boats came upon some scattered ice which Shackleton thought might prove troublesome in the dark. He gave the order to heave to. Worsley urged that they continue under oars, but Shackleton refused. They tried to find a floe they could tie up to for the night. But there was none—not even a piece large enough to accommodate Green and his stove. The best they could find was a small floe to which the *Docker* was made fast, with the *Wills* behind her and the *Caird* last. Even this was difficult in the heavy swell which made both the boats and the floe pitch violently. It was almost an hour before the job was done.

Canvas from the tents was stretched over each boat and with great difficulty the small primus stoves were lighted so that some milk could be heated. They drank it scalding hot, huddled together under the flapping canvas of the tent cloths. They were enjoying the luxury of a moment's warmth, when a new menace appeared. Large blocks of ice began to drift around the edges of the floe to the lee side where the boats were tethered.

The tent cloths were thrown aside, and the men, using every available oar and boathook, positioned themselves around each boat and poled off the approaching chunks of ice, or held them at bay so that the boats would not be dashed against them in the swell. The struggle might have gone on all night. But about nine o'clock, in the space of only a few minutes, the wind suddenly veered around to the southwest. Immediately the floe ceased to provide a shelter and became instead a windward shore; the boats were being driven toward its jagged edge. Shackleton shouted to get away, and the oarsmen hurriedly got into position. It had happened so fast, and the wind was so strong, that there wasn't time even to get in the *Docker's* bow line that had secured them to the floe; it had to be cut. They pulled frantically until at last they were clear of the floe.

Again a thick, wet snow had begun to fall. The temperature, too, began to drop, with the wind blowing up from the pole.

Before long, the surface of the sea was freezing into rubbery patches that would later become "pancake ice."

Shackleton ordered the *Docker* into the lead. The *Caird* was made fast to her stern, and the *Wills* brought up the rear. Two oars were put out from the *Docker* to keep the line of boats head up into the wind, and to prevent them from bumping into one another. By ten o'clock they were in position.

For the second night running, there was no sleep, though a few men snuggled together in hopes of generating enough warmth to drop off for a moment. But it was achingly cold. Hussey's thermometers were packed away so that no actual temperature reading could be taken, but Shackleton estimated it to be 4 below zero. They could even hear the water freezing. The snow fell on the newly formed ice with a tiny crackling sound, and the ice itself made a creaking hiss as it rose to the swell.

The clothes the men wore, now that they were sitting almost motionless, froze stiff. Not only were their garments wet from the spray and the snow, they were also worn and saturated with the oil secreted from the men's own bodies during six months of constant wear. If a man shifted his position, even slightly, his skin came in contact with a new, unwarmed surface of his clothing. Everyone tried to sit still, but it could not be done. The weariness, the lack of food, the exertion, and the worry had weakened them so that the harder they tried to sit still, the more they shivered—and their own shivering kept them awake. It was better to row. Shackleton in the *Caird* doubted that some men would survive the night.

A hundred times, it seemed, Worsley was asked what time it was. Each time, he reached under his shirt and took out the chronometer he carried slung around his neck to keep it warm. Holding it up close to his face, he read its hands in the feeble light of the moon, shining through the thin snow clouds. In time, it became a kind of gruesome game—seeing who could hold out the longest before asking again what time it was. When finally somebody succumbed to the temptation, every head rose to await Worsley's answer.

But the dawn did come—at last. And in its light the strain of the long dark hours showed on every face. Cheeks were drained and white, eyes were bloodshot from the salt spray and the fact that the men had slept only once in the past four days. Matted beards had caught the snow and frozen into a mass of white. Shackleton searched their faces for an answer to the question that troubled him most: How much more could they take? There was no single answer. Some men looked on the point of breaking, while others showed an unmistakable determination to hold out. At least, all of them had survived the night.

Shortly after sunrise, the wind swung around to the southeast and freshened considerably. Shackleton called to Worsley to bring the *Docker* alongside the *Caird*. After a hurried conference, they announced that, for the fourth time, the destination was changed. In view of the southeast wind, they would run for Elephant Island once more, now 100 miles to the northwest—and pray God the wind held fair till they arrived.

After redistributing the stores so that the *Wills* was less crowded, the boats hoisted sail and set off with the *Caird* in the lead. They worked their way through the floes, and the men took turns leaning over the bows, trying to fend off the ice. Even so, there were a number of collisions, and the *Caird* was stove in slightly when she ran into a particularly large piece. Fortunately the hole was above the waterline, but Shackleton ordered the boats to reduce sail to avoid further damage.

The primus stoves were lighted once more and a ration of hot milk was prepared. In addition, Shackleton said that all hands could eat all they wanted to make up for the cold and lack of sleep. It offered no enticement for some men, to whom seasickness was an additional misery. Orde-Lees was worst off, or at least he complained the most. But there was little sympathy for him. He had done less than the others ever since they had taken to the boats. Often when it came his turn to row, he pleaded with Worsley to let him off, claiming that he was sick or that he didn't know how to row well enough. As usual, Worsley found it diffi-cult to be stern, and since there were always plenty of volunteer oarsmen wanting to get warm, Orde-Lees was frequently allowed to skip his turn. On the rare occasions when he was ordered or shamed into taking up an oar, he managed to exhibit an inepti-tude which won him a speedy relief. Several times when he was rowing ahead of Kerr, he kept just enough out of ryhthm so that when he leaned back after every stroke he smashed into Kerr's fingers behind him. Curses, threats—nothing had any effect on him. He seemed not even to hear. Finally Kerr would ask Worsley to replace Orde-Lees.

When Shackleton gave the order that unlimited food would be permitted, the men in the *Docker* taunted Orde-Lees by mak-ing sure he saw them eating their fill in the hope that it would sicken him further.

Toward eleven o'clock, the scattered pack began to thin out, though the boats were still faced with large patches of newly fro-zen slush. At one point the pancake ice was littered with thou-sands of dead fish about seven inches long, which apparently had been killed by a cold current. Vast numbers of fulmars and snow petrels swooped down to pick them off the ice.

All the while the wind was increasing. By late morning it had risen almost to gale force and was driving the boats along at a re-markable clip.

Just before noon they burst from the line of pack into the open sea.

The change was breathtaking. The northwest swell, which had been cushioned by the pack, now advanced upon the boats in undisguised immensity. Their course lay directly into it, and within minutes they were struggling up a hill of water whose face was a quarter mile long. At its summit the wind shrieked, blowing the spray into thin, feathery lines. Then they started down, a slow but steep descent into the valley leading to the next swell. Over and over again the cycle was repeated. Before long the pack was lost from sight, and occasionally one or another of the boats disappeared behind one of these enormous rolling hills of water.

It was as if they had suddenly emerged into infinity. They had an ocean to themselves, a desolate, hostile vastness. Shackleton thought of the lines of Coleridge:

> *Alone, alone, all, all alone,*
> *Alone on a wide wide sea.*

They made a pitiable sight—three little boats, packed with the odd remnants of what had once been a proud expedition, bearing twenty-eight suffering men in one final, almost ludicrous bid for survival. But this time there was to be no turning back, and they all knew it.

The men clung to the sides of the pitching boats as they drove forward. Though they were making excellent headway, their progress was hard won. Both the *Docker* and the *Wills* were shipping water continually. The crews sat facing aft, with the wind directly in their faces—a position only slightly preferable to facing forward, where they would have been stung by the spray breaking over the side.

By midafternoon, the wind had risen even more, so Shackleton ordered a second reef taken in the sails, and they proceeded this way until dusk. At sunset, Worsley drew the *Docker* alongside the *Caird* and urged that they continue, but Shackleton flatly refused. It was difficult enough, he said, to keep the boats together in daylight; at night it would be impossible. He even rejected Worsley's suggestion that they join up and row during the night.

Shackleton was convinced that their best chance of reaching safety was to remain together. Both the *Caird* and the *Wills* were largely dependent on Worsley's skill as a navigator, and Shackleton was acutely aware that the *Wills* needed constant looking after. Not only was she the least seaworthy of the three boats, but Hudson, who was commanding her, was one of those less equal to the strain, and he was obviously weakening, both physically and mentally. Shackleton was certain the *Wills* would be lost if she got separated from the others.

He decided that the three boats would spend the night hove to. He ordered the *Docker* to rig a sea anchor, and the *Caird* made fast to the *Docker's* stern with the *Wills* behind her. Working with stiffening fingers, Worsley, Greenstreet, and McLeod lashed three oars together and stretched a piece of canvas across them. The contrivance was then made fast to a long piece of line and pitched over the side. They hoped the sea anchor would act as a brake, holding the bows of the boats up into the wind as it was dragged through the water. When it was in position, the crews of all three boats settled down to wait for morning.

Never was there a worse night. As the darkness deepened, the wind increased and the temperature dropped ever lower. Again an actual reading was impossible, but it was probably at least as low as 8 below. It was so cold that the seas that broke over them froze almost as soon as they hit. Even before the darkness was complete, it became apparent that the sea anchor could not hold them up into the wind effectively. The boats continually dropped off into the trough of the waves where they were swept broadside by the seas. The boats, the men—everything was soaked, then frozen. Most of the men tried to shelter themselves under the tent cloths, but the wind repeatedly tore them loose.

On the *Caird* they managed to make enough room for four men to huddle together at one time in the pile of sleeping bags in the bow, and they took turns trying in vain to sleep. On the *Docker,* however, there was only room enough for the men to sit upright, huddled together with their feet squeezed between the cases of stores. The seas that came on board ran down into the bottom of the boat, and since most of the men were wearing felt boots, their feet were soaked all night in the icy water. They did what they could to keep the boats bailed dry, but the water sometimes rose ankle-deep. To keep their feet from freezing, they worked their toes constantly inside their boots. They could only hope that the pain in their feet would continue, because comfort, much as they yearned for it, would mean that they were freezing. After a time, it took extreme concentration for them to keep wiggling their toes—it would have been so terribly easy just to stop.

As the hours dragged by and their agony deepened, the men in the *Docker* fought back with the single pitifully ridiculous weapon they had—curses. They cursed everything cursable—the sea, the boat, the spray, the cold, the wind, and often one another. There was a kind of pleading tone to their curses, though, as if they were prayerfully appealing for deliverance from this wet and freezing misery. Most of all they cursed Orde-Lees, who had got hold of the only set of oilskins and refused to give them up. He maneuvered himself into the most comfortable position in the boat by shoving Marston out, and he would not move. He either ignored or was oblivious to the oaths flung at him. After a while, Marston gave up and made his way to the stern where he sat down alongside Worsley at the tiller. For a time there was only the moaning of the wind through the rigging.

Then, to give vent to his rage, Marston began to sing. He sang one song, then waited, and then another. Finally he repeated over and over in a tired, thin voice, a song whose chorus went:

> *Twankedillo, Twankedillo,*
> *And a roaring pair of bagpipes*
> *Made from the green willow.*

Throughout the night the men were troubled by the need to urinate frequently. Certainly the intense cold was a factor in this condition, and the two physicians believed it was aggravated by the fact that they were continually wet so that they absorbed water through their skin. Whatever the reason, it required a man to leave the slight comfort of the sheltering canvas and make his way to the lee side of the boat several times during the night. Most of the men also had diarrhea from their diet of uncooked pemmican, and they would suddenly have to rush for the side and, holding fast to a shroud, sit on the frozen gunwale. Invariably, the icy sea wet them from beneath.

By far the worst off of the boats was the *Wills*. The water she was shipping was sometimes almost kneedeep. Little Wally How, the seaman, found it impossible to drive from his mind the fear that a killer whale would upset them into the water. Stevenson, the fireman, periodically buried his face in his hands and wept. Blackboro, who had insisted on wearing leather boots to save his felt pair for what he thought would be the future, lost all feeling in his feet after several hours. And Hudson, who had been at the tiller for almost seventy-two hours straight, developed a pain in his left buttock which became increasingly intense as the part began to swell. After a time he had to sit hunched sideways, and the rolling of the boat was agony to him. He was also suffering from severe frostbite in his hands.

The line between the *Wills* and the *Caird* alternately tightened and slacked, dropping into the water and rising into the bitter cold air each time. As the hours passed, it accumulated an ever-thickening coat of ice. The lives of the eight men aboard the *Wills* depended on that line. If it parted, and it seemed almost certain to, the *Wills* would fall off into the trough of the sea and be swamped long before her crew could beat the ice off the sail and hoist it.

All the boats were thick with ice, but the *Wills* was weighted down like a log. The seas poured on board her, flowing over the pile of sleeping bags in the bow and leaving them sheathed in ice. Ice formed in masses around her bow as she dipped into each sea, weighting her down that much more, so that every half hour or oftener, men had to be sent forward to beat the ice off her bow lest she go under.

Finally, for all the party, there was thirst. They had left the pack so abruptly and unexpectedly that they had failed to take on board any ice to be melted into water. There had been nothing to drink since the previous morning, and the men were beginning to crave water desperately. Their mouths were dry and their half-frostbitten lips began to swell and crack. Some men, when they tried to eat, found it impossible to swallow, and their hunger brought on seasickness.

CHAPTER 4

Toward 3 A.M., the wind began to fall, and by five o'clock it had dropped to a gentle breeze. Gradually the sea grew calmer.

The sky was clear, and finally the sun rose in unforgettable brilliance through a pink mist along the horizon, which soon melted into flaming gold.

It was more than just a sunrise. It seemed to flood into their souls, rekindling the life within them. They watched the growing light quenching the wild, dark misery of the night that now, at last, was over.

As the sun climbed a fraction higher, they saw off the starboard bow the peaks of Clarence Island, and a little later, Elephant Island, dead ahead—the Promised Land, no more than 30 miles away. In the joy of that moment, Shackleton called to Worsley to congratulate him on his navigation, and Worsley, stiff with cold, looked away in proud embarrassment.

They would land by nightfall—provided that not a moment was lost. Shackleton, impatient to be on the move, gave the order to get underway immediately. But it was not that simple. The light of dawn revealed the results of the night. Many faces were marked by the ugly white rings of frostbite, and almost everyone was afflicted with salt-water boils that gave off a gray, curdlike discharge when they broke. McIlroy called to Shackleton from the *Wills* that Blackboro's feet apparently were gone because he had been unable to restore circulation in them. And Shackleton himself looked haggard. His voice, which was usually strong and clear, had grown hoarse with exhaustion. Both the *Docker* and the *Wills* were severely iced up, inside and out. It took more than an hour to chip away enough to make them fit for sailing.

When it came time to haul in the sea anchor, Cheetham and Holness leaned over the bow of the *Docker* trying to untie the icy knot in the rope with fingers so stiff they would hardly move. While they worked, the *Docker* rose to a sea, then pitched downward. Holness failed to pull his head away, and two of his teeth were knocked out on the sea anchor. Tears welled in his eyes, rolled down into his beard, and froze there. The two men gave up trying to untie the sea anchor; they cut it loose and brought it, ice and all, on board.

The oars were frozen to the sides of the boats and had to be broken free. The men then tried to knock off their coating of ice, but two of them remained so slippery that they slid through the oarlocks and fell overboard. Fortunately the *Caird* managed to retrieve one, but the other drifted away.

The boats were finally underway at seven o'clock. A ration of nut food and biscuits was issued, but the men's thirst was now so intense that few of them could eat it. Shackleton suggested that they try chewing seal meat raw in order to swallow the blood. Pieces of the frozen meat were quickly handed out, and after several minutes of chewing and sucking, the men obtained enough of the bloody juice so they could at least swallow. But they went at it so voraciously that Shackleton realized the supply would soon be exhausted, so he ordered that the seal meat be given out only when thirst seemed to be threatening the reason of any individual.

The sails were set and they put out the oars and rowed at the same time, aiming for the west edge of Elephant Island to offset the gentle southwest wind that was blowing.

In the *Docker*, both Macklin and Greenstreet took off their boots and found their feet frostbitten, Greenstreet's much worse than Macklin's. Surprisingly, Orde-Lees offered to massage Greenstreet's feet. He worked over them for a long time; then he opened up his shirt and placed Greenstreet's half-frozen feet against the warmth of his bare chest. After a while, Greenstreet began to feel pain as the blood flowed back into the constricted vessels.

Hour after hour they rowed, and the outline of Elephant Island slowly grew larger. At noon, they had covered almost half the distance; by one-thirty they were less than 15 miles away. They had had no sleep for almost eighty hours, and their bodies had been drained by exposure and effort of almost the last vestige of vitality. But the conviction that they had to land by nightfall gave rise to a strength born of desperation. It was pull or perish, and ignoring their sickening thirst, they leaned on their oars with what seemed the last of their strength.

By 2 P.M., the snowy, 3,500-foot peaks of Elephant Island rose steeply out of the water dead ahead, probably no more than ten miles off. But an hour later, the island was still in the same position, hanging there, no closer and yet no farther away. Row as they might, they were standing still, apparently caught in a strong tidal current setting offshore. The wind had shifted to the north, so that they were also bucking a headwind, and the sails had to be lowered.

Shackleton, who was becoming progressively more anxious to get the party ashore, called the boats together and had them made fast one behind the other, with the *Docker* in the lead. He seemed to think it would increase their speed. It didn't. About four o'clock, the wind swung around to the west. Hurriedly they took in their oars and hoisted sail, trying to beat up into the wind. But for the *Wills* it was an impossible task, so the *Caird* had to take her in tow. They made almost no headway against the current.

Toward 5 P.M., the wind fell off. Immediately they took to the oars once more and pulled frantically in the gathering dusk, hoping to make a landing before night. But half an hour later the wind suddenly sprang up out of the wsw, and within fifteen minutes it was blowing nearly 50 miles an hour. Worsley brought the *Docker* alongside the *Caird*. Screaming to make himself heard above the wind, he told Shackleton he thought it would be best if the boats separated to try to make land independently along the southeast shore of Elephant Island.

Shackleton, for once, agreed to the separation; at least, he granted Worsley permission to proceed independently. The *Wills*, however, was kept fast astern of the *Caird*, and Shackleton admonished Worsley to do everything in his power to stay within sight. It was dark by the time the *Docker* cast off. The island was close, but just how close was now impossible to tell—maybe 10 miles, probably less. High in the sky was a ghostly, pale white image, the light of the moon shining through the clouds and reflecting back up from the glaciers on the island. It was all they had to steer by as the boats pounded forward into the cross sea. At times the wind was so strong they had to let go the lines holding the sails to avoid capsizing. The men in the *Caird* crouched low to escape the driving spray, but in the *Docker,* and especially the *Wills,* there was no escape.

Those who were steering took the worst punishment of all, and about eight o'clock, the strain began to tell on Wild, who had been at the *Caird's* tiller for twenty-four hours without relief. Shackleton ordered McNeish to take over, but the carpenter himself was very nearly exhausted. After about half an hour at the tiller, though the icy wind tore at his clothing and the spray stung him in the face and soaked him through, McNeish's head slumped forward and he fell asleep. Instantly, the *Caird's* stern swung to leeward and a huge wave swept over them. It awakened McNeish, but Shackleton ordered Wild to resume the helm.

Their immediate goal was the southeast corner of the island. Once around that, they would have the protection of the land; then they could look for a place to beach the boats. About nine-thirty, the reflection in the sky looked very close, and they knew they were almost on top of the land. But then, inexplicably, they began to lose ground. Looking over the sides of the boats they could see that they were traveling rapidly through the water, yet ever so gradually, the land was slipping from their grasp. There was nothing to do but to push on.

About midnight, Shackleton glanced to starboard and saw that the *Docker* was gone. He jumped to his feet and peered intently across the stormy waters, but there was no sign of her. Anxiously, he ordered the candle in the compass binnacle lighted and then had the binnacle hoisted up the mast so that it shone on the *Caird's* sail. But no answering light appeared in the distance.

Shackleton called for a box of matches. He instructed Hussey to light one every few minutes and hold it so that it flared against the sail. One at a time, Hussey struck the matches as Shackleton peered into the darkness. Still there was no signal from the *Docker*.

But she tried to answer. She was hardly more than a half mile away, and her men had seen the *Caird's* signal in the dark. On Worsley's instructions they took their only candle under the tent cloth and lighted it. Then they tried to hold it so that its light would show through the canvas in reply to Shackleton's signal—but the reply was never seen.

A moment later, all thought of trying to signal the *Caird* was forgotten as the *Docker* suddenly lurched violently in the grip of a fierce tide rip. Worsley was barely able to keep control of the boat. The crew hurriedly took in the sail and even unstepped the mast, which threatened to snap off in the wildly pitching boat. They put out the oars and tried to hold her steady by rowing. One moment she collided with a solid, unseen wave, then the water opened beneath her and she dropped into a dark chasm.

Worsley ordered Orde-Lees to take up an oar, but Orde-Lees begged to be let off, claiming that he was not a fit rower for such a perilous time, and that it was too wet for him. The two men screamed at one another in the darkness, and from every corner of the boat men cursed Orde-Lees. But it was no use, and finally Worsley disgustedly waved him forward. Orde-Lees immediately crawled into the bottom and refused to move, even though his weight unbalanced the boat.

Greenstreet, Macklin, Kerr, and Marston were at the oars, and they had about reached the limit of their endurance. After a time, Worsley decided to risk hoisting sail again. He swung the *Docker* into the teeth of the wind, holding her as close to it as she would go, so that they were taking the seas more or less head on. He put all the skill of twenty-eight years at sea into holding her in that delicate position, but she was very nearly uncontrollable. Furthermore, she was becoming sluggish under her increasing burden of water. Orde-Lees, who had been lying in the bottom, sat upright. He seemed suddenly to realize that the boat was sinking, and he grabbed a pot and began to bail. Cheetham joined him, and together they worked furiously, hurling the water over the side. In time, the *Docker* rose again to the seas.

It was now about three o'clock, and Worsley himself began to fail. He had faced the wind so long that his eyes refused to function properly, and he found it impossible to judge distance. Try as he might, he could no longer stay awake. They had been in the boats now for five and a half days, and during that time almost everyone had come to look upon Worsley in a new light. In the past he had been thought of as excitable and wild—even irresponsible. But all that was changed now. During these past days he had exhibited an almost phenomenal ability, both as a navigator and in the demanding skill of handling a small boat. There wasn't another man in the party even comparable with him, and he had assumed an entirely new stature because of it.

Now, seated at the tiller, his head began to nod. Macklin saw him going and offered to take over. Worsley agreed, but when he tried to go forward he found he could not straighten out his body. He had sat for almost six days in the same position. McLeod and Marston came aft and pulled him out of the stern, dragging him over the seats and cases of stores. Then they laid him down in the bottom of the boat and rubbed his thighs and stomach until his muscles began to loosen. But by then he was asleep.

Greenstreet, too, had taken a moment's exhausted rest, but now he awoke and took over the tiller from Macklin. Neither of them had any idea where they might be. But they shared the same dread as everybody else—the open sea. Between Elephant and Clarence Islands there is a gap about 14 miles wide, beyond which lies the Drake Passage. The last time the boats had been sure of their position was at dusk, when Elephant Island lay only about 10 miles away. But since then the wind had been out of the southwest—straight toward that fateful gap. If they were blown through, the chances of beating back to windward toward the island would be virtually nonexistent. Nevertheless, Greenstreet and Macklin admitted frankly to one another that very likely the *Docker* had already been driven out to sea.

The *Docker's* compass had been smashed some time earlier, and all that remained to steer by was Worsley's little silver pocket compass. The two men spread the tent cover over their heads, and Macklin struck matches while Greenstreet tried to read the compass. But even under the shelter of the canvas, the wind snuffed out the matches almost as soon as they were lit. Macklin then took his knife and split the individual match heads to make them flare long enough so that Greenstreet could see the compass.

Every few minutes they ducked under the tent cloth and took a reading, hoping to hold the *Docker* on a southwest course so that at least she would not be blown farther out to sea.

As they seemed on the very brink of exhaustion, and as the wind screamed to new heights, the palest hint of light showed in the eastern sky and began to brighten, very slowly. There was no telling how long it took to get light enough to see, but it was a long, long time. Even their raging thirst, after forty-eight hours without water, was forgotten as they waited for the sun to reveal their fate. Secretly, each man tried to prepare himself for the shock of seeing only an empty sea, or at best a distant island far away to windward and unreachable.

Gradually, the surface of the sea became discernible. And there, dead ahead, were the enormous gray-brown cliffs of Elephant Island rising out of the mists, sheer from the water, high above the boat—and less than a mile away. The distance seemed no more than a few hundred yards. There was no great joy in that moment. Only a feeling of astonishment which soon gave way to a sense of tremendous relief.

Just then, without an instant's warning, offshore gusts of wind swept down off the cliffs, striking the surface of the sea at perhaps 100 miles an hour. A moment later a wall of water as high as the boat rolled toward the *Docker*.

Greenstreet shouted to drop the sail. The oars were hurriedly put out and they pulled head-on into the blasts that shrieked down off the mountaintops. Somehow they managed to hold the *Docker's* head up into it, but the exertion required them to put forth strength they no longer really had. Looking forward, they saw a new wave, possibly 6 feet high, bearing down upon them.

Somebody shouted to wake up Worsley, and McLeod shook him violently, trying to rouse him. But Worsley was like a dead man, sprawled over the cases of stores midships with the soaking wet tent cloth spread over him. McLeod shook him again, and when Worsley failed to stir, McLeod kicked him, again and again; finally Worsley opened his eyes. He sat up, and instantly he realized what was happening.

"For God's sake," he shouted, "get her around—get away from it! Hoist the sail!"

Greenstreet put the tiller over, and the men struggled feverishly to raise the sail. She had just caught the wind when the first wave hit them and rolled over the stern. Greenstreet was almost knocked off his seat. A moment later, the second wave engulfed them. The *Docker*, half-filled with water, slumped under the burden and lost most of her headway. Everything else was forgotten. The men seized the first thing that came to hand and began to bail. They threw the water over the side with mugs, hats, even their cupped bare hands. Gradually they got the *Docker* emptied out. Worsley took the tiller and turned north to run before the gale, with the seas pursuing the boat from astern. He guided her close inshore, just under the lofty glaciers fringing the island. Pieces of ice floated amongst the waves, and the men leaned over the sides as the boat drove past and scooped them up with their hands.

A moment later they were chewing and sucking greedily, and the delicious water was running down their throats.

CHAPTER 5

Throughout the night, Shackleton on board the *Caird* had kept watch for the *Docker*. And as the hours passed, his anxiety mounted. He had faith in Worsley's seamanship, but such a night demanded something more than skill.

However, there was more than enough to keep him occupied with the *Caird*. Wild remained at the tiller, and as the southwest gale increased, he held them on a course as nearly into the wind as possible so that they wouldn't be blown past the island. Spray burst over the bow and swept across the dark forms of the men hunddled in the bottom of the boat. Hussey tried tending the line to the mainsail, but several times the wind tore it from his grasp, and Vincent had to take over for him.

On board the *Wills,* towed astern of the *Caird,* conditions were even more miserable. The pain in Hudson's side had become almost intolerable, and it was more than he could bear to stay at the tiller. Tom Crean took over for him, and occasionally Billy Bakewell had a turn at steering. Rickenson, a slight individual, seemed on the point of collapse, and sat by himself off to one side. How and Stevenson, when they weren't bailing, clung to one another seeking to generate some bit of warmth between their bodies.

The bow of the *Wills* plunged into almost every sea, so that the men sat kneedeep in water. Ironically, this was almost a comfort, for the water was warmer than the air. Blackboro's feet were long since beyond the point of hurting. He never complained, though he knew that it was only a matter of time until gangrene set in. Even if he lived, it seemed unlikely that this youngster who had stowed away a year and a half before would ever walk again. Once during the night, Shackleton called to him in an attempt to raise his spirits.

"Blackboro," he shouted in the darkness.

"Here, sir," Blackboro replied.

"We shall be on Elephant Island tomorrow," Shackleton yelled. "No one has ever landed there before, and you will be the first ashore."

Blackboro did not answer.

Shackleton sat in the stern of the *Caird* alongside Wild, with his hand on the line between them and the *Wills*. Before dark, he had instructed Hudson that if the *Wills* got adrift, he was to make for land to leeward, probably Clarence Island, and wait there until a rescue boat could be sent to pick up the men. But the order had been merely a routine pretense. Shackleton knew that if the *Wills* broke loose, she would never be seen again. And now, as he sat in the stern, he could feel the *Wills* seize up on the towline as she rose unwillingly to each wave. Looking back he could just see her in the darkness. Several times the line went slack and she disappeared from sight only to reappear suddenly, outlined against the whiteness of a breaking wave.

When at last the first gray tinge of dawn appeared, the *Wills*, by some marvelous caprice of luck, was still doggedly astern of the *Caird*. And there was land, too, looming on top of them off the port bow—great black headlands appearing through the mists, scarcely a quarter mile away. Immediately, Shackleton ordered them to put about and head west across the wind. And in the space of fifteen minutes, possibly less, the wind suddenly eased off. They had passed the northeast tip of the island—and they were under the lee of the land at last. They held to a westerly course with the hulking cliffs and glaciers rearing up alongside them. Dominican gulls screamed in flight along the rock faces that rose sheer from the water, great masses of volcanic formations against whose sides the seas broke furiously. But there was no sign of a landing place—not even the smallest cove or beach.

There was ice, though. Large pieces of glaciers that had tumbled into the water floated on the surface. The men snatched up small chunks and thrust them into their mouths. For nearly an hour they searched the shoreline for a foothold, however small. Then somebody spied a tiny, shingled beach, half-hidden behind a chain of rocks. Shackleton stood up on one of the seats and saw that it was a treacherous place. He hesitated for a moment, then ordered the boats to make for it.

When they were a thousand yards off, Shackleton signaled the *Wills* to come alongside and take him on board. Of the two boats, she had the shallower draft, and Shackleton wanted to approach the beach in her first to see if the *Caird* could negotiate the seething channel between the rocks.

At that exact moment, the *Docker* was driving westward along the coast, looking for a place to land. Since sunrise, by Worsley's estimate, they had gone 14 miles, past point after point, without seeing a single site fit to beach the boat on. During all that distance, there had not been a glimpse of the other two boats, and it was now almost nine-thirty. The *Docker's* crew were sure that they alone had survived the night. "Poor blighters," Greenstreet whispered to Macklin. "They're gone."

Then they rounded a tiny spit of land, and there, dead ahead, were the masts of the *Caird* and *Wills*, bobbing in the backwash from the breakers. By some incredible coincidence, the *Docker's* inability to find a suitable place to land had reunited her with the rest of the party. Had there been a haven somewhere in those 14 miles behind her, the two groups might now have been miles apart, each assuming the other had been lost.

The men aboard the *Docker* gave three hoarse cheers to their shipmates, but the noise of the breakers drowned them out. A few minutes later, their sail was sighted from the *Caird,* and just then Shackleton himself looked up and saw the *Docker* bearing down upon them. By then the *Wills* was close inshore. A shallow reef lay across the opening, and heavy rollers foamed over it. Shackleton waited for his moment, then gave the order to pull, and the *Wills* rolled safely over the reef. With the next wave, her bow ground against the shore.

Shackleton, remembering his promise, urged Blackboro to jump ashore, but the lad failed to move. He seemed not to comprehend what Shackleton was saying. Impatiently, Shackleton took hold of him and lifted him over the side. Blackboro dropped to his hands and knees, then rolled over and sat down with the surf surging around him.

"Get up," Shackleton ordered.

Blackboro looked up. "I can't, sir," he replied.

Shackleton suddenly remembered Blackboro's feet. In the excitement of the landing he had forgotten, and he felt ashamed. How and Bakewell jumped overboard and pulled Blackboro farther up the beach.

The stores were rapidly unloaded, and the *Wills* was rowed out to the *Docker.* Stores and men were transferred and ferried ashore. Then the *Caird* was unloaded enough so she could negotiate the reef.

As the boats were being pulled to safety, Rickenson suddenly turned pale, and a minute later collapsed of a heart attack. Greenstreet's frostbitten feet would hardly support him, and he hobbled ashore and lay down alongside of Blackboro. Hudson pulled himself through the surf, then sank down on the beach.

Stevenson, a vacant expression on his face, was helped ashore, out of reach of the water.

They were on land.

It was the merest handhold, 100 feet wide and 50 feet deep. A meager grip on a savage coast, exposed to the full fury of the sub-Antarctic Ocean. But no matter—they were on land. For the first time in 497 days they were on land. Solid, unsinkable, immovable, blessed land.

PART V

CHAPTER 1

Many of the men half-stumbled about aimlessly, scuffling their feet in the pebbles, or bending down to pick up a handful of rocks; some even dropped full length to the ground to feel its sublime solidity beneath them. For a time a few men simply sat down, shivering uncontrollably and mumbling gibberish to themselves.

Just then the sun came out. In its light their faces showed dead white from exhaustion and frostbite, and from being continually soaked with water. The circles around their eyes were so deep their eyes seemed to have sunk slightly into their heads.

Green readied some milk as quickly as he could, and each man's mug was filled. They drank it almost boiling hot and its heat spread throughout their bodies, setting their nerves to tingling as if their blood had suddenly been thawed and begun to flow again.

From where they stood around the blubber stove, the cliffs of their side of the island were less than 15 yards away. They rose straight up 800 feet into the air, leveled off for a bit, then climbed skyward again to a height of perhaps 2,500 feet. But their little niche of gravel was relatively thick with life—"a land of fatness, Antartically speaking," James noted. Farther down the beach, ten seals lay basking in the sun a short distance from the water. There was also a small rookery of ringed penguins high up on a rock to one side, and periodically little bands of gentoo penguins waddled up out of the water to survey these strange creatures who had come in from the sea. There were birds, too—skua gulls, paddies, cormorants, and Cape pigeons.

Shackleton stood in the center of the group. He had removed his helmet and his long, uncut hair hung down over his forehead. His shoulders were bent with care, and his voice was so hoarse from shouting that he was unable to speak above a whisper. Yet he felt a profound sense of satisfaction and accomplishment to be standing at last on land, surrounded by his men.

The men themselves spoke very little as they drank their milk. Each seemed absorbed in his own thoughts. Most of them were extremely unsteady, both from exhaustion and from the fact that they had fought the motion of the boats so long that their equilibrium was temporarily unbalanced. When they had finished their milk, a party was sent to bring in some seals. They brought back four, which were immediately stripped of blubber, and cut into thick steaks. Green set to work frying up all the steaks his pots could hold while the rest of the men pitched the tents and piled the stores well clear of the water.

Finally the food was ready, and they ate. It was neither breakfast nor lunch nor dinner. It was one long intermittent meal. As soon as they had finished the first round of steaks, Green put more on the fire. When these were ready the men stopped whatever they were doing and ate again. It wasn't until nearly 3 P.M. that they had eaten all they could hold.

Then it was time to sleep. They unrolled their soaked sleeping bags and wrung out what water they could; the dampness that remained made little difference. James wrote: "Turned in and slept, as we had never slept before, absolute dead dreamless sleep, oblivious of wet sleeping bags, lulled by the croaking of the penguins." It was the same for all of them. "How delicious," wrote Hurley, "to wake in one's sleep and listen to the chanting of the penguins mingling with the music of the sea. To fall asleep and awaken again and feel this is real. We have reached the land!!"

Most of the men were awakened once during that glorious night to stand an hour's watch, and even this was almost pleasure. The night was calm, and the sky was clear. The moon shone on the little pebbled beach, washed by the waves, a scene of utter tranquility. Furthermore, wrote Worsley, the watchmen, during their 1-hour tour of duty, "feed themselves, keep the blubber fire going, feed themselves, dry their clothes, feed themselves, and then feed themselves again before turning in."

Shackleton permitted the men to sleep until nine-thirty the next morning. But at breakfast an ugly rumor began to circulate, and when they had finished eating, Shackleton confirmed the almost shocking truth of it. They would have to move.

There could hardly have been a more demoralizing prospect. Having barely escaped the sea's hungry grasp a scant twenty-four hours before, now to have to return to it. . . . But the need was indisputable. They could see that only great good fortune had permitted them to land where they were. The cliffs at the head of the beach bore the marks of high tides and the scars of storm damage, indicating that the entire spit was frequently swept by seas. The place was obviously tenable only in good weather and while the tides were moderate.

Shackleton ordered Wild to take a crew of five seamen in the *Wills* and sail west along the coast to look for a more secure campsite. The *Wills* set out at eleven o'clock. The rest of the party worked at a leisurely pace throughout the day. The tents were struck, then pitched again as high up on the beach as a shelf could be found that would accommodate them. The stores were piled even higher, in case of a sudden storm.

But most of the day was spent simply enjoying life. They were all still crippled from the six days spent in cramped positions in the boats, and now for the first time they began to realize the incredible tension they had been under for so long. They became conscious of it, strangely, by a mounting awareness of a long-forgotten feeling. It was something they knew now they had not really experienced since abandoning the *Endurance*. It was security. The knowledge that, comparatively at least, there was nothing to fear. There was still danger, of course, but it was different from the imminent threat of disaster which had stalked them for so long. In a very literal way, it seemed to release a portion of their minds which hitherto had been obsessed with the need to remain ceaselessly alert.

It was a joy, for example, to watch the birds simply as birds and not for the significance they might have—whether they were a sign of good or evil, an opening of the pack or a gathering storm. The island itself was a sight worthy of more than casual observation. Along the coastline, the cliffs looked like an enormous wall thrown up against the sea. Glaciers crept down their sides all the way to the water, where the action of the waves constantly wore away at the ice. Now and again, a small piece or a section almost as big as a berg would plunge into the water.

The ferocity of the land apparently spawned similarly forbidding weather. For some strange meteorological reason, savage, tornadolike downdrafts periodically swooped down from the heights above and fairly exploded when they struck the water, whipping the seas close inshore into a frenzy of spindrift and froth. Hussey thought they were the "williwaws," sudden bursts of wind peculiar to coastal areas in polar regions. It was one of these, apparently, that had nearly caught the *Docker* the morning before.

They waited throughout the day for Wild and his party to return, but darkness came and there were still no signs of them. The other men ate supper and turned in, leaving the blubber stove burning with the door to the firebox open and facing seaward to act as a beacon. Hardly had they fallen asleep when the watchman heard a shout from seaward. It was the returning *Wills*. All hands were roused, and they went down to the water's edge. Wild brought the *Wills* through the breakers and she was soon hauled well up onto the beach.

Wild and his five exhausted men confirmed the fact that this was truly an inhospitable place. In nine hours of looking, they had found only one seemingly secure place to camp—a fairly sheltered spit of beach, about 150 yards long and 30 yards wide, some 7 miles along the coast to the west. There was a good-sized penguin rookery there, Wild said, and his men had also sighted a number of seals and some few sea elephants. A nearby glacier would keep them supplied with ice for melting into water.

Shackleton was satisfied, and he announced that they would break camp at dawn. The party was awakened at 5 A.M., and they ate their breakfast in the light from the blubber stove. When dawn came it was clear and still. The boats were launched and everything was loaded except ten cases of sledging rations and some paraffin, which were left behind in a very high crevice to minimize the weight in the boats. The supplies could be sent for later if the need arose. The tide came in very slowly, so it wasn't until eleven o'clock that there was enough water over the reef to get away.

The *Wills* had been lightened by transferring Blackboro to the *Caird* and Hudson to the *Docker*, and for the first 2 miles the boats made fair progress. Then, with hardly an instant's warning, the elements seemed to go berserk. All at once, the wind was shrieking in their ears, and the sea, which a moment before had been nearly calm, was torn into froth. They were caught in one of the violent downdrafts from the cliffs. It lasted only three or four terrifying minutes, and then was gone. But it heralded a change in weather, for within a quarter hour the wind had moved from the south to the southwest and quickly risen in force from breeze, to gale, to storm, then hurricane. The boats, under the lee of the land, should have been protected from the gale by the towering 2,000-foot cliffs alongside them. But instead, the cliffs sucked down on winds passing overhead so that they shrieked down upon the boats, and roared out to sea.

Only by staying very close up against the land could the boats avoid being blown offshore. To port, the land rose so sheer that it looked as if it were hanging over them. Great drunken green waves were flung against the cliffs, and spray filled the air. To starboard, the sea was whipped into a maelstrom by the wind. Between, there was a meager corridor of safety; and along this passage the boats crept forward. And their progress was creeping at best. Shortly after noon, the tide turned and the current began to flow against them. They could gauge their progress against the land, and at times they seemed to advance only by inches or even to be standing still. To hoist sail was unthinkable; they could only row. The *Caird* still had its full quota of four oars, but the *Docker* and the *Wills* had been reduced to three apiece.

The temperature had fallen perhaps 15 degrees since the change of wind, and now hovered around 5 degrees. The spray combined with the snow to freeze into a mushy coating over the insides of the boats, and on the heads and shoulders of the men. During the loading of the stores, Greenstreet had given his mittens to Clark to hold. But then in the hurry to get away while the tide was favorable, Clark had gone off in the *Caird,* leaving Greenstreet in the *Docker* with nothing to protect his hands as he rowed. Now his hands began to freeze. Frostbite blisters developed in his palms, and the water in them also froze. The blisters became like hard pebbles inserted into his flesh.

Somewhat after one o'clock, when they had covered half the distance to the new camp, they came to a towering rock protruding from the water about a quarter-mile offshore. The *Caird,* with

Wild at the tiller, and the *Wills* under the command of Crean made the obvious decision to pass inland of the rock. But Worsley, acting on one of his unpredictable impulses, elected to pass outside of it. The *Wills* and the *Caird* struggled on toward the beach, but the *Docker* was lost from sight.

By going to seaward of the rock, she had ventured too far offshore and been caught by the full violence of the wind. Here the surface of the water was torn into foam and the wave tops were ripped off and blown downwind. Worsley knew at once that he had acted unwisely, and he swung the *Docker* back toward the coast. "Put your backs into it!" he shouted at the rowers. But it was almost all the oarsmen could do to hold their own against the wind, and it was doubtful how much longer they could do even that.

Worsley suddenly jumped up and shouted for Greenstreet to take the tiller; then he took over Greenstreet's oar. Worsley was fresh, and he set a tremendous pace. Somehow, Macklin and Kerr on the other oars managed to keep up, and slowly, foot by foot, they pulled their way closer to the rock and finally reached it. They had gained a lee only to be caught in the surge of the seas against the rock. "Back water! Back water!" Worsley screamed.

They held her off—but only barely. Three times the *Docker* was lifted up and hurled toward the rock, but then the wind eased down momentarily, and they were able to pull clear. Greenstreet resumed his oar, and they continued toward the land.

In the midst of the struggle, the mitten on Macklin's right hand had slipped off, and he saw now that his exposed fingers were turning white with frostbite. But he dared not stop rowing even long enough to cover them.

By now it was after three o'clock. The *Caird* and the *Wills* had landed safely. Two seals found lying on the beach had been killed and stripped of blubber to start a fire. Shackleton stood looking out across the storm-driven sea for a glimpse of the *Docker*.

Finally, around a point of land, a speck appeared through the gray mists. It was the *Docker*, toiling into the wind toward the beach. It looked as if she were going to make it, when suddenly another blast tore down from the cliffs.

Worsley again took over Greenstreet's place, and this time old McLeod put out the stump of a broken oar and added its feeble pulling power to the others. It made a difference, though—just enough to gain the reefs. Worsley quickly grabbed the tiller and guided her through the rocks.

The moment her bow touched, Greenstreet swung his numbed feet over the side and hobbled ashore through the surf. He spied the vapor rising from the freshly killed seals, stumbled toward where they lay, and thrust his frozen hands into their blood-warm bowels.

CHAPTER 2

O nce more they were all on land, and safe. But the wondrous joy that had marked the landing only thirty hours before was absent now. They realized, as one man said, that "Elephant Island had flattered only to deceive." She had revealed her true face to them, and the sight of it was ugly.

Moreover, an examination of the new campsite raised serious doubts about whether it had been worth the trouble to move. It was a rocky spit about thirty yards across, extending to seaward like a tongue stuck out from an enormous glacier 150 yards inland. The spit rose steeply from the water, and its upper reaches appeared to be above the high water mark. But otherwise it was completely naked. Except at the shoreline, there was not a boulder or even a small rock that might protect a man from the wind.

"A more inhospitable place could scarcely be imagined," wrote Macklin. "The gusts increased in violence and became so strong that we could hardly walk against them, and there was not a lee or a scrap of shelter anywhere." As the forecastle hands were setting up No. 4 tent, the wind got under it and ripped a 4-foot rent in its threadbare material. A few minutes later, No. 5, the old hoop tent, was caught by a blast of wind that very nearly tore it to shreds. The men made no effort to repair their tents, for by now it was dark and nobody really cared anyhow. They simply spread the tent cloths as best they could and weighted them down with rocks. Then they spread out their sleeping bags, which had been soaked anew during the trip in the boats, then lay down and fell asleep.

Throughout the night the wind continued to shriek down from the mountains. It got hold of the *Docker,* the heaviest of the boats, and swung her completely around. During his watch, McIlroy looked on helplessly as the wind picked up a large bag of ragged old blankets and carried it out to sea. The men who were sleeping on the ground were slowly covered by an accumulation of snow. And by four o'clock, everyone was sleeping on the ground, because the tents had threatened to blow away, and had to be taken down.

The blizzard persisted throughout that day, and into the next. Hardly a man stirred from the meager protection of his sleeping bag until 11 A.M., when Shackleton ordered all hands out to kill penguins. Orde-Lees wrote: "The blizzard was, if anything, worse. It was impossible to face the wind. The driving snow rushed down one's throat as one breathed and choked one." There were about 200 penguins altogether, and of that number they managed to secure a total of seventy-seven. "Skinning them with our already partially frostbitten hands was painful work," Orde-Lees continued, "for to bare the hand for very few minutes in such a blizzard means almost certain frostbite. We sought shelter as we could find . . . but it was only the warmth of the dead penguins that saved our hands."

The weather cleared briefly during the night, and the hulking cliffs of the island stood out in silhouette against the star-filled sky. By morning, a fresh blizzard had begun, but it was not quite so bad as the last one.

It was April 20, a day notable for only one reason: Shackleton finally made official what everyone had expected for a long time.

The floe starts to crack, revealing the extent of the helm damage
(Royal Geographic Society)

Last great attempt to cut the *Endurance* free of the icepack
(Royal Geographic Society)

The *Endurance* is crushed between the floes, October 24, 1915
(Royal Geographic Society)

Frank Wild surveys the wreck of the *Endurance* on November 8, 1915, during their last official visit to the wreck (Royal Geographic Society)

(*Top*) Ernest Shackleton and Frank Wild at Ocean Camp. Hurley's boxes of photography equipment are arranged beside the doorway to Shackleton's tent (Royal Geographic Society). (*Bottom*) Ocean Camp in the distance (Royal Geographic Society)

Relaying the *James Caird* across the ice, after a successful test in the water (Royal Geographic Society)

Lionel Greenstreet, after exercising the dogs in weather so cold his breath froze (Scott Polar Research Institute)

Ernest Shackleton and Frank Hurley prepare dinner at Patience Camp
(Royal Geographic Society)

Hubert Hudson, navigating officer (Scott Polar Research Institute)

Elephant Island, enjoying their first hot drink and food after a harrowing seven-day journey (Royal Geographic Society)

(*Top*) The Snuggery: the *Stancombe Wills* and the *Dudley Docker* are made into a hut for shelter. After this photo, a stove and chimney were made and installed for heat (Royal Geographic Society). (*Bottom*) Unsuccessful attempts to dig a cave for shelter on Elephant Island (Royal Geographic Society)

Launching the *James Caird* from Elephant Island, April 24, 1916
(Royal Geographic Society)

(*Above*) Sending off the *James Caird*. This original print was later altered by Hurley to instead depict the rescue (Royal Geographic Society). *(Lower right)* The triumphant *Yelcho* returns to Elephant Island for the rest of the crew, almost two years after the *Endurance* first set sail from England (Royal Geographic Society)

The rescued crew of the *Endurance* in Punta Arenas, September 3, 1916. Hussey was the only crewmember Shackleton allowed to shave before reaching port (Scott Polar Research Institute)

He would take a party of five men and set sail in the *Caird* for South Georgia to bring relief. They would leave as soon as the *Caird* could be made ready and provisioned for the trip.

The news came as no surprise to anyone. In fact a formal announcement was unnecessary. The subject had been discussed openly even long before the party had left Patience Camp. They knew that whatever island they might ultimately reach, a boat journey of some sort would be necessary to bring rescue to the party as a whole. Even the destination, illogical as it might look on a map, had been settled to everyone's satisfaction.

There were three possible objectives. The nearest of these was Cape Horn, the island of Tierra del Fuego—"Land of Fire," which lay about 500 miles to the northwest. Next was the settlement of Port Stanley in the Falkland Islands, some 550 miles very nearly due north. Finally there was South Georgia, slightly more than 800 miles to the northeast. Though the distance to South Georgia was more than half again as far as the journey to Cape Horn, weather conditions made South Georgia the most sensible choice.

An easterly current, said to travel 60 miles a day, prevails in the Drake Passage, and almost incessant gales blow in the same direction. To reach either Cape Horn or the Falkland Islands would mean beating to windward against both of these colossal forces; it was enough to dare a 22-foot boat on these storm-wracked waters without trying to drive her to windward. En route to South Georgia, on the other hand, the prevailing winds would be generally astern—at least in theory.

All this had been discussed and discussed again. And though the *Caird's* chances of actually reaching South Georgia were remote, a great many men genuinely wanted to be taken along. The prospect of staying behind, of waiting and not knowing, of possibly wintering on this hateful island was far from attractive.

Shackleton had already made up his mind, after long discussions with Wild, not only as to who should be taken, but who should not be left behind. Worsley would be indispensable. They would travel perhaps a thousand miles across the stormiest ocean on the globe. The ultimate goal was an island no more than 25 miles wide at its widest point. To guide an open boat that distance, under conditions that were frightening even to contemplate, and then to strike a pinpoint on the chart was a task that would sorely tax even Worsley's skill as a navigator. After him, Shackleton chose Crean, McNeish, Vincent, and McCarthy.

Crean was tough, a seasoned sailor who did as he was told. And Shackleton was not sure that Crean's rough, tactless nature would lend itself well to a period of enforced and perhaps long waiting. McNeish was now fifty-seven years old, and really not up to the journey. But both Shackleton and Wild felt that he was still a potential troublemaker and not a good man to be left behind. Furthermore, if the *Caird* were damaged by ice—a possibility which was far from remote—McNeish would prove invaluable. Jack Vincent bore the same stigma as McNeish—his compatibility under trying conditions was open to doubt, and he might fare badly if left behind. On the positive side, he had behaved well during the journey from Patience Camp, and his simple strength was in his favor. By contrast, Timothy McCarthy had never caused anyone a moment's trouble, and he was universally liked. Shackleton picked him for no more complicated reasons than that he was an experienced seaman, and that he was built like a bull.

As soon as Shackleton made the decision official, McNeish and Marston went to work removing the planks that had been added to the *Docker* in order to fashion a sort of decking over the *Caird*. The blizzard made working conditions miserable.

The rest of the men were busy trying to create some degree of comfort. A new shelter was made for the galley out of packing cases, rocks, and some pieces of canvas. Because of the physical conditions of Blackboro and Rickenson, who was still weak from his heart attack, Shackleton granted permission for the *Docker* to be upended to form a shelter for the members of No. 5 tent. The men did what they could to make this shelter weatherproof by packing snow and mud along one side, and draping blankets, coats, and odd bits of canvas from the other. But nothing could be done to dry the ground beneath the boat, which was a stinking mess of melted snow in which penguin guano had dissolved. The discomfort was so intense that even sleeping was almost impossible. The blizzard had continued for three days and nights. The winds, which Hussey estimated reached 120 mph, had driven the dustlike snow into everything—even to the very foot of their sleeping bags, which had never even begun to dry out from the boat journey.

The strength of the wind made it perilous at times even to venture outside. Occasionally small blocks of ice were hurled through the air. Once a 10-gallon cooking pot was whisked from alongside the galley and carried almost out of sight before it was dropped into the sea. The forecastle hands lost their hoosh pot when it was put down on a rock for a moment; it simply disappeared. Another time McLeod spread out his Burberry parka to dry with two stones "as large as his head on top of it." When he turned his back for a moment, the wind blew the rocks off, then snatched the parka away. Some men had their mittens blown off. Though a canvas covering was placed over the pile of stores and anchored down by a circle of large rocks, the wind seemed to reach underneath and snitch away small articles.

In spite of these miserable conditions, the work of preparing the *Caird* for her journey went on the following day. McNeish, Marston, and McLeod attached the runners of a dismantled sledge across the upper sides of the boat to form a framework for decking her over. Pieces of plywood from the cases of stores were nailed over these, and a canvas covering of sorts was begun. The mainmast was removed from the *Docker* and lashed inside the *Caird's* keel in the hope that she would not break in two when she encountered bad weather.

Periodically Worsley climbed to a ledge of rock about 150 feet high near the penguin rookery to observe the ice formation. A narrow belt of broken floes lay offshore, but it did not look too thick to get through. However, Worsley's primary concern was the continuing thick weather which prevented him from obtaining a sight with which to check his only remaining chronometer. Without a sight they would have to rely on the hope that the chronometer was accurate.

Greenstreet's frostbitten hands had recovered somewhat, and he and Bakewell were given the job of providing the *Caird* with ballast. Together they sewed shale into canvas sacks, about a hundred pounds to each sack. The canvas was frozen, and they had to thaw it out a foot at a time by holding it close to the blubber stove. The heat and the rough stones caused the frostbite blisters in Greenstreet's hands to break and then bleed.

There were other significant preparations for the journey. Hurley buttonholed Shackleton, who signed the following letter in Hurley's diary:

21st April, 1916

To whom this may concern viz. my executors assigns etc. Under is my signature to the following instructions.

In the event of my not surviving the boat journey to South Georgia I here instruct Frank Hurley to take complete charge & responsibility for exploitation of all films & photographic reproductions of all films & negatives taken on this Expedition

*the aforesaid films & negatives to become the property of Frank
Hurley after due exploitation, in which, the moneys to be paid
to my executors will be according to the contract made at the
start of the expedition. The exploitation expires after a lapse
of eighteen months from date of first public display.*

I bequeath the big binoculars to Frank Hurley.

E. H. Shackleton

*Witness
John Vincent*

The next day the blizzard rose to new heights. Several men
were cut on the face by bits of flying ice and rock. All work except the simplest cooking was out of the question, and the men
stayed in their sleeping bags all day. Wild predicted that if conditions didn't improve shortly, some of the weaker men would
not survive. And Shackleton met secretly with Macklin to ask
how long he thought the men who were remaining behind
could hold out under such conditions. Macklin said he thought
about a month. Fortunately the wind eased considerably during
the night, though a heavy snowfall continued. The temperature
dropped sharply. In the morning McNeish got busy once more
with the *Caird*. All that remained was to finish the canvas decking. Alf Cheetham and Timothy McCarthy were put to sewing
the bits of canvas together, but in the bitter cold it was so stiff
they had to pull the needle through it with a pair of pliers at
every stitch.

At the same time, the welfare of the men who would be left
behind was under consideration. For a while they thought of
building a hut of stones, but all the available rocks had been worn
by the action of the sea until they were very nearly round; since

there was nothing to use for cement this plan had to be abandoned. Instead, a party of men with picks and shovels began to dig a cave in the face of the glacier at the head of the spit. But the ice proved to be almost rock-hard and it was slow work.

Shackleton spent the day supervising the various activities. He saw that the *Caird* was very nearly finished, and announced that she would sail as soon as the weather permitted. As evening came on and the weather looked more promising, Shackleton ordered Orde-Lees and Vincent to melt ice to fill the two water casks to be carried aboard the *Caird*. They made every effort to find fresh-water ice from the glacier, but all of it had been tainted slightly by salt water spray that had frozen against the face of the glacier. When it was ready, Orde-Lees took a sample of the melted water to Shackleton, who tasted it. He noted the trace of salt, but he said it would do all right.

Shackleton spent almost the whole night talking with Wild about a hundred different subjects, ranging from what should be done in the event that a rescue party failed to arrive within a reasonable length of time to the distribution of tobacco. When there was nothing more to discuss, Shackleton wrote a letter in his log, which he left with Wild:

April 23rd, 1916 Elephant Island

Dear Sir

In the event of my not surviving the boat journey to South Georgia you will do your best for the rescue of the party. You are in full command from the time the boat leaves this island, and all hands are under your orders. On your return to England you are to communicate with the Committee. I wish you, Lees & Hurley to write the book. You watch my interests.

*In another letter you will find the terms as agreed for lecturing
you to do England Great Britain & Continent. Hurley the
U.S.A. I have every confidence in you and always have had,
May God prosper your work and your life. You can convey
my love to my people and say I tried my best.*

Yours sincerely

E. H. Shackleton

Frank Wild

CHAPTER 3

Throughout the night the successive watchmen kept a close watch for a break in the weather; it came during the very early morning hours. The wind moderated considerably. Shackleton was immediately notified and he ordered that all hands be called at the first streak of light. The men were turned out just before 6 A.M.

McNeish went to work putting the finishing touches on the *Caird's* canvas decking, while Green and Orde-Lees began to render some blubber into oil to be poured on the sea in the event that they had to heave to because of extremely bad weather. Others collected stores and equipment for the boat.

The *Caird* party was to take a six weeks' supply of food, consisting of three cases of the scrupulously hoarded sledging ration, two cases of nut food, a supply of biscuits, and powdered milk and bouillon cubes to provide the party with hot drinks. The cooking would be done on a Primus stove, and two were to be taken so they would have a spare. What little extra clothing could be found in the way of socks and mittens was rounded up, along with six of the reindeer sleeping bags.

For equipment, the *Caird* would carry one pair of binoculars, a prismatic compass, a small medicine chest originally intended for a sledging party, four oars, a bailer, the pump that Hurley had made, a shotgun and some shells, a sea anchor and a fishing line, plus a few candles and a supply of matches. Worsley had gathered together all the navigational aids he could find. He took his own sextant and another which belonged to Hudson, along with the necessary navigational tables and what charts were to be had. These were packed into a box that was made as watertight as possible. He still carried his sole chronometer slung around his neck. Out of twenty-four on board the *Endurance* when she sailed from England, this one alone had survived.

A farewell breakfast was prepared, for which Shackleton permitted two extra biscuits and a quarter pound of jam per man. For the most part, the men stood around joking. McCarthy was admonished by the other forecastle hands not to get his feet wet during the voyage. Worsley was cautioned against overeating when he reached civilization, and Crean was forced to promise that he would leave some girls for the rest of the party after they were rescued. But the tension in the air was unmistakable. Both groups knew they might never see one another again.

Shortly after breakfast the sun came out. Worsley grabbed his sextant and quickly obtained a sight, which, when he had worked it out, proved his chronometer to be fairly accurate. It seemed like a lucky omen.

Toward nine o'clock, Shackleton went with Worsley up the lookout point to survey the ice conditions offshore. They saw a band of floes parallel to the coast about 6 miles out, but there was an opening through which the *Caird* could pass easily. They returned to camp and found that McNeish was finished and the boat was ready.

Under the circumstances McNeish had done a magnificent job. The entire boat was decked over with canvas except for an open hatchway aft that was about 4 feet long and 2 feet wide.

Yoke lines like reins ran back to the rudder for steering. So far as appearances went, she looked seaworthy enough.

All hands were mustered to launch her. She was lying with her stern toward the sea, and there was a long line attached to her bow. The men tried to shove her off the beach, but the heavy, volcanic grit at the shoreline held her fast. Marston, Greenstreet, Orde-Lees, and Kerr waded into the icy surf up to their knees, and with the rest of the men shoving, attempted to rock her free. She still refused to move. Wild tried to pry her bow free, using an oar as a lever, while all hands pushed. But the oar broke and the boat was fast as ever. The *Caird's* crew, except for Shackleton, scrambled on board in the hope of poling her off with oars; as they did so, a large wave broke on the beach, and she rode out on its backwash into deeper water.

The moment she was afloat, the weight of the five men sitting on the decking made her top-heavy and she rolled heavily to port. Vincent and McNeish were thrown into the sea. Both men made their way ashore, cursing furiously. Vincent traded with How for a semidry pair of underwear and trousers, but McNeish refused to exchange clothes with anybody and climbed back on board the boat.

The *Caird* was then paddled out past the reef, and she waited at the end of her bowline while the *Wills* was launched and loaded with about half a ton of ballast. This cargo was rowed out and transferred to the *Caird;* on her second trip, the *Wills* took out another quarter ton of ballast sacks, and an extra 500 pounds of large rocks.

Shackleton was now ready to go. He had spoken to Wild for the last time and the two had shaken hands. The provisions were placed on board the *Wills,* and Shackleton and Vincent climbed aboard and she pulled away from the beach.

"Good luck, Boss," the shore party called after him. Shackleton swung around and waved briefly.

When they reached the *Caird,* Shackleton and Vincent jumped on board, and the stores were rapidly passed across.

The *Wills* then returned for her final load—the two 18-gallon casks of water and several pieces of ice, weighing perhaps 125 pounds altogether, which were intended to supplement the boat's supply of water. Because of their weight, the casks were made fast astern of the *Wills,* and she towed them out. But just as she was clearing the reef, a huge swell rose beneath her and swung her broadside to the surf. She got across, but one of the water casks was torn loose and went drifting toward the beach. The *Wills* quickly delivered her load and went after the stray water cask. She picked it up just as it was about to wash up on the beach, and returned with it to the *Caird.*

For a few minutes, the two boats lay alongside one another, bumping heavily. Shackleton was terribly anxious to get away, and he was urgently directing the stowage of ballast and equipment. Finally the two crews leaned across and shook hands. Again there were several nervous jokes. Then the *Wills* let go and headed for the beach.

It was just twelve-thirty. The three little sails on the *Caird* were up when the men ashore saw McCarthy in the bow signaling to cast off the bow line. Wild let go of it, and McCarthy hauled it in. The party on shore gave three cheers, and across the surging breakers they heard three small shouts in reply.

The *Caird* caught the wind, and Worsley at the helm swung her bow toward the north.

"They made surprising speed for such a small craft," Orde-Lees recorded. "We watched them until they were out of sight, which was not long, for such a tiny boat was soon lost to sight on the great heaving ocean; as she dipped into the trough of each wave, she disappeared completely, sail and all."

CHAPTER 4

For the twenty-two men who turned their faces inland, the excitement was past and the trial by patience had begun. Their helplessness was almost total, and they knew it. The *Caird* had sailed, taking with her the best of everything they had.

After a while they pulled the *Wills* farther up onto the beach, then turned her over and crawled underneath. "As we sat there, cramped, crowded and wet," wrote Macklin, "we wondered how we were going to face the month ahead of us, which was the . . . very least we could hope for before relief." And this, he admitted, was a "most optimistic" expectation, based upon a half-dozen assumptions—the first among them being that the *Caird* would actually get through.

On this score, their general feeling, at least outwardly, was confident. But how else might they have felt? Any other attitude would have been the equivalent of admitting that they were doomed. No matter what the odds, a man does not pin his last hope for survival on something and then expect that it will fail.

Supper was served early, and the men turned in almost immediately. They awoke the following morning to a bleak, forbidding day of half mist, half snow. The bad weather only made it the more imperative that some sort of shelter be devised, so all able hands returned to the work of excavating the ice cave in the face of the glacier. They kept at it all that day, and the next, and the next. But by the morning of the twenty-eighth, four days after the *Caird* had sailed, it was obvious that the idea would have to be abandoned. Whenever they were inside the cave, which was now large enough for several men to enter, the heat given off by their bodies would melt the interior so that streams of water ran down the walls and along the bottom.

Only one possibility remained—the boats. Greenstreet and Marston suggested that they might be inverted to form the roof of a hut, and Wild agreed. They began to collect rocks to build a foundation. It was exhausting toil. "We are all ridiculously weak," Orde-Lees wrote. "Stones that we could easily have lifted at other times we found quite beyond our capacity, and it needed two or three of us to carry some that would otherwise have been one man's load. . . . Our weakness is best compared with that which one experiences on getting up from a long illness."

Unfortunately, most of the suitable stones lay at the seaward end of the spit, which meant they had to be carried nearly 150 yards to the site chosen for the shelter. Finally, when the foundation walls were about 4 feet high, the boats were placed on top, side by side. It took more than an hour to chock up the wall a little here, and lower it somewhat there. The few scraps of wood that remained were laid across the upended boats from keel to keel, and a tent was stretched over the whole affair; its ropes were anchored at each side to serve as guys. As a final touch, pieces of canvas were lashed around the foundation so that the wind might not find its way in between the stones. There was a gap in the foundation on the shoreward side to serve as an entrance, and two overlapping blankets were hung there to keep the weather out.

At last Wild pronounced the hut ready for occupancy, and the men gathered up their sodden sleeping bags and crawled inside. They were allowed to select whatever spot they wanted, and some men immediately crawled up into the upper story formed by the inverted seats of the boats. Other men took positions on the ground, wherever it looked the snuggest, or the driest, or the warmest. Supper was issued at 4:45 P.M., and the men wearily crawled into their bags the moment they had eaten. For the first several hours, they lay in dreamless, exhausted sleep. But shortly after midnight, a new blizzard blew up, and from then until dawn their sleep was fitful at best. The gale screaming down from the peaks inland shook the hut, and it seemed that each new gust would knock the boats off their foundation. And the force of the wind penetrated every chink, so that snow whistled in through a thousand tiny openings. But somehow when dawn came the shelter was still intact.

" . . . then what a miserable getting up," wrote Macklin. "Everything deeply snowed over, footgear frozen so stiff that we could only put it on by degrees, not a dry or warm pair of gloves amongst us. I think I spent this morning the most unhappy hour of my life—all attempts seemed so hopeless, and Fate seemed absolutely determined to thwart us. Men sat and cursed, not loudly but with an intenseness that showed their hatred of this island on which we had sought shelter."

But if they were to survive there was work to be done. In spite of the cold and the wind, which was sometimes so furious that they had to duck inside until the gusts eased off, they set about making the shelter more secure. Some men rearranged the tent over the roof and lashed down the guy ropes more solidly. Others tucked in bits of blankets around the foundation and packed wet grit from the beach against the whole affair to seal it up.

But again that night the blizzard raged on. Snow once more found its way inside, though not nearly so much as the night before. On the morning of April 30, James, Hudson, and Hurley, who had been trying to sleep in their tent, gave up and moved into the shelter with everybody else. Hurley wrote: "Life here without a hut and equipment is almost beyond endurance." But little by little, as the wind revealed their vulnerable spots, they sealed them up, and each day the shelter became just a little more livable.

They tried cooking their meals inside, but after two days Green succumbed to smoke-blindness and had to be relieved temporarily by Hurley. They remedied the problem of smoke to a large degree by extending a chimney up through the roof between the two boats. But then, some wild caprice of wind would frequently rush down the chimney, expelling great, thick masses of smoke into the hut, and making the air inside so dense that the men would be forced into the open, half-choked, with tears running down their cheeks.

During the day enough light filtered through the canvas roofing so that the men could make their way about, but long before dusk the hut grew much too dark to see anything. Marston and Hurley experimented and found that, by filling a small container with blubber oil and draping pieces of surgical bandage over the edge as a wick, they could obtain a feeble flame by which a man might read if he were not more than a few feet away. By such methods they gradually eliminated one little misery after another.

At last on May 2, eight days after the *Caird* had sailed, and more than two weeks after their arrival, the sun came out. The men hurriedly carried their sleeping bags outside to spread them out to dry. It was clear again on the third, and on the fourth. Even after three days of sunshine, their sleeping bags were not completely dry, though the improvement was a notable one. " . . . we are already much drier than we ever expected to be again," James wrote.

There were lengthy debates about how long it would take the *Caird* to reach South Georgia, and how long after that it would be before a rescue ship arrived. The most optimistic figured that by May 12, a week hence, they might expect to see a ship. More conservative guesses said that it would be June 1 before there could be any thought of rescue. But again it was a matter of fighting back hope. Even as early as May 8, long before they could expect anything to have happened, all of them were already worrying about whether the ice conditions around the island might prevent a relief ship from approaching.

This anxiety had a solid basis in fact. The month of May—the equivalent to November in the Northern Hemisphere—was already one quarter over. Winter was only a matter of weeks, possibly days, away. When it did arrive, there was a strong possibility that ice might form completely around the island and thwart any attempts to bring a ship in. On May 12, Macklin wrote: "Wind from E. Expect we will get the Pack into the bay again—we do not want this just now, with daily hope of the Relief Ship."

There was plenty to keep them occupied—though they worked with one eye kept to seaward. There were penguins to be killed, and once in a while a seal, and there was ice to be gathered for water. They spent long hours trying to snare paddies—small pigeonlike scavenger birds which flitted around the pile of meat. An oar was made into a flagstaff and placed on the highest accessible point. From it, incongruously enough, the Royal Yacht Club burgee stood out before the Elephant Island gales as a signal to the anticipated relief ship.

Macklin and McIlroy were kept busy with patients. Kerr developed a bad tooth and Macklin had to pull it for him. "And a grimy quack of a dentist I must have looked," wrote Macklin. "Not much refinement here—'Come outside and open your mouth'—no cocaine or anesthesia."

Wordie's hand became infected, and Holness was troubled with a sty. Rickenson was slowly recovering from the heart attack he suffered the day they landed, but the salt water boils on his wrists stubbornly refused to heal. Greenstreet's feet, which had been frostbitten in the boats, did not improve and he was confined to his sleeping bag.

Hudson seemed in a serious way. His hands showed definite signs of healing, but the pain in his left buttock which had begun in the boats had developed into a very large abscess which pained him constantly. Mentally, too, the scars of the boat journey apparently were still with him. Much of the time he lay in his sleeping bag for hours without speaking, and he seemed disinterested and detached from what was going on around him.

The most serious invalid was Blackboro. His right foot appeared to be recovering, and there was hope that it might even be saved. But in the toes of his left foot gangrene had already set in. McIlroy, who was attending him, was chiefly concerned with preventing the afflicted parts from developing what is called "wet gangrene," in which the dead flesh remains soft and is likely to spread infection to other parts of the body. In dry gangrene, the parts turn black and become brittle. In time, the body builds up a wall separating the living tissue from the dead, and the threat of infection is greatly reduced. McIlroy was intent on seeing that Blackboro's foot remained dry so that the separation would be complete before any operation was undertaken.

More and more, as the days wore on, they fell inescapably into the routine of their existence. Each evening before supper they would take one final long look to seaward to make certain that the dark shape of a ship or a wisp of smoke on the horizon had not been overlooked. But when they had satisfied themselves that no relief vessel was to be seen, they would go into the hut for supper.

Afterward Hussey would often play the banjo for a time. But the short period in the evening before the blubber lamps were extinguished was devoted mostly to talk. Almost anything could serve as a topic of conversation or debate, though their rescue was the primary subject, with food running a close second.

Marston had a *Penny Cookbook*, and it was in constant demand. Each night he would loan it out to one group of men or another, and they would pore over it, planning the imaginary meals they would have when they got home. Orde-Lees wrote one night: "We want to be fed with a large wooden spoon and, like the Korean babies, be patted on the stomach with the back of the spoon so as to get in a little more than would otherwise be the case. In short, we want to be overfed, grossly overfed, yes, very grossly overfed on nothing but porridge and sugar, black currant and apple pudding and cream, cake, milk, eggs, jam, honey and bread and butter till we burst, and we'll shoot the man who offers us meat. We don't want to see or hear of any more meat as long as we live."

On May 17, McIlroy conducted a poll of the hut, asking each man what he would have if he were permitted any one dish of his choice. The results revealed that Orde-Lees was right—the craving for sweets was almost unanimous, and the sweeter the better. A sampling:

Clark	Devonshire dumpling with cream
James	Syrup pudding
McIlroy	Marmalade pudding and Devonshire cream
Rickenson	Blackberry and apple tart with cream
Wild	Apple pudding and cream
Hussey	Porridge, sugar and cream

Green	Apple dumpling
Greenstreet	Christmas pudding
Kerr	Dough and syrup

There were a few men, however, whose first choice went to something other than sweets:

Macklin	Scrambled eggs on toast
Bakewell	Baked pork and beans
Cheetham	Pork, apple sauce, potatoes, and turnips

And Blackboro simply wanted some plain bread and butter.

Green found himself the subject of much interest because he had once been employed as a pastry cook, and the men never seemed to tire of asking him about it—especially whether he had been permitted to eat all he wanted on the job.

One night Hurley, lying in his sleeping bag, heard Wild and McIlroy discussing food.

"Do you like doughnuts?" Wild asked.

"Rather," McIlroy replied.

"Damned easily made, too," Wild said. "I like them cold with a little jam."

"Not bad," said McIlroy, "but how about a huge omelette?"

"Bally fine."

Later two of the forecastle hands were overheard by Hurley "discussing some extraordinary mixture of hash, apple sauce, beer and cheese." Then Marston, referring to his cookbook, got into a heated debate with Green over whether bread crumbs should form the base for all puddings.

Through one means or another, they kept their spirits up— mostly by building dreams. But each day the ever-shortening hours of daylight told of the approach of winter. The sun now rose a little after nine o'clock and set about 3 P.M. Since they were more than 300 miles north of the Antarctic Circle, they did not have to face the prospect of the sun disappearing altogether. But the weather was becoming increasingly cold.

Macklin wrote on May 22: "There is a big change in the scenery about here—everything is now covered with snow, and there is a considerable ice foot to both sides of the spit. For the last few days ice has been coming in, and dense pack extends in all directions as far as the eye can reach, making the chances of a near rescue seem very remote. No ship but a properly constructed iceship would be safe in this pack; an iron steamer would be smashed up very soon. Besides this there is very little daylight now. . . . "

Indeed, the realization was spreading that, logically at least, a rescue before winter was becoming increasingly improbable, if not impossible. On May 25, one month and one day after the *Caird* had sailed, Hurley wrote: "Weather drifting snow and wind from east. Our wintry environment embodies the most inhospitable and desolate prospect imaginable. All are resigned now and fully anticipate wintering."

CHAPTER 5

They were not resigned, though—not by any means. Perhaps logically there was so little chance for a ship to get through that it would be best to adopt an attitude of stoic resignation. But there was simply too much at stake.

"Every morning," Macklin wrote on June 6, "I go to the top of the hill, and in spite of everything I cannot help hoping to see a ship coming along to our relief." Even Hurley, who had been so positive, recorded that "all [hands] scour the skyline daily in the expectancy of a mast or plume of smoke."

And though day after day no ship appeared, they attributed it to a dozen different reasons—the ice, the gales, the fog, arrangements for getting a proper ship, official delays—and all or any of these factors combined. There was almost never any mention of the most probable reason of all . . . the *Caird* had been lost.

In an entry notable for its candor, Orde-Lees wrote: "One cannot help but be a bit anxious about Sir Ernest. One wonders how he fared, where he is now and how it is that he has not yet been able to relieve us. [But] the subject is practically taboo; everyone keeps their own counsel and thinks different, and no one knows just what anyone else thinks about it, and it is quite obvious that no one really dare say what they really do think."

But whatever each of them might think, there was nothing to do but to wait and hope. Each day one man took his turn as "stoker," and it was his duty to tend the fire all day, keeping it going with penguin skins—and a minimum of smoke. There was also the job of "outside Peggy," which entailed bringing in ice for water and gathering the necessary supplies of frozen meat to be cooked. Both tasks were tedious, and there was a fair amount of trading in order to escape them. Half a penguin steak would usually buy the services of a substitute stoker for one day.

There was also a good deal of bartering in the matter of rations, and several food pools were formed. Typical of these was the "sugar pool" in which each man who belonged passed up one of his three lumps of sugar each day in order to partake of a feast when his turn came around every sixth or seventh day. Wild made no objection to this sort of thing. In fact he permitted a wide range of flexibility in most matters. It served to avoid friction and it gave the men something to occupy their minds.

There was, on the whole, an astounding absence of serious antagonisms, considering the conditions under which they were attempting to exist. Possibly it was because they were in a state of almost perpetual minor friction. Arguments rambled on the whole day through, and they served to let off a great deal of steam which might otherwise have built up. In addition, the party had been reduced to an almost classless society in which most of them felt free to speak their minds, and did. A man who stepped on another man's head trying to find his way out at night was treated to the same abuse as any other, regardless of what his station might once have been.

This matter of going outside at night to relieve themselves was possibly the most disagreeable aspect of their existence. A man had to pick his way amongst the sleepers by the light of only a single blubber lamp, kept burning specifically for this purpose. It was almost physically impossible to avoid stepping on somebody somewhere. Then came the crawl through the hut entrance and out into weather which often approached blizzard conditions. Frequently a man could scarcely keep his feet outside. Pieces of rock and bits of ice flew unseen through the blackness. Rather than face such a prospect, the men came to practice bladder control to the limits of bodily endurance.

After a time, however, Wild succumbed to mounting pressure and a 2-gallon gasoline can was made into a urinal for use at night. The rule was that the man who raised its level to within 2 inches of the top had to carry the can outside and empty it. If a man felt the need and the weather outside was bad, he would lie awake waiting for somebody else to go so that he might judge from the sound the level of the can's contents.

If it sounded ominously close to the top he would try to hold out until morning. But it was not always possible to do so, and he might be forced to get up. More than once, a man would fill the can as silently as possible, then steal back into his sleeping bag. The next man to get up would find to his fury that the can was full—and had to be emptied before it could be used.

The unfortunate victim, however, could expect very little sympathy. Most of the men looked on this as a kind of practical joke, and anyone who really lost his temper about it was so roundly ridiculed by the others that he soon gave it up.

But there were definite fluctuations in morale, in accordance with the weather and whether the pack was in or out. When the sun did shine, the island became a place of rugged beauty, with the sunlight shimmering off the glaciers, producing indescribably vivid colors that were constantly changing. For all the party, it was difficult to be unhappy on days like this. But most of the time the island was far from beautiful. Though the gales were fewer, there were long stretches of wet, gloomy weather, resulting in the kind of outlook Greenstreet recorded one evening: "Everyone spent the day rotting in their bags with blubber and tobacco smoke—so passes another goddam rotten day."

Throughout May, the more pessimistic members of the party—championed by Orde-Lees—had predicted that one day the penguins would migrate and never be seen again until the end of the winter. Orde-Lees felt so strongly, in fact, that he made a number of bets on the matter. Then one day early in June he lost three, all at the same time.

He had wagered (1) that there would not be a single penguin on that day; (2) that no more than ten would appear on any one day after June 1, and (3) that no more than thirty would be secured during the entire month. On that particular day they killed 115.

Food was thus not a cause for immediate concern. But there were other matters that needed attention—notably Blackboro's foot. Early in June McIlroy was satisfied that the separation between the dead and the living tissue was complete, and it would be dangerous to postpone the operation any longer. A rescue in time to get Blackboro to a hospital where the amputation might be done properly was now obviously out of the question. The operation would have to take place on the next warm day.

June 15 dawned mild and misty. McIlroy, after consulting with Wild and Macklin, decided to proceed. Blackboro had long before resigned himself to the operation. What few surgical supplies they had were made ready, and as soon as breakfast was over, the hoosh pot was filled with ice which was melted into water and brought to a boil to sterilize the instruments. A number of packing cases were placed side by side close to the stove and covered with blankets to serve as an operating table.

When everything was ready, the men were herded outside to wait until the operation was over. The two other invalids, Hudson and Greenstreet, remained in the hut. Hudson lay at the far end, but Greenstreet's berth across the seats of the *Docker* was directly over the operating scene. Wild and How both stayed inside to assist, and Hurley remained to stoke the fire. As soon as the men had left, he began to pile penguin skins onto the blaze.

As the temperature started to rise, Blackboro was lifted onto the operating table. Every available blubber lamp was lighted, and the dingy interior of the hut grew fairly light in the little circle around the stove. When it was warm enough, McIlroy and Macklin stripped to their undershirts, the cleanest garments they had.

The anesthetic was to be chloroform—not a very good anesthetic, especially close to an open fire. But it was all they had, and there were only 6 ounces of that. Macklin, who was to administer it, waited for the hut to get warm enough so that the chloroform would vaporize. As Hurley fed skins into the stove, the temperature crept upward. Within twenty minutes it had reached a sweltering 80 degrees, and Macklin uncorked the bottle of chloroform and poured a small amount onto a piece of surgical gauze. Then he patted Blackboro's shoulder reassuringly and held the gauze across his face. He instructed Blackboro to close his eyes and breathe deeply, and Blackboro obediently did as he was told. Within five minutes he was unconscious, and Macklin nodded to McIlroy that he could begin.

Blackboro's foot was propped up and extended over the edge of the packing cases. A large empty tin can was placed underneath. When the bandage was removed, the flesh of Blackboro's toes looked almost mummified, black and brittle. Wild removed a scalpel from the hoosh pot sterilizer and handed it to McIlroy.

At the far end of the hut, Hudson turned his face away so that he wouldn't have to watch. Greenstreet, however, peered down from his perch, thoroughly absorbed in what was going on beneath him.

McIlroy cut across the end of Blackboro's foot, then peeled the skin back. Macklin glanced at Wild and saw that he never flinched. "A hard case," Macklin thought to himself.

McIlroy then asked for a pair of forceps, and Wild removed them from the boiling water. To Greenstreet they looked like a pair of tin snips. Carefully, McIlroy reached well up under the flap of skin to where the toes joined the foot. Then one at a time he cut them off. Each dropped with a metallic clatter into the empty tin can below.

Next McIlroy meticulously scraped away the dead, blackened flesh, and when the wound was clean, be carefully stitched it up. Finally it was done; Blackboro's foot had been neatly trimmed off just at the ball joint. Altogether it had taken fifty-five minutes.

Before long Blackboro began to moan, and in a little while he opened his eyes. He was groggy for a time, but then he smiled up at the two doctors. "I'd like a cigarette," he said.

So McIlroy tore a page out of the *Encyclopaedia Britannica*, rubbed up some plug tobacco and rolled a cigarette for his patient. The tension in the hut eased, and Wild, seeing the hoosh pot full of water, suggested that they use it to wash. McIlroy and Macklin were delighted with the idea. A tiny scrap of soap was found, and they removed their undershirts and washed themselves as best they could down to their waists. Still a small amount of hot water remained, so they borrowed three lumps of sugar from the next day's ration and brewed themselves some hot sugar water.

The rest of the men, meanwhile, had sought shelter in the cave which had been dug in the face of the glacier. They had spent the time cutting one another's hair.

CHAPTER 6

Though the winter's pack ice on most days extended all the way to the horizon, and the relief ship—even, if it had come—would have been held several miles offshore, there were rare occasions when the pack moved out. Thus the possibility that a rescue vessel might just slip through could never be entirely ruled out. So there was always that niggling little ray of hope which kept them climbing the lookout bluff religiously each day. But it also served to slow the passage of time.

One by one the wearisome days crept by. There was only one high point—Midwinter's Day on June 22. They celebrated it with a hearty breakfast in the morning and a marvelous nut-food pudding for supper consisting of twenty-three biscuits, four sledging rations, two boxes of powdered milk, and twelve pieces of nut food.

Afterward, as they lay in their sleeping bags, a lively program of twenty-six different acts was presented. Many of the men had worked for days on the topical verses they would present, and as it turned out, most of the barbs were directed toward Green and Orde-Lees.

Hussey, of course, played the banjo, and Kerr, as he had a year before on the *Endurance*, sang *Spagoni the Toreador*—"especially out of key to oblige." James, however, delivered the hit song of the evening to the tune of *Solomon Levi:*

> My name is Frankie Wild-o; my hut's on Elephant Isle.
> The wall's without a single brick, the roof's without a tile.
> But nevertheless, you must confess, for many and many
>   a mile,
> It's the most palatial dwelling place you'll find on Elephant
>   Isle.

The evening ended with a toast to the sun's return, and to the Boss and the crew of the *Caird.* It was drunk in "Gut Rot, 1916," a mixture of water, ginger, sugar, and methylated alcohol taken from the supply for the Primus stoves. "Horrible taste," wrote Macklin. "It served only to turn most of us teetotalers for life, except for a few who pretended to like it. . . . Several felt ill after."

With the passage of Midwinter's Day, however, there was no longer any definite event to look forward to—nothing but the interminable waiting . . . and wondering.

"We are still enduring our existence here with patience," Macklin wrote on July 6, "and time really passes fairly quickly in spite of the dreadful tedium. My mind is becoming terribly blank—I lie for hours without even so much as thinking in a sort of vacuous state."

And a few days later Orde-Lees wrote: "Wild is always saying that 'the ship' will be here next week; but, of course, he says this just to keep up the spirits of those who are likely to become despondent. Optimism it is, and if not overdone, it is a fine thing. . . . He says . . . that he will not get uneasy about Sir Ernest until the middle of August."

Hurley recorded on July 16: "Go for my Sunday promenade. The well beaten 100 yards on the spit. This one would not tire of provided we knew Sir E. and the crew of the 'Caird' were safe and when relief could be definitely expected. We speculate about the middle of August. . . . "

This, then, became the target date—the time, as it were, when they might begin to worry officially. Wild purposely made it as remote as he reasonably could to keep their hopes alive as long as possible.

But it was far from easy. Little by little, conditions were becoming increasingly primitive. The treasured nut food had been finished, and the powdered milk, too. And though these were sorely missed, their lack could hardly be compared with the tragedy when the tobacco finally ran out. It did not happen all at once. Some men had been more frugal with their ration than others, who had gone ahead and smoked up their allotment in the belief that they would not be marooned for more than a month or so.

Jock Wordie, with typical Scottish thrift, had stretched his supply so that he was the last man to run out, and during the week or so when his small hoard was all that remained, he found himself the center of almost ceaseless bargaining. The seamen scoured the spit for any sort of even mildly interesting bit of rock that might excite Wordie's geological interest. Then, clutching it so as not to let him see, they would barter with him for a pipeful . . . half a pipeful, a quarter pipeful—two puffs? And though Wordie had himself gone over the spit minutely a dozen times for any rock specimens there might be, his curiosity would invariably get the better of him.

In time even his supply was exhausted, and there followed a period of depression that amounted almost to mourning. But the desire to smoke was so strong that before long experiments were begun to find a substitute. McLeod started it all by removing the sennegrass insulation from his boots, then filling his pipe with it.

"The smell," wrote James, "is like that of a prairie fire rather than of tobacco."

Nevertheless, the habit caught on, and soon a good many men were smoking sennegrass. Bakewell thought up a scheme for imparting the proper flavor to it. He borrowed as many pipes as he could, and boiled them together with some sennegrass in the hoosh pot. Theoretically, after the grass had been dried out, it should have had something of a tobaccolike flavor—but "the result obtained," James noted, "was no adequate reward for the trouble of preparation."

"Lichen has also been tried," James continued, "and we live in fear that some one will start on seaweed."

There were a number of other minor annoyances, including the matter of snoring. Hurley wrote: "Wild has devised an ingenious arrangement for the cure of chronic snorers. Lees, who continually disturbs our peaceful slumbers by his habitual trumpeting, was the first offender for the experiment. A slip noose is attached to his arm which is led by a series of eyelets across the bunks to [Wild's] vicinity. As the various sleepers are disturbed they vigorously haul on the line—much as one would do to stop a taxi. It might do the latter—but Lees is incorrigible, scarcely heeding our signals. It has been suggested that the noose be tried around his neck. I'm sure many would exert their full man power."

During most of July the weather was comparatively reasonable, and only on a few occasions did the familiar williwaws shriek down from the cliffs. But one menace which was a never-ending threat was the glacier at the head of the inlet. Periodically without an instant's warning, sections would break or "calve" from its surface. Orde-Lees described one particularly large calving:

"An immense chunk, big as a church, long pending from the glacier, fell off with a report like several bursts of thunder. It raised a mighty wave, quite forty feet high, which made straight for our hut and would have wiped it out had not the brash in the bay damped it sufficiently. . . . As it was it flung huge chunks of ice weighing tons, almost right across the spit.

"Marston was so convinced that it would inundate, if not overwhelm the hut that he hollered out a 'stand by,' but it was unnecessary and only served to rather alarm the two poor invalids, Hudson and Blackboro."

And though they were spared the fate of being dramatically swept off the spit, the island did its best to flood them away. They discovered early in July that water had filtered up through the rocks forming the floor of the hut. It was difficult to tell exactly where it came from, but apparently it was the result of natural drainage running down under their foundation.

When they first became aware of it, they tried to make a drain through one of the side walls, but this was not noticeably effective. And once the condition had begun, it seemed to get progressively worse. They soon found that to avoid being flooded away, they had to dig a hole about 2 feet deep at the lowest spot inside the hut. This immediately filled with water and they were thus able to bail it out. The first time they removed more than 70 gallons. Thereafter they had to be constantly alert whenever the weather was warm or wet. James recorded on July 26:

"About midnight awakened by pleas of men that water in hut was up to stones. Only thing to do to get up and bail or else get soaked. Hurley, McIlroy, Wild and Self rose and got out 50 gallons. About the same amount had to be taken out at 5 A.M. and yet more before breakfast."

Not only was it an irksome task, but the water itself was a nauseating liquid, soupy with penguin guano. As luck would have it, the sump-hole from which they bailed was located directly in front of the cooking stove.

Over the months the interior of the hut had become filthy to the point of squalor. Indeed, they usually referred to it as "The Sty" or the "Snuggery." When they could, they brought in fresh stones to cover the floor, but a great deal of the time the only available stones outside were frozen in place. In the subterranean gloom inside the place, small pieces of food had dropped unnoticed onto the floor. And now, with the combination of water and heat, the food began to rot, contributing yet one more disagreeable odor.

Near the end of July, the abscess on Hudson's buttock had grown to the size of a football. McIlroy disliked the idea of opening it because of the risk of infection, but Hudson was in such severe pain that it had to be done. McIlroy finally performed the operation without an anesthetic, and removed more than two pints of foul-smelling liquid.

"It is hard to realize one's position here," Macklin wrote, "living in a smoky, dirty, ramshackle little hut with only just sufficient room to cram us all in: drinking out of a common pot . . . and laying in close proximity to a man with a large discharging abscess—a horrible existence, but yet we are pretty happy. . . . "

And later, "I have given Blackboro my piece of reindeer skin which I brought from Ocean Camp . . . His bag is rottener than mine; poor chap, he gets very little chance of getting out of it."

As July drew to a close, the feeling of anxiety, so long suppressed, became increasingly difficult to fight back.

Hurley wrote on the thirtieth: "Today seems to be particularly monotonous, and the wild magnificence of the precipitous cliffs that limit us to the circumscribed confines of Cape Wild loom through the mist like prison walls, sinister and inaccessible. If there were only some duties, useful or otherwise, to be performed, the burden of time would be more pleasant and at present our sole exercise is to promenade up and down the 80 yards of the spit, or climb to the lookout and scan the misty skyline for a mast. We look forward anxiously to the forthcoming month, when relief is anticipated. One grows weary of continually estimating the days from the 'Caird's' departure to the hoped for arrival of the [relief ship]."

In varying degrees it was the same with all of them. In their interminable discussions of when and how they might be rescued, there had been one possibility that was rarely mentioned—the loss of the *Caird*. It was considered somehow bad luck even to discuss it, and any man who brought it up was looked upon as speaking out of turn and in bad taste, almost as if he had sullied something that was sacred.

And though they were still hesitant to suggest openly that the *Caird* could be lost, they could no longer avoid admitting, at least tacitly, that something quite possibly might have happened. Shackleton had been gone for ninety-nine days . . . and there was a kind of creeping awareness that they might be watching for something that would never come.

If so, Macklin finally conceded in his diary on July 31, "it means a journey in the 'Stancomb Wills' to Deception I. This will be an arduous journey, but I hope I will be picked one of the party if it comes to this."

Still there was the deadline they had set for themselves—the middle of August. But time seemed almost to come to a standstill.

August 1 was the anniversary of the day, two years before, when the *Endurance* had sailed from London, and one year before, when she had sustained her first serious pressure. Hurley summed it up:

The memories of everything up to now, he wrote, "flit through our minds as a chaotic, confused nightmare. The past twelve months appear to have passed speedily enough and though we have been dwelling here in a life of security for nearly 4 months, this latter period seems longer than the preceding balance of the year. This doubtless is occasioned by our counting the days and the daily expectations of deferred relief, as well as our having no . . . work to perform. . . . The watching day by day and the anxiety for the safety of our comrades of the Caird lay a holding hand on the already retarded passage of time."

Each day they spent a little longer atop the lookout bluff, searching for a sign of the relief ship. On August 3, Orde-Lees wrote: " . . . still surrounded by close pack. . . . We are pretty short of both fuel and meat but no one seems to care very much. . . . Sir Ernest's non-return is now openly discussed. No one likes to think that he could possibly have failed to reach South Georgia, but it is significant of the current of thoughts that Wild has given orders that every scrap of cord and wool and all nails are to be carefully kept in view of the possibility of our having to make a boat journey to Deception Island. . . . "

For such a journey, they were desperately short of equipment. The only sail remaining was the *Wills'* ridiculous little jib, so they would have to contrive some sort of mainsail out of sewn-together pieces of the rotten tent cloths. There was not even a mast from which it might be hoisted. The mast from the *Wills* had been taken to make a mizzenmast for the *Caird*, and the *Docker's* had been sacrificed to strengthen the *Caird's* keel. But something probably could be done with the five oars they still had.

And so it went.

August 4 (James): "Monotony of existence extreme."

August 5 (Hurley): " . . . sitting like an invalid in one's sleeping bag and re-reading the same few books."

August 6 (Hurley): "It would be ideal weather for the ship to arrive."

August 7 (Macklin): "Hudson was up and out for a little while today; he was very groggy, and on attempting to wave his hand to McIlroy he fell on his back."

August 8 (Orde-Lees): " . . . we had to bale out four times . . . rather more than usual."

August 9 (Greenstreet): "Wordie discovered an old newspaper (or part of one) date Sept. 14, 1914, which is being eagerly read and reread by all."

August 10 (Macklin): "I have been watching the snow petrels—they are wonderful little birds. Sometimes they get caught by a breaker and dashed on the shore, but they soon recover and go off again to their fishing."

August 11 (Orde-Lees): "Marston was out at 5 A.M., but the coast was clear . . . "

August 12 (Macklin): "I cannot help worrying about my people at home. If only I could be sure that they had got news I should not mind; but I know how they will worry. . . . "

August 13 (James): "Beginning to look anxiously for the ship. This is about the time. . . . "

August 14 (James): "We have been eating seaweed lately, boiled. The taste is peculiar but anything for a change."

August 15 (Orde-Lees): "It snowed at intervals during the day."

August 16 (Macklin): " . . . eagerly on the lookout for the relief ship—and most of us go up the hill and eagerly scan the horizon for any sign of her. Some of the party have quite given up all hope of her coming. . . . "

August 17 (Hurley): "The ice has put in a reappear-
ance . . . "

August 18 (Greenstreet): "Both bays full of pack and
heavy pack as far as the eye can see."

August 19 (Orde-Lees): "There is no good in deceiving
ourselves any longer."

PART VI

CHAPTER 1

Monday April 24th . . . We took Good bye with our
companions. & set sail on our 870 miles to South
Georgia for assistance at 12-30 & at 2 P M we came
to a stream of ice which we managed to get through
in about an hour. Then we were in the open sea wet
through but happy through it all.

    —McNeish's log.

Monday, 24th. April.

Wild Camp for Rating Chron. 192/262

Took departure in James Caird at 12-30 p.m.
Steered N.N.E. 8 miles, then E. 1 mile to a break
in the stream ice here running E and W

Wind: to 4 p.m. WNW 6 [approx. 30 MPH] . . .

    —Worsley's log.

The little group of dark figures waving good-by were silhou-etted against the white snow, and they made a pathetic pic-ture from the *Caird* as she lifted to the increasing swell.

Worsley held her on a northerly course and Shackleton stood beside him, alternately peering ahead at the approaching ice, and turning again to look at the men he was leaving behind. It was only a short time, it seemed, until they were no longer discernible.

Before long the whole of Elephant Island widened out astern, its great craggy headlands and glacier walls catching the sun. Off to the right, tiny Cornwallis Island, rising steeply out of the sea, came into view from behind Cape Valentine; and a little while later the snowy peaks of Clarence Island could be seen, delicately half-hidden by the violet-tinted mists. In the water, an occasional seal or a small flock of penguins swam past, looking curiously at this strange creature that was moving across the surface of the sea.

It was just two o'clock when the *Caird* reached the ice, which proved to be a thick line of ancient floes that had been broken and melted into a myriad of different shapes. They rose to the long westerly swell in stately cadence, producing a hoarse, rus-tling noise.

Worsley swung the boat east, parallel with the ice, to search for the opening that he and Shackleton had seen from the spit earlier in the day. It took them almost an hour to reach it, and they discovered that it was nearly clogged with floe fragments and patches of brash ice. Nevertheless Worsley brought the *Caird's* bow around and they started through.

Almost at once the boat was dwarfed by weird shapes of ice, some of them twice the height of the mast. They swayed and bowed in the lazy movement of the sea. Above the water they were pure, snowy white; beneath it they shaded into ever deepen-ing blue.

Worsley tried to steer the boat safely amongst the lumps, but several times, turning to avoid one fragment they bumped into another, and Shackleton decided they had better row.

The sails were dropped and the men carefully crawled up onto the decking and put out their oars. Rowing was extremely awkward, sitting as they were, flush with the oarlocks. Fortunately the wind died down. Shackleton had taken over the helm and he urged the rowers on. It was after four o'clock and the light was beginning to fail.

However, after almost an hour the ice began to thin out and they soon came to the northern edge of the pack, then emerged once more into the open sea. The rowers happily scrambled back inside the cockpit and everyone was enormously relieved.

The wind had gradually swung around to the southeast, the perfect direction for driving them north. Shackleton ordered the sails set, and after they were up, he sent Crean, McNeish, Vincent, and McCarthy forward to get some sleep, saying that he and Worsley would stay on duty throughout the night to watch for ice.

When everything was squared away, Shackleton turned and looked astern. It was just possible to make out Elephant Island as a hulking, shadowy mass. For several minutes he stared without speaking.

A forbidding-looking place, certainly, but that only made it seem the more pitiful. It was the refuge of twenty-two men who, at that very moment, were camped on a precarious, storm-washed spit of beach, as helpless and isolated from the outside world as if they were on another planet. Their plight was known only to the six men in this ridiculously little boat, whose responsibility now was to prove that all the laws of chance were wrong—and return with help. It was a staggering trust.

As the darkness deepened, ten thousand stars pricked through the blue-black sky, and the little wisp of a pennant that fluttered from the *Caird's* mainmast described an irregular circle across the sparkling heavens as the boat rolled before the quartering sea.

The two men sat side by side, Worsley steering and Shackleton huddled close up against him. The southerly wind was cold and the sea was picking up. Their primary concern was ice, and Shackleton and Worsley kept a sharp lookout. They passed an occasional lump early in the evening, but by ten o'clock the sea appeared to be clear.

From time to time Shackleton rolled cigarettes for both of them, and they spoke of many things. It was obvious that the burden of responsibility Shackleton had borne for sixteen months had nibbled away somewhat at his enormous self-confidence. He wanted to talk and to be assured that he had acted wisely.

He confided to Worsley that the decision to separate the party had been a desperately difficult one, and he abhorred having to make it. But somebody had to go for help, and this was not the sort of responsibility which could be delegated to another person.

As for the journey itself, he seemed strangely doubtful, and he asked Worsley's opinion of their chances. Worsley replied that he was sure that they would make it, but it was evident that Shackleton was far from convinced.

The truth was that he felt rather out of his element. He had proved himself on land. He had demonstrated there beyond all doubt his ability to pit his matchless tenacity against the elements—and win. But the sea is a different sort of enemy. Unlike the land, where courage and the simple will to endure can often see a man through, the struggle against the sea is an act of physical combat, and there is no escape. It is a battle against a tireless enemy in which man never actually wins; the most that he can hope for is not to be defeated.

It gave Shackleton a feeling of uneasiness. He now faced an adversary so formidable that his own strength was nothing in comparison, and he did not enjoy being in a position where boldness and determination count for almost nothing, and in which victory is measured only in survival.

But more than anything he was dreadfully tired, and he wanted simply for the journey to be over, and as quickly as possible. If only they could make Cape Horn, he said to Worsley, they would cut one-third off the distance they had to go. He knew it was impossible, but he asked Worsley whether he thought the southeast wind just might hold long enough for them to do so. Worsley looked at him sympathetically and shook his head. Not a chance, he replied.

Just before six o'clock, the first light of dawn crept across the sky and as it grew brighter, both men relaxed. Now if they came upon any ice, at least they could see it.

Shackleton waited until seven o'clock and then he called the other men. Crean rigged the Primus, and after a considerable amount of trouble getting it to light and keeping the hoosh pot in place, they finally had breakfast.

When they had finished, Shackleton announced that the watches would begin, four hours on and four hours off. Shackleton said he would take the first trick with Crean and McNeish, and Worsley would have the other with Vincent and McCarthy.

CHAPTER 2

To classify the dangers they faced in order of magnitude would have been impossible, but of the known threats, the greatest undoubtedly was ice—especially at night. One single collision with an unseen fragment could have ended the journey in a moment. Thus Shackleton's plan was to get north with all possible speed before turning east toward South Georgia.

And for the next two days they were lucky. The wind held steady out of the southwest—much of the time almost at gale force. By noon on April 26, they had logged a total of 128 miles from Elephant Island without encountering a sign of ice.

However, those two days were an ordeal during which they were introduced, one at a time, to the endless miseries which constituted life on board the boat. Always and forever there was the water—the all-pervading, inescapable water. Sometimes it was just a shower of spray thrown up from the bow and flung astern by the wind, which caused no real suffering except to the man at the helm. Much worse were the quieter, solid seas dipped up by the bow that poured aft and sloshed into the cockpit. And worst of all were the occasions when the boat plunged down just as a wave broke. Then green, foaming water rolled across the decking, splashed into the cockpit and drained down into the boat in icy streams through a score of openings in the canvas decking, as rain might pour through the roof of some dilapidated shack. Within twenty-four hours after leaving Elephant Island, the decking had begun to sag so that there were a dozen pockets to hold the water.

The man at the helm, of course, suffered the most, and each of them took his turn at the yoke lines for an hour and twenty minutes during each watch. But the other two men on duty were better off only by comparison. When they weren't bailing or tending the sails or shifting ballast by moving the rocks in the bottom, they spent their time trying to avoid the streams coming from above. It was of little use, though. Invariably they wound up huddled over with the water pouring off their backs.

All of them were dressed more or less the same way—heavy wool underwear, woolen trousers, a thick, loose sweater, with a pair of light gabardine Burberry overalls on the outside. Their heads were covered with knitted, woolen helmets and Burberry outer helmets, tucked in at the neck. On their feet they wore two pairs of socks, a pair of ankle-high felt boots and finneskoes— reindeer-skin boots with the hair side out, though every trace of hair had long since worn off, leaving them bald and limp. There was not a set of oilskins on board.

Such clothing was intended for wear in intense, dry cold—not on board a pitching, spray-drenched boat. Here it had an almost wicklike action, soaking up every icy drop until the saturation point was reached, then maintained.

The best that could be done was to live with this trial by water, as they had on the trip to Elephant Island—to sit as still as possible after each soaking so as to avoid contact with the newly drenched area of clothing. But to sit motionless in a 22-foot boat in a heavy sea can be difficult indeed.

The boat had to be pumped out at fairly frequent intervals, usually two or three times each watch, and the job required two men—one to operate the plunger while the other held the icy brass cylinder down into the water in the bottom of the boat. Even with mittens, the hands of the man gripping the cylinder would go numb within the space of five minutes, and they would trade places.

Nor was the discomfort on board limited to the men on watch. They realized from the very beginning that even sleeping had a special brand of unpleasantness all its own. The sleeping bags were located in the bow, nominally the driest part of the boat. To reach them involved a tortuous crawl on hands and knees over the rocks in the bottom. The closer a man got to the bow, the more restricted the space became, until finally he had to get down on his belly and slither forward, insinuating himself between the underside of the seats and the ballast.

When at last he had reached the bow, there was the job of getting into his bag, then finally the problem of going to sleep. Fatigue helped, of course, but even so, the action of the boat in the bow was more violent than anywhere else. At times they were heaved bodily upwards, only to fall down onto the rocks again, or perhaps to be slammed from beneath as the boat was pitched aloft by a new wave. The *Caird* had been equipped with six sleeping bags so that each man might have his own. But Shackleton soon suggested that they share three bags and use the others as mattresses, to protect them from the rocks. Everyone quickly agreed.

They discovered, too, that under the decking there was not quite enough room to sit upright. For the first couple of meals they tried to eat half bent over, with their chins pressed down against their chests. But this position greatly interfered with swallowing, and the only thing to do was to stretch out on the rocks in the bottom.

But no matter what position they assumed—sitting, reclining, or lying in their sleeping bags—the struggle against the motion of the boat was ceaseless. The 2,000 pounds of ballast in the bottom gave the *Caird* a particularly vicious action, and she jerked upright after every wave. Worsley thought she was over-ballasted and he urged Shackleton to throw some of the rocks overboard. But Shackleton took a characteristically cautious view of the matter. The only way to see if Worsley was right was to dump the ballast—and then it would be gone forever. It was better, Shackleton felt, to put up with the wicked motion of the boat than to risk being light.

They had sailed from Elephant Island in rather high spirits, knowing that they were embarked at last for civilization. As McNeish had recorded—"wet through, but happy through it all."

But after two days of uninterrupted misery, their cheeriness had worn away. And by noon on April 26, after Worsley had fixed the position at 128 miles from Elephant Island, the ordeal to which they were committed had become altogether too real. There was only the consolation that they were making progress—at the agonizingly slow rate of about 1 mile every half hour or so.

The actual position on April 26 was 59°46′ South, 52°18′ West, and it put the *Caird* a scant 14 miles north of the 60th parallel of latitude. Thus they had just crept over the line separating the "Raving Fifties" from the "Screaming Sixties," so called because of the weather that prevails there.

This, then, was the Drake Passage, the most dreaded bit of ocean on the globe—and rightly so. Here nature has been given a proving ground on which to demonstrate what she can do if left alone. The results are impressive.

It begins with the wind. There is an immense area of persistent low pressure in the vicinity of the Antarctic Circle, approximately 67° South latitude. It acts as a giant sump into which high pressure from farther north continually drains, accompanied by almost ceaseless, gale-force, westerly winds. In the prosaic, often studiously understated language of the U.S. Navy's *Sailing Direction for Antarctica*, these winds are described categorically:

"They are often of hurricane intensity and with gust velocities sometimes attaining to 150 to 200 miles per hour. Winds of such violence are not known elsewhere, save perhaps within a tropical cyclone."

Also in these latitudes, as nowhere else on earth, the sea girdles the globe, uninterrupted by any mass of land. Here, since the beginning of time, the winds have mercilessly driven the seas clockwise around the earth to return again to their birthplace where they reinforce themselves or one another.

The waves thus produced have become legendary among seafaring men. They are called Cape Horn Rollers or "graybeards." Their length has been estimated from crest to crest to exceed a mile, and the terrified reports of some mariners have placed their height at 200 feet, though scientists doubt that they very often exceed 80 or 90 feet. How fast they travel is largely a matter of speculation, but many sailormen have claimed their speed occasionally reaches 55 miles an hour. Thirty knots is probably a more accurate figure.

Charles Darwin, on first seeing these waves breaking on Tierra del Fuego in 1833, wrote in his diary: "The sight . . . is enough to make a landsman dream for a week about death, peril and shipwreck."

As viewed from the *Caird,* the sight of these rollers constituted ample reason for such thoughts. In the rare moments when the sun shone, they were cobalt blue, which gave them the appearance of being infinitely deep—as indeed they were. But most of the time the sky was overcast, and then the whole surface of the sea turned a somber, lifeless gray.

There was no sound to the relentless advance of these cliffs of water except the hiss of their foaming brows when they rose to such a height or charged forward so fast that they lost their balance and their crests tumbled to the force of gravity.

Once every ninety seconds or less the *Caird's* sail would go slack as one of these gigantic waves loomed astern, possibly 50 feet above her, and threatening, surely, to bury her under a hundred-million tons of water. But then, by some phenomenon of buoyancy, she was lifted higher and higher up the face of the onrushing swell until she found herself, rather unexpectedly, caught in the turmoil of foam at the summit and hurtling forward.

Over and over again, a thousand times each day, this drama was re-enacted. Before long, to the men on board the *Caird,* it lost all elements of awesomeness and they found it routine and commonplace instead, as a group of people may become inured to the perils of living in the shadow of an active volcano.

Only very occasionally did they think about South Georgia. It was so remote, so Utopian that it was almost depressing to contemplate. No man could have endured with just that to keep him going.

Instead, life was reckoned in periods of a few hours, or possibly only a few minutes—an endless succession of trials leading to deliverance from the particular hell of the moment. When a man was awakened to go on watch, the focal point of his existence became that time, four hours away, when he could slither back into the cold, wet rockiness of the sleeping bag he was now leaving. And within each watch there were a number of subdivisions: the time at the helm—eighty eonic minutes, during which a man was forced to expose himself to the full wickedness of the spray and the cold; the ordeal of pumping, and the awful task of shifting ballast; and the lesser trials which lasted perhaps two minutes— like the interval after each numbing spray struck until a man's clothes warmed enough so that he could move once more.

Again and again the cycle was repeated until the body and the mind arrived at a state of numbness in which the frenzied antics of the boat, the perpetual cold and wet came to be accepted almost as normal.

On April 27, three days out from Elephant Island, their luck turned bad. About noon a raw and penetrating mistlike rain began to fall, and the wind slowly started to move around toward the north—dead ahead.

They were now perhaps 150 miles north of Elephant Island and still well within the zone where they might encounter ice. Thus they could not afford to be blown a single mile to the south. Shackleton and Worsley spent several minutes discussing the possibilities and finally decided there was no choice but to hold the *Caird* up into the wind as best they could.

And so the struggle began, swinging from one tack to the other and taking a wearisome pounding in the process. It was all the more unpleasant because they were simply absorbing punishment while doing nothing more than holding their own. But about 11 P.M., to their great relief, the wind eased down and moved into the northwest. By the time Worsley's watch took over at midnight they were able to resume the course to the northeast.

At dawn on April 28, only a light northwest breeze was blowing; actually, it was the best weather they'd had since leaving Elephant Island, four days before. But there were dangerous signs of deterioration, both among the men and in their equipment. Shackleton noticed with apprehension that the familiar pains of the sciatica he had suffered at Ocean Camp were coming back. And all of the men were bothered by an increasing sensation of discomfort in their feet and legs—a feeling of tightness.

About mid-morning, McNeish suddenly sat down in the center of the cockpit and peeled off his boots. His legs, ankles, and feet were puffy and dead white, apparently from lack of exercise and from being continually soaked. When Shackleton saw the condition of McNeish's feet, he suggested that the other men remove their footgear—and they were all the same. Vincent was in far the worst condition, apparently suffering from rheumatism. Shackleton looked in the medicine chest and gave him the only remedy which seemed likely to help—a small bottle of witch hazel.

The damage to Worsley's navigational books by the constant soaking was an even more serious problem. The destruction of these books could mean losing the way across this forsaken waste of ocean. And though every effort was made to protect them, they had to be taken out whenever a sight was taken.

Both covers of the logarithm book were soggy, and the wet was beginning to spread to the inside pages. The *Nautical Almanac,* with its tables of sun and star positions, was in even worse shape. It was printed on cheaper paper and was fast approaching a state of pulpiness. Its pages had to be carefully peeled apart to separate them.

In the matter of taking sights, Worsley at first tried bracing himself inside the cockpit. But it was no good. To remain upright was difficult enough; to get an accurate reading was impossible. He found that it was best to kneel on the helmsman's seat, with Vincent and McCarthy holding him around the waist.

Early in the afternoon of April 28, the relatively good weather from the northwest came to an end as the wind slowly moved to the west and began to freshen. By dusk it had inched to the ssw and risen almost to gale force. Night came on and an overcast blotted out the stars. The only way to steer was by watching the pennant on the mainmast blown out before the wind and holding to a course which kept it pointed just off the port bow.

Only once in the night was a positive check on the direction permitted, and then a flaming match was lighted so they could see the compass for a moment to make certain that the wind was still out of the same quadrant. They had only two candles which were being strictly preserved for that time that now seemed so far away—the landfall at South Georgia.

The dawn of the fifth day, April 29, rose on a lumpy sea under a dull sky. Low, troubled clouds skudded past, almost touching the surface of the water. The wind was nearly dead astern, and the *Caird* labored forward like a protesting old woman being hurried along faster than she cared to go.

Just before noon a rift appeared in the sky, and Worsley hurriedly got his sextant. He was just in time, for a few minutes later the sun smiled down for one wintry flicker and then was gone. But Worsley had his sight, and Shackleton had recorded the chronometer reading. When the position was worked out, it put the *Caird* at 58°38' South, 50°0' West—they had covered 238 miles since leaving Elephant Island, six days before.

They were almost one-third of the way.

CHAPTER 3

One-third of the sentence had been served.

Throughout the day and into the night, the southwesterly wind continued, growing ever stronger. By the time the bleak gray sky grew light on the morning of April 30, the surface of the sea was torn into foam, and the frenzied screech of the gale through the rigging rose and fell hysterically as the *Caird* was lifted to each successive swell. The temperature had dropped very close to zero, and the bitterness of the wind suggested that it was blowing straight off pack ice that was not very far away.

As the morning hours passed, it became more and more of a struggle to steer the boat. The 60-knot gale drove her head down into the seas, and the huge waves that rolled up astern constantly threatened to slew her around broadside. By midmorning she was wallowing more than sailing, running off to one side and then the other, and taking seas on board with almost every wave. The pump was not adequate to handle the water, and extra hands had to be called to bail. Toward noon the boat began to ice up.

The decision was inevitable, but Shackleton put it off as long as he dared. They pumped and bailed and beat the ice off her—all the while fighting to hold her stern up into the wind. Noon . . .

one o'clock . . . two o'clock. But it was no use. The sea was more than she could take. Shackleton reluctantly gave the order to come about. The sails were dropped, and the sea anchor, a cone-shaped piece of canvas about 4 feet long, was put over on the end of a long bow line. It dragged through the water and thus brought the *Caird's* bow up into the wind.

Almost at once conditions improved. At least less water came on board. The boat, however, behaved like a thing possessed. She staggered drunkenly upward over each new wave, then plunged sideways only to have her bow jerked violently around as she seized up on the sea anchor. There was never a moment—not even an instant of repose. The only thing to do was to hang on, and endure.

It was not long before the furled sails started to collect ice, and with each burst of spray their load grew heavier. Within an hour, they were frozen into a solid mass, and the action of the boat was growing sluggish as she began to get top heavy. The sails had to be removed, so Crean and McCarthy were sent forward, and after knocking off the ice, they brought the sails below and stuffed them into the already crammed space under the decking.

But then a heavy coating began to accumulate on the oars. There were four of them lashed against the shrouds. As the ice built up, they became like miniature bulwarks which prevented the water from spilling overboard before it froze. Shackleton watched anxiously, hoping that the load of ice on deck might not grow too heavy. But in the failing light of dusk he saw that it would be dangerous to let it go until morning. He ordered Worsley, Crean, and McCarthy to go with him up onto the pitching deck.

With great effort they clubbed the ice off the oars, then pitched two of them over the side. The remaining pair was lashed to the shrouds about 18 inches above the deck so that the water would run off.

It took more than twenty minutes, and by the time they were finished it was dark and they were utterly drenched. They crept back into the cockpit—and the night began.

Each of the watches shivered through their four hideous hours, cringing beneath the decking, sodden and half-frozen, trying to remain upright against the wild lurching of the boat while perched on the despised rocks in the bottom.

For seven painful days the rocks had made eating difficult; they had interfered with bailing; they had vastly complicated the simple act of getting about, and they had made sleeping all but impossible. But it was moving them that was worst of all. Periodically they had to be shifted in order to ballast the boat properly, which meant lifting them while crouched over and kneeling, often painfully, on other rocks. By now, every sharp corner and every slippery surface was intimately known and utterly detested.

Then, too, there were the reindeer hairs. They moulted from the insides of the sleeping bags, and at first they had been only a petty annoyance. But no matter how much hair was shed, the supply seemed inexhaustible. And they were everywhere . . . the sides of the boat, the seats, the ballast. They clung in wet clumps to faces and hands. The men breathed them as they slept, and occasionally woke up choking on them. The hairs ran down into the bottom and clogged the pump, and little clusters of them were turning up more and more frequently in the food.

Gradually, as the long hours of the night crept by, a subtle change could be detected in the boat. For one thing, the trickles of water through the decking became smaller, then finally ceased altogether. At the same time her behavior was growing noticeably less violent, and instead of pitching wildly, she rose to the seas with increasing restraint.

The first light of dawn told why. The entire boat above the waterline was encased in ice, half a foot thick in places, and the rope to the sea anchor had grown to the size of a man's thigh. Under the weight of it, she was riding at least 4 inches deeper, like a waterlogged derelict rather than a boat.

Worsley was on watch and he immediately sent McCarthy to awaken Shackleton, who hurried aft. When he saw the situation, he excitedly ordered all hands called. Then he himself took a small axe and cautiously crawled forward.

With extreme care so as not to puncture the decking, he began to knock the ice away with the back side of the axe. Periodically a wave burst against the boat and swept over him, but he kept at it for nearly ten minutes while the others anxiously looked on. By then he was so stiff with cold that he could no longer trust his grip or balance. He crawled back into the cockpit with the water dripping from his clothes and his beard frozen half-stiff. He was shivering noticeably as he handed the axe to Worsley to continue the job, cautioning him to use extreme care while he was on the decking.

And so each of them took his turn at chipping for as long as he could endure it, which was rarely more than five minutes. First they had to knock off enough ice to get a handhold and a place to put their knees. To stand up on that glassy, rolling deck would have been to commit suicide, for had a man fallen overboard, the others could never have got in the sea anchor and hoisted sail in time to rescue him.

Below, Shackleton discovered that ice was forming even inside the cockpit. Long icicles hung from under the decking, and the water in the bottom was very nearly frozen.

He called for Crean, and together they managed to get the Primus stove alight in the hope that it would give off enough heat to warm the cockpit above the freezing point. Unless the water in the bottom could be thawed enough so it could be pumped out, there was danger that it would simply sink the boat under them.

It took an hour of agonizing work on deck before they felt the *Caird* begin to regain her buoyancy. But they kept at it until they had succeeded in getting rid of most of the ice except a large chunk on the sea-anchor line which they simply could not risk attempting to reach.

Shackleton then called them below to have some milk. They gathered around the stove, almost sick with cold. It seemed inconceivable that their numbed bodies could have given off any warmth, but apparently they did, for after a while the icicles under the decking began to melt and drip down onto them. Not long afterward the water in the bottom had thawed enough so they could pump it out.

Shackleton still had Crean keep the Primus stove alight, but toward noon the acrid fumes it gave off had made the air almost unbreathable and it had to be extinguished. It took several minutes for the atmosphere to clear, and then they became aware of a new smell—a fetid, sweet-sour sort of odor, like spoiled meat. McNeish discovered it came from the sleeping bags, which in fact had begun to rot. A closer examination disclosed that two of them actually were slimy inside.

Throughout the afternoon the coating of ice steadily built up again. And late in the day Shackleton decided there was too much at stake to gamble on the chance that the *Caird* would survive until morning. Once more, he ordered that the boat be cleared. It took more than an hour, but finally it was done, and after a ration of hot milk they settled down to wait for morning.

The southwesterly gale screamed on, showing not the slightest sign of fatigue. The watches of that night were like a tally sheet of infinity. Every individual minute had to be noted, then lived through and finally checked off. There was not even a crisis to relieve the tortured monotony. When at last, about six o'clock, the sky to the east began to brighten they could see that once again the boat was carrying a dangerously heavy burden of ice. As soon as the light permitted she had to be chipped clear for the third time.

It was May 2, and the beginning of the third day of the gale. The weather throughout had been overcast so that no position could be obtained. Now the anxiety of not really knowing where they were was added to everything else.

Some time after nine o'clock, the wind eased ever so slightly, though nowhere near enough to get under way. A few minutes later the *Caird* rose to a particularly high sea, and just then she was struck by a breaking wave. The smallest quiver—a gentle shock—passed through her, and the wave rolled on. But this time she didn't swing back up into the wind. The sea anchor was gone.

CHAPTER 4

There was a moment of confusion, then they felt her roll sickeningly to starboard as she fell off into the trough of the sea and they knew instinctively what had happened.

Both Shackleton and Worsley scrambled to their feet and looked forward. The frayed end of the bow line was dragging through the water. The lump of ice was gone—and the sea anchor with it.

Shackleton thrust his head below and shouted for the others to get the jib. They hauled it out, frozen into a rumpled mass. Crean and McCarthy crept forward over the heavily rolling deck, dragging the sail with them. The rigging, too, was frozen and had to be beaten into compliance. But after a long minute or two they got enough ice off the halyards to hoist the jib to the mainmast as a storm trysail.

Slowly, grudgingly, the *Caird's* bow once more swung around into the wind, and all of them felt the tension go out of their muscles.

The job of the helmsman now was to hold her as close to the wind as she would go, swinging from one tack to the other. It required constant vigilance, and it could hardly have been more unpleasant, facing into the breaking seas and the piercing wind.

Fortunately the gale continued to diminish, and by eleven o'clock Shackleton decided to risk hoisting sail. The jib was removed from the mainmast, and the reefed lugsail and mizzen were run up. Then, for the first time in forty-four hours, the *Caird* was under way again toward the northeast, and the journey was resumed. But it was a slovenly course, with the boat running before the enormous following sea, her bow half buried by the force of the wind astern.

Shortly after noon, as if from nowhere, a magnificent wandering albatross appeared overhead. In contrast to the *Caird,* it soared with an ease and grace that was poetic, riding the gale on wings that never moved, sometimes dropping to within 10 feet of the boat, then rising almost vertically on the wind, a hundred, two hundred feet, only to plunge downward again in a beautifully effortless sweep.

It was perhaps one of nature's ironies. Here was her largest and most incomparable creature capable of flight, whose wingspread exceeded 11 feet from tip to tip, and to whom the most violent storm was meaningless, sent to accompany the *Caird,* as if in mockery of her painful struggles.

Hour after hour the albatross circled overhead, and there was an elegance of motion to the bird's flight that was very nearly hypnotic. The men could hardly avoid a feeling of envy. Worsley remarked that the albatross could probably have covered the distance to South Georgia in fifteen hours or less.

As if to emphasize their wretchedness, Worsley recorded: "Reindeer bags in such a hopeless sloppy slimy mess, smelling badly & weighing so heavily that we throw two of the worst overboard." Each of them weighed about 40 pounds.

Later he wrote: "Macty [McCarthy] is the most irrepressible optimist I've ever met. When I relieve him at the helm, boat iced & seas pourg: down yr neck he informs me with a happy grin 'It's a grand day sir' I was feeling a bit sour just before. . . . "

Throughout the afternoon and evening the weather gradually grew less violent; and by dawn on May 3, the wind had fallen off to a moderate southwesterly breeze. As noon approached, the clouds started to thin out. Before long patches of blue sky appeared, and soon the sun was shining down.

Worsley took out his sextant, and it was no task at all to get a sight. When he had worked it out, the fix put their position at 56°13′ South, 45°38′ West—403 miles from Elephant Island.

They were just more than halfway to South Georgia.

Thus, in the space of only an hour, or maybe a little more, the outlook on board the *Caird* was completely altered. The battle was half won, and a warm sun was overhead. The off-duty watch no longer huddled in the dismal confines of the forecastle. Instead the sleeping bags were hauled out and run up the mast to dry. The men peeled off various articles of clothing, and boots, socks, and sweaters were tied onto the shrouds and backstay.

The sight that the *Caird* presented was one of the most incongruous imaginable. Here was a patched and battered 22-foot boat, daring to sail alone across the world's most tempestuous sea, her rigging festooned with a threadbare collection of clothing and half-rotten sleeping bags. Her crew consisted of six men whose faces were black with caked soot and half-hidden by matted beards, whose bodies were dead white from constant soaking in salt water. In addition, their faces, and particularly their fingers were marked with ugly round patches of missing skin where frostbites had eaten into their flesh. Their legs from the knees down were chafed and raw from the countless punishing trips crawling across the rocks in the bottom. And all of them were afflicted with salt water boils on their wrists, ankles, and buttocks. But had someone unexpectedly come upon this bizarre scene, undoubtedly the most striking thing would have been the attitude of the men . . . relaxed, even faintly jovial—almost as if they were on an outing of some sort.

Worsley took out his log and wrote:

> Moderate sea, Southerly swell
> Blue sky; passing clouds.
> Fine. Clear weather.
> Able to reduce some parts of our
>   clothing from wet to damp.
> To Leith Harb. 347. m [miles]

By evening the sun had done a wonderful job of drying, and when they crawled into their sleeping bags that night the sensation was distinctly pleasant—at least by comparison.

The good weather held throughout the night and into the following day, May 4; and again the gear was distributed among the rigging. The wind was out of the southeast at no more than 15 knots. Only an occasional sea splashed on board so that they had to pump only twice during the day.

Worsley's sight at noon put the position at 55°31′ South, 44°43′ West, a run of 52 miles in twenty-four hours.

Two days of good weather had worked their magic, and among the entire crew there was a growing feeling of confidence, subtle but unmistakable. In the beginning, South Georgia had existed only as a name—infinitely distant and lacking in reality.

But no more. They were even at this moment less than 250 miles from the nearest point on South Georgia. And having already covered 450 miles, the distance that remained was at least conceivable. Three days more, or maybe four at the most, should see them there, and then it would all be over. And so that peculiar brand of anxiety, born of an impossible goal that somehow comes within reach, began to infect them. Nothing overt, really, just a sort of added awareness, a little more caution and more care to insure that nothing preventable should go wrong now.

The wind remained steady out of the southeast during the night, though it grew considerably stronger, with occasional squalls to almost 40 knots. With the coming of light on May 5 the weather had returned to its old familiar pattern—overcast sky with a nasty, lumpy sea running. The wind was on the starboard beam so that the spray broke over almost at will. By nine o'clock, everything was as wet as it had ever been.

Otherwise, it was a notably uneventful day, distinguished only by the fact that toward evening the wind shifted slowly to the north and then the northwest. It increased in velocity, too, and by dark was blowing a gale.

Steering was difficult that night. The sky was overcast, and the pennant on the mainmast by which the course had once been kept had blown away, bit by bit, in successive gales. Now they had to steer by the feel of the boat and by watching the shadowy white line of a breaking sea ahead.

At midnight, after a drink of hot milk, Shackleton's watch took over, and Shackleton himself assumed the helm while Crean and McNeish stayed below to pump. His eyes were just growing accustomed to the dark when he turned and saw a rift of brightness in the sky astern. He called to the others to tell them the good news that the weather was clearing to the southwest.

A moment later he heard a hiss, accompanied by a low, muddled roar, and he turned to look again. The rift in the clouds, actually the crest of an enormous wave, was advancing rapidly toward them. He spun around and instinctively pulled his head down.

"For God's sake, hold on!" he shouted. "It's got us!"

For a long instant nothing happened. The *Caird* simply rose higher and higher, and the dull thunder of this enormous breaking wave filled the air.

And then it hit—and she was caught in a mountain of seething water and catapulted bodily forward and sideways at the same time. She seemed actually to be thrown into the air, and Shackleton was nearly torn from his seat by the deluge of water that swept over him. The lines to the rudder went slack, then suddenly seized up again as the boat was viciously swung around like some contemptible plaything.

For an instant, nothing existed but water. They couldn't even tell whether she was upright. But then the instant was over; the wave had rolled on, and the *Caird,* though stunned and half dead under a load of water that rose nearly to the seats, was miraculously still afloat. Crean and McNeish seized the first implements that came to hand and began to bail furiously. A moment later, Worsley's watch fought their way out of the sleeping bags and joined the struggle, throwing water over the side with a wild urgency, knowing that the next wave would surely be the finish unless they could lighten her before it struck.

Shackleton at the helm kept looking astern for another telltale streak of brightness. But none appeared, and ever so slowly, as they frantically pumped and bailed and ladled the water overboard, the *Caird* lifted to the seas again.

The ballast had shifted and the glass on the compass was broken—but they apparently had won. It took more than two hours to get her emptied out, and much of the time they were working in icy water to their knees.

Crean started a search for the Primus stove. He found it at last, wedged up against the ribs of the boat, but it was completely clogged. For a half hour he worked over it in the dark, his patience slowly ebbing away. Finally, through clenched teeth, he swore at the stove. Then it lit and they had some hot milk.

CHAPTER 5

The dawn of May 6 revealed an ugly scene. The wind was blowing nearly 50 knots from the northwest, and the *Caird* was straining into it, trying to hold to a northeasterly course. As every wave passed, some portion of it poured on board the boat.

But it seemed really not to matter too much. They had been pounded and bruised and drenched almost to the point of insensibility. Furthermore, the wave during the night had somehow changed their attitude. For thirteen days they had suffered through almost ceaseless gales, then finally a huge rogue sea. They had been the underdog, fit only to endure the punishment inflicted on them.

But sufficiently provoked, there is hardly a creature on God's earth that ultimately won't turn and attempt to fight, regardless of the odds. In an unspoken sense, that was much the way they felt now. They were possessed by an angry determination to see the journey through—no matter what. They felt that they had earned it. For thirteen days they had absorbed everything that the Drake Passage could throw at them—and now, by God, they deserved to make it.

Their resolve was strengthened when Worsley worked out the position. It put them at 54°26′ South, 40°44′ West. If this figure was accurate, they were a scant 91 miles from the western tip of South Georgia, and very soon there should be a sign of land—a bit of seaweed or a piece of driftwood.

As if to mock their determination, though, the sea rose menacingly throughout the morning. By noon it had grown so treacherous that Shackleton felt it was foolhardy to press on, though Worsley urged him to do so. At one o'clock, Shackleton gave the order to heave to. They came about and dropped the sail. The jib was run up the mainmast and they began once again to tack back and forth into the wind.

All of them fell sullen—even Shackleton, who from the beginning had required of the men that they make every effort to remain cheerful in order to avoid antagonisms. But it seemed too much—to be so close, possibly only one good day's run, and to have to stop.

The strain on Shackleton was so great that he lost his temper over a trivial incident. A small, bob-tailed bird appeared over the boat and flew annoyingly about, like a mosquito intent on landing. Shackleton stood it for several minutes, then he leaped to his feet, swearing and batting furiously at the bird with his arms. But he realized at once the poor example he had set and dropped back down again with a chagrined expression on his face.

The rest of the afternoon passed without incident until almost dusk when Crean started to prepare the evening hoosh. A minute or two later, he called for Shackleton to come below. Crean handed him a mug of water to taste, and Shackleton took a small sip; then a grave expression came over his face. The second cask of water—the one that had got adrift during the launching of the *Caird* from Elephant Island—was foul. It had the unmistakable brackish taste of sea water that apparently had seeped into it. Not only that, but the cask was hardly half full, indicating that a great deal of the water had leaked out.

Crean asked Shackleton what he should do, and Shackleton, rather snappishly, replied that there was obviously nothing they could do—it was the only water they had, and they would have to use it.

Crean went ahead and made the hoosh. When it was ready the men sampled it cautiously, and found that it was disagreeably salty.

For Shackleton, the discovery meant simply that the need for haste had now become acute. As soon as it was dark and Worsley was at the helm, he went aft and the two men discussed the situation. Their food, Shackleton said, should last two weeks. But they had less than a week's supply of water—and that was brackish. Thus a landing had to be made, and soon.

The inevitable question then became—would they hit South Georgia? Shackleton asked Worsley how accurate he thought their navigation had been. Worsley shook his head. With luck, he said, maybe within 10 miles, but it was always possible to make a mistake.

They both knew that except for one or two tiny islands, the Atlantic Ocean eastward beyond South Georgia is a void all the way to South Africa, nearly 3,000 miles away. If, through a miscalculation or because of a southerly gale, they missed the island, there would be no second chance. The land would then lie to windward of them, and they could never beat back toward it. They dared not miss.

Fortunately, as the night wore on, the northwesterly gale diminished slightly, and the sky began to clear. At 1 A.M., Shackleton decided it was safe to get under way, and they again set their course for the northeast.

The all-important thing now was to learn the position, but soon after dawn a foglike mist moved in. They could see the sun, but only as a hazy outline. Worsley kept his sextant handy all morning, hoping that the fog would clear. After several hours, he took his notebook and, partly in desperation, he scribbled: "Most unfavourable conditions for Obs. Misty with boat jumping like a flea. . . ."

Normally, in taking a sight, the perimeter of the sun is brought down to the horizon with the sextant. Now the best that Worsley could do was to peer through the mists at the sun's blurred image and try to estimate its center. Again and again he took sights on the theory that when he averaged them out he might come up with a reasonably accurate fix. He finally put the position at 54°38′ South, 39°36′ West, 68 miles from the tip of South Georgia. But he warned Shackleton not to put much stock in it.

The original plan had been to round the western tip of South Georgia, passing between Willis and Bird Islands, then swing east and run along the coast to the whaling station at Leith Harbor. But that had assumed reasonably decent navigating conditions, and had not taken into account the shortage of water. Now it no longer mattered where they landed, just so long as they did land. So they altered course to the east, hoping to hit anywhere on the west coast of the island, and it was of very little consequence where.

It turned out, too, that the water situation was considerably more serious than they had first imagined. Not only was the water brackish, but it was polluted with sediment and reindeer hairs which had somehow gotten into the cask. This noisome liquid, that had to be strained through gauze from the medicine chest, was drinkable—but just barely so, and it only aggravated their thirst. Furthermore, Shackleton had reduced each man's ration to about a half-cup per day, and the serving of hot milk at the beginning of each watch during the night had been eliminated. That afternoon, Shackleton informed them that for the rest of the voyage, they could only afford to have hoosh twice a day.

Throughout the afternoon there had been a mounting air of expectancy that they would sight some indication that the land was close by—birds or kelp or something. But there was none. And with the approach of evening, the attitude of expectancy gave way to one of apprehension—of a strangely paradoxical sort.

By Worsley's estimate they should have been a little more than 50 miles off the coast. But Worsley's calculations were admittedly crude, and they could easily have been much closer.

On the west coast of South Georgia there was not the smallest settlement, much less a beacon light or even a buoy to guide them. In fact, even to this day, the west coast of South Georgia is only sketchily charted. Thus it was entirely conceivable that they might come upon the coast in the dark—suddenly and disastrously.

On the other hand, their fear of running onto the island was oddly counterbalanced by the dread awareness that they might just as easily miss it altogether—run by it in the night, and never know it was there. Indeed, they might already have done so.

The darkness was now complete, and the *Caird* pounded forward on an ENE course with the wind on her port beam. The men peered ahead into the night with salt-rimmed eyes for the shadowy image of a headland; and they strained their ears for any unusual noise, perhaps the sound of surf pounding on a reef. But visibility could hardly have been worse—an overcast blotted out the stars, and the foggy mist still swept across the surface of the water. The only sounds that could be heard were the moaning of the wind through the stays and the surge of the heavy confused sea that was running.

Thirst, of course, heightened their expectation and prolonged each anxious minute. But in spite of the discomfort and uncertainty, there was an undercurrent of suppressed excitement. Each of the watches made wild, speculative guesses about how soon they would reach the whaling station and what it would be like to bathe and have clean clothes and sleep in a real bed and actually eat food served on a table.

Gradually the hours crept by, though there was nothing to indicate that they were nearing the coast. At 4 a.m., when Worsley's watch came on, Shackleton remained with him at the helm to keep a lookout for the land. They were making about 3 knots, and by six o'clock they should have been less than 15 miles offshore—but there was not a sign of it—not the smallest bit of ice or shred of seaweed.

Seven o'clock came—12 miles from the island, and yet no trace. The air of anticipation was slowly being replaced by a feeling of increasing tension. Some of the peaks on South Georgia were nearly 10,000 feet high. Surely they would be visible by now.

At eight o'clock, Shackleton's watch was due to take over. But nobody thought about watches. Instead all hands crowded into the cockpit, searching ahead and to each side in an atmosphere of competition, of hoping, of anxiety—all at once. But there was only the sea and sky, just the same as there had always been.

Toward nine o'clock, Shackleton sent Crean below to prepare some hoosh. When it was ready they ate it hurriedly in order to return to their lookout posts.

It was a strange time, a time of eagerness and expectation—underscored by grave, unspoken doubts. It was all so nearly over. An occasion for excitement, even jubilation. And yet, in the back of their minds was a nagging voice which refused to be silent—they might very well be looking in vain. If the island was there, they should have sighted it hours before.

Then, at just after ten-thirty, Vincent spotted a clump of seaweed, and a few minutes later a cormorant was sighted overhead. Hope flared anew. Cormorants rarely ventured farther than 15 miles from land.

Soon the foggy mists began to break up, though ever so slowly. Ragged clouds still scudded along close to the surface of the water.

But visibility was better. At noon the fog was almost gone. But the interminably heaving sea stretched in every direction.

"Land!"

It was McCarthy's voice, strong and confident. He was pointing dead ahead. And there it was. A black, frowning cliff with patches of snow clinging to its sides. It was just visible between the clouds, possibly 10 miles away. A moment later the clouds moved like a curtain across the water, shutting off the view.

But no matter. It was there, and they had all seen it.

CHAPTER 6

S hackleton was the only one who spoke.

"We've done it," he said, and his voice was strangely unsteady.

Not a sound came from the others. They simply stared ahead, watching for the land to reappear, just to be sure. And in a minute or two, when the clouds had blown away again, it did. Feeble, foolish grins spread across their faces, not of triumph or even joy, but simply of unspeakable relief.

They held the *Caird* on a course straight for the point they had first seen and within an hour they were close enough to make out the general contour of the land. Worsley took out his notebook and drew a rough sketch of it.

He then compared it with the chart and it appeared to correspond to the area of Cape Demidov. If so, it meant that his navigation had been very nearly faultless. They were only about 16 miles from the western tip of the island, the point for which they had originally been aiming.

By two-thirty, the *Caird* was a little more than 3 miles off the coast and it was possible to see patches of green lichens and areas of yellow-brown tussock grass showing through the snow on the steep sides of the headlands. Growing things—the first they had seen in more than sixteen months. And they would be standing amongst them in an hour or a little more.

Everything seemed perfect. But not for long. Within a few minutes, the deep rumbling sound of breakers reached them. Then dead ahead and off to the right an occasional spout of bursting spray shot skyward. As they drew closer they could see the backs of great seething combers hurtling shoreward as the Cape Horn graybeards blindly advanced to their destruction on uncharted reefs.

The whole complexion of things was suddenly changed. There could be no thought of a landing, not here at least, for the boat would not have lived ten seconds in those breakers. It was something they didn't deserve—a needless cruelty. The land lay just in front of them, and they had earned it. Yet now that the journey was done, sanctuary was ironically denied them.

They could not even hold to this course much longer. Crean hurriedly took over the helm from Worsley who spread the chart out so that he and Shackleton might study it. A decision had to be made quickly.

If the point ahead was Cape Demidov, and it appeared almost certain now that it was, their chart showed two possibilities of finding shelter. One was King Haakon Bay, some 10 miles east along the coast to starboard. The other was Wilson Harbor, just to the north of the point for which they were now making.

But King Haakon Bay lay in a generally east-west position, and was therefore almost totally exposed to the northwesterly wind that was blowing. Furthermore, it would take them until night even to reach its entrance and whatever reefs guarded the opening would have to be negotiated in the dark.

Wilson Harbor, on the other hand, though it was only about 4 miles away, and possibly would have offered a somewhat better shelter, unfortunately lay just enough to windward to put it out of reach in view of the sea that was running.

Consequently, although there were two theoretical choices, there was really none worthy of the risk. By three o'clock the land was only 2 miles distant. They could easily have reached it in less than forty-five minutes. But they would have died doing so.

Thus, at 3:10 P.M., Shackleton gave the order to come about. They swung onto the starboard tack and headed seaward once again to lay off until morning in the hope that they could then make a better approach or perhaps find a way through the reefs.

Worsley took out his navigation book again and wrote this:

" . . . Heavy westerly swell.

Very bad lumpy sea.

Stood off for night; wind increasing . . . "

They set a course for the SSE, intending to get far enough offshore so that they might safely heave to and wait for daylight. As the boat heeled to port before the following wind, hardly a one of them spoke. Individually they were fighting somehow to console their awful disappointment. But there was now, truly, but one more night to go.

Toward five o'clock the light began to fail, and the sky off the *Caird's* starboard quarter was kindled into vivid, almost angry shades of orange and red that slowly faded. It was dark by 6 P.M.

Overhead a heavy bank of clouds rolled in, and the wind gradually increased and began to move toward the west. Crean prepared some hoosh, but they were nearing the bottom of the spoiled cask, and the food seemed particularly foul. A deliberate effort was required to swallow it.

The wind had an ominous sound, and it was rising with every hour. At eight o'clock, rain began to fall. Before long the rain turned into sleet, then hail that drummed across the decking. By 11 P.M., the storm had reached gale force, and the *Caird* was caught in a cross sea that drove in from every direction, hurling the boat one way, then slamming her another.

They ran before the quartering gale until midnight; and though they had not the slightest idea where they might be, Shackleton decided they must be far enough offshore to heave to. Crean and McCarthy cautiously made their way forward in the dark and removed the mainsail and jib, then set the jib on the mainmast. The Caird's bow was brought up into the wind, and the long wait for daybreak was begun.

The remainder of that night was an eternity, composed of seconds individually endured until they merged into minutes and minutes finally grew into hours. And through it all there was the voice of the wind, shrieking as they had never heard it shriek before in all their lives.

The dawn of May 9 finally came, but there was no real dawn. Instead the wild blackness of the night slowly gave way to a thick gray pall. Only an estimate could be made of the wind's actual speed, though it was at least 65 knots. The cross sea was the worst it had been, and added to it there was now a mountainous westerly swell sweeping inland before the gale. The rollers that raced shoreward were perhaps 40 feet high, maybe more.

The Caird, with her miserable little rag of a trysail blown stiff by the wind, rose to the top of each onrushing swell and there she quivered before the fury of the gale. It seemed strong enough almost to peel the canvas decking off her. There, too, it was difficult even to breathe. The atmosphere was a saturated substance, composed less of air than of rain and snow, and mostly wind-driven mist, torn from the surface of the water.

Visibility was reduced to a hazy sphere surrounding the boat. Beyond that was only a blinding sameness that screamed by without interruption.

And though they had not the vaguest idea where they might be, they knew one thing all too well: somewhere off to leeward the black cliffs of South Georgia were waiting, steadfastly hurling back this colossal onslaught of water. They wished they knew how far.

It seemed inconceivable, but during the morning hours the wind actually rose, and by noon it was probably close to 80 knots out of the southwest. To prepare food was out of the question, but they had almost no appetites for eating anyhow. Their tongues were swollen with thirst, and their lips cracked and bleeding. Any man who wanted it could have all the cold sledging ration he could eat, and a few of them tried to gnaw on bits of it, but they lacked the saliva to swallow properly.

The *Caird's* bow was kept pointed into the wind. But it was astern that they looked, trying to catch a glimpse of the island or the treacherous reefs that had kept them at bay the previous afternoon. All morning they heard it getting closer. Deep below the high-pitched shriek of the wind and the tormented upheaval of the sea, there was a thudding bass heartbeat, more felt than heard—the impact of successive waves breaking on the coast, transmitted through the water as a series of muddled shocks which struck the boat.

Then, at just about two o'clock, they saw where they were. A quirk of wind tore the clouds apart, and two wicked peaks loomed above a line of cliffs and the perpendicular faces of glaciers that dropped sheer into the sea. The coastline looked to be about a mile away, perhaps a little more.

But vastly more important, in that single glimpse they saw to their terror that they were only a short distance outside the line of breakers, the point at which the seas ceased to behave like swells and became combers instead, rushing faster and faster toward their own destruction against the land. As each swell passed under them they could feel it tugging momentarily at the boat, trying to get hold of her and hurl her toward the beach. It seemed now that everything—the wind, the current, and even the sea itself—were

united in a single, determined purpose—once and for all to anni-
hilate this tiny boat which thus far had defied all their efforts to
destroy it.

No choice remained but to hoist sail and try to claw their way
offshore into the teeth of this fiendish gale. But it could not be
done. No boat—least of all the *Caird*—could beat to windward
under conditions like these.

Shackleton rushed aft and took over the lines of the tiller from
Crean. Then Crean and Worsley crawled up onto the decking and
pulled themselves forward on their bellies. Had they stood upright, they would have been knocked or simply blown overboard.
Finally they reached the mainmast, and hugging onto it, they cautiously got to their feet. The wind was so strong they could hardly
get the jib off. But after several minutes' work they succeeded,
and the *Caird's* bow instantly fell off into the trough. The two
men lunged forward and hurriedly secured the jib to the forestay.

McCarthy was needed to help with the mainsail, for had the
wind got hold of it, their combined strength could not have kept
it from being ripped out of their hands.

But at last it was made fast and reefed, and the mizzen, too.
Then Shackleton pulled the *Caird's* bow around to the southeast,
and the wind, like a solid object, struck her a shuddering blow
that all but capsized her. Shackleton shouted excitedly to McNeish
and Vincent below to shift ballast. They, kneeling on the rocks
and working as feverishly as their strength permitted, piled the
boulders against the starboard side, and the Caird righted herself
somewhat.

She moved forward half a boat-length before the first sea
struck her and stopped her dead. Solid water was flung over the
masthead, and the strain was so great that her bow planks opened
up and little lines of water squirted in through the seams. Once
more she moved ahead, and once more the sea clubbed her to a

halt. Over and over again the process was repeated until it seemed certain that she would burst her planking, or have the masts torn out of her.

The water now was coming in both from above and below. It was rising so fast that two men working constantly could not handle it, so Shackleton put all hands to the task—three men on the pump and one bailing with the 2-gallon hoosh pot. That left one man to relieve whoever showed the first signs of exhaustion.

But for all their efforts they seemed only to be standing still. Occasionally the clouds were ripped aside, revealing the coast off the port quarter, just as close as ever. After more than an hour they had demonstrated the truth of what they first suspected—it could not be done. No boat could beat to windward in such a storm.

Shackleton was sure the end was very near.

But actually they were making headway. Gauged against the indistinct outline of the coast, it was imperceptible—but it was real, nonetheless.

They became aware of it suddenly just after four o'clock when a rift in the storm showed a great, craggy peak off the port bow. It was Annenkov Island, a 2,000-foot mountaintop shoved up out of the sea some 5 miles off the coast. And they realized at once that it lay directly in their path.

Though the *Caird's* bow was pointed well to seaward, she was powerless to prevent the gale from driving her downwind. Thus her actual course was more sideways than forward. Nor was there any way to turn. Astern lay the coast, and the chart showed that off to port was a successive line of reefs. Only to starboard was there open sea—and that was surely the one direction she could not go, for that was the direction from which the wind was blowing.

There was nothing to do, therefore, but to hold to the south-easterly course, as close into the wind as possible, and pray God that somehow she could edge by the island—if she held together that long. Neither was at all likely.

By now it was getting dark, though the sky was somewhat clearer, and Annenkov Island was plainly visible most of the time as a black shape against the sky.

The sight it presented was the more awesome by contrast. While they were literally enveloped in the wild ferocity of the storm, struggling simply to remain afloat—off to port lay this huge, resolute bulk which was implacably creeping closer through the darkness. Before long they could hear the deep booming of the surf against the cliffs.

Only the man at the helm actually could see what was happening, for the others dared not pause in their bailing for fear that the water would get ahead of them. Periodically they changed tasks in order to get some relief. Thirst had long since ceased to matter, along with everything else except the fight to keep the boat under them. Each helmsman in turn, mindful of the anxiety of those below, shouted down to them reassuringly, "She'll clear it—she's doing it."

But she wasn't. By seven-thirty they were on top of the island, and the sheer mass of it now dominated everything to leeward. The sound of the seas against its side virtually drowned out even the screaming of the wind. The foaming backwash of the breakers thrown back from the cliffs swirled around the *Caird*, and the towering, snowy peak above them was so close they had to crane their necks to see it.

Worsley thought to himself of the pity of it all. He remembered the diary he had kept ever since the *Endurance* had sailed from South Georgia almost seventeen months before. That same diary, wrapped in rags and utterly soaked, was now stowed in the forepeak of the *Caird*. When she went, it would go, too. Worsley thought not so much of dying, because that was now so plainly inevitable, but of the fact that no one would ever know how terribly close they had come.

He waited at the helm, silent and tense—braced for the final, shattering impact when the Caird's bottom would be torn out against some unseen rock. As he watched, the water streaming down his face and dripping from his beard, the sky to the east crept into view.

"She's clearing it!" he screamed. "She's clearing it!"

The bailers stopped and everybody looked up and saw the stars shining to leeward. The island was no longer in the way. They had no idea how, even why—perhaps some unexpected eddy of the tide had driven them offshore. But no one then stopped to seek an explanation. They knew only one thing—the boat had been spared.

Now only one obstacle remained—Mislaid Rock—three-quarters of a mile beyond the western tip of Annenkov Island. So they clung to the southeasterly course, close into the wind. But somehow it all seemed easier. The roar of the breakers grew fainter, and by nine o'clock they knew that they were safely past everything.

All at once they felt inexpressibly weary, numb, even indifferent. The gale, too, appeared exhausted by the struggle, or perhaps it knew that it had lost, for the wind rapidly died off, and within the short space of thirty minutes it had swung around to the ssw.

They came about and set a course for the northwest, giving South Georgia a wide berth. The sea was still high, but the viciousness had gone out of it.

They had to continue to bail almost until midnight before they had reduced the *Caird's* burden of water to the extent that three men could handle it. Then Worsley's watch was sent below to get some sleep, while Shackleton, Crean, and McNeish remained on duty.

Once more their thirst returned, much worse than it had ever been. But only a pint or two of water remained, and Shackleton decided to save it until morning.

At three-thirty, Worsley's watch took over and toward seven o'clock, South Georgia came into view again, about 10 miles off to starboard.

They set a course straight for the land, but the *Caird* had hardly settled onto it when the wind shifted to the northwest and fell very light. Thus, throughout the morning their progress was steady but painfully slow. At noon they were almost abeam of Cape Demidov once more, and dead ahead were two inviting glaciers which held the promise of ice to be melted into water. But it was evident that they could not reach them before dark.

Consequently they came about to head for King Haakon Bay. For twenty minutes they made good progress, but then the damnable wind swung around to head them off, blowing from the east—straight out of the bay.

The sails were lowered, and with Shackleton at the helm, the other men took turns rowing, two at a time. Before long the tide turned and began to set to the south, thus aiding the wind in keeping them offshore. And it soon became apparent that they were doing little more than holding their own. However, by three o'clock they had managed to pull close enough to see relatively calm water in the bay beyond the reefs—and they also saw what appeared to be a safe passage. But they could not possibly get through before dark—not under oars.

It was time for a last desperate attempt. Another night, this time without a drop of water, and possibly another gale—they simply did not have it in them.

Hurriedly they ran up every sail to its full height and headed for the narrow opening in the reefs. But it meant sailing straight into the wind, and the *Caird* simply could not do it. Four times they lay off, and four times they tried to tack into the wind. Four times they failed.

It was well after four o'clock, and the light was beginning to go. They ran the *Caird* a mile to the south, trying to get the wind as much abeam as possible. Then they came about once more onto the starboard tack. This time she just managed to slip through.

Instantly the sails were dropped and the oars were put out. They rowed for about ten minutes, then Shackleton spotted a small cove in the cliffs to starboard.

The entrance was protected by a small reef of its own over which the surge of the swell was breaking. But they saw an opening—though it was so small the oars had to be taken in at the last moment.

About 200 yards beyond was a steep, bouldered beach. Shackleton stood in the bow, holding the frayed remains of the sea-anchor line. Finally the *Caird* rose up on a swell and her keel ground against the rocks. Shackleton jumped ashore and held her from going out.

As quickly, as they could, the other men scrambled after him.

It was five o'clock on the tenth of May, 1916, and they were standing at last on the island from which they had sailed 522 days before.

They heard a trickling sound. Only a few yards away a little stream of fresh water was running down from the glaciers high above.

A moment later all six were on their knees, drinking.

PART VII

CHAPTER 1

It was a curiously quiet moment, almost devoid of rejoicing. They had accomplished the impossible, but at a staggering price. Now it was over, and they knew only that they were unutterably tired—too tired even to savor much more than the dim awareness that they had won. They managed, however, to shake hands all around. It seemed somehow the thing to do.

Yet even in that small moment of victory, tragedy threatened. The surf inside the cove was especially heavy. It had swung the *Caird's* stern around, and she was pounding against the rocks.

They stumbled back down the beach, but the rocks were rough and their legs were rubbery with weakness. By the time they reached the boat her rudder had already been torn off. She had to be raised clear of the water—and that meant unloading her. So they formed themselves into a chain and began the laborious job of passing the stores up the beach. When that was done the hated rock ballast was thrown over the side.

But when it came time to get the *Caird* onto safer ground, the real extent of their weakness became evident. Exerting every ounce of their combined strength, they could hardly do more than rock the boat back and forth, and after about six tries Shackleton saw that it was no use to continue until they had rested and had something to eat.

A piece of light rope was made fast to the *Caird's* bow and secured to a boulder. They left the boat at the water's edge, pounding against the rocks.

What appeared to be a small cave had been sighted about 30 yards off to the left, and they dragged their sleeping bags and a small amount of stores up to it. It proved to be hardly more than a hollow in the cliffs. But enormous icicles, at least 15 feet high, had collected across its face, forming a front wall. They crawled inside and found that the cave was about 12 feet deep, with ample room to shelter them.

Crean lighted a fire and prepared some hoosh. It was eight o'clock by the time they had finished eating, and Shackleton instructed all of them to turn in, saying that they would stand one-man watches over the *Caird.* He agreed to take the first. The others crawled into their wet, but blissfully motionless sleeping bags, and within seconds they were truly unconscious.

Everything went well until about 2 A.M. Tom Crean was on watch when a particularly heavy sea caught the *Caird* and she broke loose. Crean managed to grab the bow line and he shouted for help. But by the time the others had awakened and made their way down to the beach, Crean had been dragged into the water almost over his head.

With all of them pulling they managed to bring her back to shore, and they tried once more to get her up the beach, this time by rolling her over. Again they lacked the strength.

They were very close to exhaustion, but even their desperate craving for sleep could not be considered when weighed against the possible loss of the boat. Shackleton decided they would have to stand by her until daylight.

They sat down to wait for morning. But there was no sleep because periodically they had to fend the *Caird* off the rocks.

Shackleton reviewed their situation in his mind. He had originally hoped to use this place only as a stopover to replenish their water and to obtain a few days' rest, then press on around the coast to Leith Harbor. But the *Caird's* rudder was now lost. Furthermore, if they were to have rest, the boat had to be pulled clear of the water. To do so, they would have to lighten her by removing the decking, since they lacked the strength to lift her as she was. Once that was done, she would hardly be fit to face the sea again.

Sitting on the rocks waiting for morning, Shackleton came to the conclusion that instead of sailing to Leith Harbor, they would remain on the south side of the island and three of the party would go overland to bring help.

By sea it would have been a voyage of more than 130 miles out around the western tip of the island and then along the north coast. By land it was a scant 29 miles in a straight line. The only difference between the two was that in the three-quarters of a century that men had been coming to South Georgia, not one man had ever crossed the island—for the simple reason that it could not be done.

A few of the peaks on South Georgia rise to somewhat less than 10,000 feet, which certainly is not high by mountain-climbing standards. But the interior of the island has been described by one expert as "a saw-tooth thrust through the tortured upheaval of mountain and glacier that falls in chaos to the northern sea." In short, it was impassable.

Shackleton knew it—and yet there was no choice. He made his announcement after breakfast, and all of the men accepted it routinely and without question. Shackleton said he would make the journey with Worsley and Crean as soon as it seemed feasible.

But there was work to be done first. McNeish and McCarthy were put to the task of removing the decking and the extra planks from the *Caird*, while Shackleton, Crean, and Worsley went to work leveling the floor of the cave with some loose stones and dry tussock grass. Vincent remained in his sleeping bag, gravely troubled with rheumatism.

By noon, McNeish had dismantled enough of the *Caird's* upperworks to lighten her considerably, so they decided to attempt to get her up. And this time they were able—but just barely so. They shoved her up the beach literally by inches, pausing every few minutes to rest. She was safely above the high water mark by one o'clock.

Later in the afternoon, Shackleton and Crean climbed a plateau at the head of the cove, and there they saw mounds of white among the rocks. These proved to be baby albatrosses on the nest. Shackleton went back for the shotgun, and they killed one adult and one chick. They ate them for supper, and Worsley wrote of the older bird: "Good eating but rather tough." McNeish noted simply: "It was a treat."

Afterwards they turned in and slept for twelve glorious hours without a single interruption. By morning they all felt infinitely better. Later in the day McNeish recorded rapturously: "We have not been as comfortable for the last 5 weeks. We had 3 young & 1 old albatross for lunch. with 1 pint of gravy which beets all the chicken soup I ever tasted. I have just been thinking what our companions [on Elephant Island] would say if they had food like this."

Shackleton and Worsley, meanwhile, had made a survey of sorts around the area and saw that it was very nearly impenetrable country. Except for the cove in which they were camped, the cliffs and glaciers rose almost perpendicularly.

Consequently, Shackleton decided they would sail the *Caird* to the head of King Haakon Bay, a distance of about 6 miles. Their chart indicated that the terrain there was somewhat more hospitable, and they would also be 6 miles closer to Stromness

Bay on the opposite side of the island where the whaling stations were situated.

Short as this journey was, Shackleton felt the men were not yet equal to it, so they spent two days recuperating and eating sumptuously. Little by little, as they gained strength and the tension went out of their nerves, a marvelous feeling of security came over all of them, dimmed only by the knowledge of the responsibility they bore to the castaways back on Elephant Island.

May 14 had been the day set for the trip to the head of the bay, but the weather in the morning was squally with rain, so the trip was postponed until the following day. In the afternoon there were encouraging signs of clearing. McNeish wrote: "I went to the top of the hill & had a lay on the grass & it put me in mind of old times at *Home* sitting on the hillside looking down at the sea."

They were up at dawn the following morning. The *Caird* was loaded and easily shoved downhill into the water. She had cleared the cove and entered the open bay at eight o'clock. A brisk northwesterly wind was blowing, and before long the sun broke through the clouds.

It was an utterly carefree journey as the *Caird* drove smartly across the sparkling water. After a while they even began to sing. It occurred to Shackleton that they could easily have been mistaken for a picnic party out for a lark—except perhaps for their woebegone appearance.

Shortly past noon they rounded a high bluff, and before them lay a sheltered, gently sloping beach of sand and pebbles. It was populated by hundreds of sea elephants, enough to keep them supplied with food and fuel indefinitely. They were ashore by twelve-thirty.

The *Caird* was hauled above the reach of the water, and then they turned her over. McCarthy shored her up with a foundation of stones and when she was ready, they arranged their sleeping bags inside. It was decided to name the place "Peggotty Camp," after the poor but honest family in Dickens' *David Copperfield.*

Shackleton was extremely anxious to begin the journey, primarily because the season was getting on and the weather was bound to turn bad before long. In addition, the moon was now full, and they were certain to need its light while traveling at night. However, the next day, May 16, dawned cloudy and rainy, keeping them confined under the *Caird* nearly all day. They spent the time discussing the journey and McNeish busied himself fixing their boots for climbing. He had removed four dozen 2-inch screws from the *Caird,* and he fixed eight of them into each shoe to be worn by the members of the overland party.

Again on May 17 the weather was not fit for travel, with squally winds and sleet blowing. Worsley went with Shackleton to the east, toward the extreme head of the bay, to reconnoiter inland as much as possible. It was not a very successful mission due to the poor visibility, though Shackleton satisfied himself that there appeared to be a snow slope leading from the head of the bay up toward the interior.

They had first thought of hauling their supplies on a small sledge, and McNeish had put together a crude affair out of pieces of driftwood. But when they tried it out, it proved to be clumsy and hard to pull, and the idea was abandoned.

May 18 was another day of disagreeable weather, and Shackleton was almost beside himself to begin the journey. They spent a tense day going over their gear once more, and watching for a break in the weather.

The decision had been made to travel light, even without sleeping bags. Each of the overland party was to carry his own allotment of three days' sledging rations and biscuits. In addition they were to take a filled Primus stove which carried enough fuel for six meals, plus a small pot for cooking and a half-filled box of matches. They had two compasses, a pair of binoculars, and about

50 feet of rope knotted together, along with the carpenter's adz for use as an ice axe.

The only superfluous item Shackleton permitted was Worsley's diary.

At dusk the break came. The sky showed signs of clearing. Shackleton met with McNeish, whom he was leaving in charge of the three men staying behind. Shackleton gave him his final instructions, and he wrote this letter in McNeish's diary:

May 18th, 1916
South Georgia

Sir

I am about to try to reach Husvik on the East Coast of this island for relief of our party. I am leaving you in charge of the party consisting of Vincent, McCarthy & yourself. You will remain here until relief arrives. You have ample seal food which you can supplement with birds and fish according to your skill. You are left with a double barrelled gun, 50 cartridges [and other rations] . . . You also have all the necessary equipment to support life for an indefinite period in the event of my non-return. You had better after winter is over try and sail around to the East Coast. The course I am making towards Husvik is East magnetic.

I trust to have you relieved in a few days.

Yours faithfully

E. H. Shackleton

CHAPTER 2

The others turned in, but Shackleton could not sleep, and he went outside repeatedly to check on the weather. It was clearing, but only very slowly. Worsley, too, got up about midnight to see how conditions were.

However, by 2 A.M., the moon was shining down brilliantly, and the air was wonderfully clear. Shackleton said the time had come.

A final hoosh was prepared and they ate as quickly as they could. Shackleton wanted to get away with the least possible fuss in order not to emphasize the significance of their leaving in the minds of those who were staying behind. It took only a few minutes to gather up their meager equipment. Then they shook hands all around and Shackleton, Worsley, and Crean crawled out from under the *Caird*. McNeish accompanied them for about 200 yards, shook each of their hands again and wished them luck, then walked slowly back to Peggotty Camp.

It was 3:10 A.M. The final journey had begun. The three men made their way along the shoreline to the head of the bay, then started upland, climbing a fairly steep, snow-covered slope.

Shackleton was in the lead, and he set a brisk pace. For the first hour or so they trudged upward without a pause. But the

snow underfoot was soft to about ankle depth, and they soon began to feel the strain in their legs. Fortunately, when they reached
a height of about 2,500 feet the slope leveled off.

On the chart they carried, only the coastline of South Georgia
was shown—and a great deal of that was missing. The interior was
blank. Thus, they could be guided only by what they could see,
and Shackleton was terribly eager to determine what lay ahead.
But about 5 A.M., a thick fog rolled in, shrouding everything
in a diffused glow of luminescence in which even the snow beneath their feet was real only when they set foot on it. Shackleton
thought it would be best if they roped themselves together for
safety.

By daybreak Worsley estimated that they had covered about
5 miles, and as the sun rose higher, the fog began to thin out.
Peering ahead they saw an enormous snow-covered lake, just
slightly to the left of their easterly course. The lake was a rare bit
of good luck because it promised the opportunity of a level route
across its entire length, and they started toward it.

For an hour they followed an easy downhill route, though
there was an increasing number of crevasses. At first these were
thin and shallow, but before long they grew wider and deeper,
and it soon became apparent that the three men were descending
the face of a glacier. It was an unusual situation because glaciers
rarely emptied into lakes—and yet there it was, stretching invit-
ingly before them.

By seven o'clock, however, the sun had risen high enough to
burn away the last traces of the fog, and they suddenly saw that
the lake extended all the way to the horizon.

They were marching toward Possession Bay—the open sea, on
the northern coast of South Georgia.

They had, in fact, covered about seven miles and almost
crossed the island at a narrow neck. But it was of absolutely no
use to them. Even if they could have descended the perpendicular

headlands below them, there was no shoreline along which they might make their way. The glacier fell sheer into the sea. There was nothing to do but to retrace their steps, and they started back upland.

The worst of it was that it cost them time. Given time, they could have probed and reconnoitered for the best route, resting when they felt the need and traveling only when they were fit, and when the weather was best. But they had dared all for the sake of speed. They had neither sleeping bags nor tents. And if they were caught in these mountains by a change of weather, they would be powerless to save themselves. The blizzards of South Georgia are considered among the worst on earth.

It took two toilsome hours to regain the ground they had lost, and then they set off again toward the east. By eight-thirty they saw that a range of small mountains lay ahead, a series of ridges and spurs—four altogether, like the knuckles of a tightly clenched fist. Worsley figured that their route lay closest between the first and the second, and they set their course in that direction.

At nine o'clock they paused for their first meal. A hole was dug in the snow and the Primus stove was placed in it. A mixture of sledging rations and biscuits was stirred up, and they ate it scalding hot. They were on the trail again by nine-thirty.

From here the ascent became increasingly steep, and they labored upward, a foot at a time, with Shackleton in the lead. They climbed what seemed to be an almost vertical slope, cutting steps in its face with the adz.

Finally, about eleven-fifteen, they gained the summit. Shackleton was the first to peer over. He saw beneath him a precipitous drop, ending in a chasm 1,500 feet below. It was strewn with the shattered fragments of ice that had plunged from where he crouched. He waved for the others to come see for themselves. There was no way down. Furthermore, to the right lay a chaotic mass of ice cliffs and crevasses—impassable territory. To the left was a steeply descending line of glaciers dropping away into the sea. But dead ahead—the direction in which their course lay—was a gently rising snow slope, stretching away for perhaps 8 miles. It was this they had to reach—if only they could get down to it.

It had taken more than three hours of strenuous effort to reach the summit, but now the only thing to do was to retreat, to retrace their steps again and try to find a different way, perhaps around the second peak.

They granted themselves five minutes' rest, then started down the way they had come. Physically the descent was relatively easy and took only an hour, but it was a disheartening business. When they reached the bottom, they skirted around the base of the mountain, making their way between the overhanging ice cliffs and a truly gigantic bergschrund—a crescent-shaped gully, a thousand feet deep and a mile and a half long, cut out by the wind.

They paused at twelve-thirty to have another ration of hoosh, and then they started up again. It was a tortuous climb, much steeper than the first, and they had to cut steps with the adz beginning halfway up the face of the slope. The height and the exertion were a terrible strain and they found it impossible to keep going steadily. Every twenty minutes or so they sprawled on their backs with their legs and arms flung out, sucking in great gulps of the rarefied air.

But finally, about three o'clock in the afternoon, they were in sight of the ridge—a cap of blue-white ice.

The view from the top revealed the descent to be every bit as frighteningly impossible as the first had been, only this time there was an added menace. The afternoon was getting on, and heavy banks of fog were beginning to form in the valley far below. Looking back, they saw more rolling in from the west.

Their situation was starkly simple: Unless they could get lower, they would freeze to death. Shackleton estimated their altitude at 4,500 feet. At such a height, the temperature at night might easily drop well below zero. They had no means for obtaining shelter, and their clothes were worn and thin.

Hurriedly Shackleton turned and started down again with the others following. This time he did his best to keep as high as possible, cutting steps in the slope and working laterally around the side of the third peak—then up again once more.

They moved as quickly as they could, but there was very little speed left in them. Their legs were wobbly and strangely disobedient.

Finally, well after four o'clock, they struggled to the top. The ridge was so sharp that Shackleton was able to sit astride it, one leg on either side. The light was fading fast, but peering warily down he saw that though the descent was steep, it was not so bad as the others had been. Toward the bottom it appeared to slope away toward level ground. But there was no telling for sure because the valley now was thick with fog and the light was very poor.

Furthermore, the fog creeping up behind them was approaching very rapidly, threatening to obliterate everything, leaving them blinded and trapped atop this razorback.

The time for hesitation was past, and Shackleton swung himself over the side. Working furiously, he began to cut steps in the face of the cliff, descending slowly, a foot at a time. A bitter chill had come into the air, and the sun was nearly down. Gradually they were getting lower, but it was maddeningly slow progress.

After thirty minutes, the ice-hard surface of the snow grew softer, indicating that the grade was not quite so steep. Shackleton stopped short. He seemed to realize all at once the futility of what he was doing. At the rate they were going it would take hours to make the descent. Furthermore, it was probably too late to turn back.

He hacked out a small platform with the adz, then called to the others to come down.

There was no need to explain the situation. Speaking rapidly, Shackleton said simply that they faced a clear-cut choice: If they stayed where they were, they would freeze—in an hour, maybe two, maybe more. They had to get lower—and with all possible haste.

So he suggested they slide.

Worsley and Crean were stunned—especially for such an insane solution to be coming from Shackleton. But he wasn't joking . . . he wasn't even smiling. He meant it—and they knew it.

But what if they hit a rock, Crean wanted to know.

Could they stay where they were, Shackleton replied, his voice rising.

The slope, Worsley argued. What if it didn't level off? What if there were another precipice?

Shackleton's patience was going. Again he demanded—could they stay where they were?

Obviously they could not, and Worsley and Crean reluctantly were forced to admit it. Nor was there really any other way of getting down. And so the decision was made. Shackleton said they would slide as a unit, holding onto one another. They quickly sat down and untied the rope which held them together. Each of them coiled up his share to form a mat. Worsley locked his legs around Shackleton's waist and put his arms around Shackleton's neck. Crean did the same with Worsley. They looked like three tobogganers without a toboggan.

Altogether it took a little more than a minute, and Shackleton did not permit any time for reflection. When they were ready, he kicked off. In the next instant their hearts stopped beating. They seemed to hang poised for a split second, then suddenly the wind was shrieking in their ears, and a white blur of snow tore past. Down . . . down . . . They screamed—not in terror necessarily, but simply because they couldn't help it. It was squeezed out of them by the rapidly mounting pressure in their ears and against their chests. Faster and faster—down . . . down . . . down!

Then they shot forward onto the level, and their speed began to slacken. A moment later they came to an abrupt halt in a snowbank.

The three men picked themselves up. They were breathless and their hearts were beating wildly. But they found themselves laughing uncontrollably. What had been a terrifying prospect possibly a hundred seconds before had turned into a breathtaking triumph.

They looked up against the darkening sky and saw the fog curling over the edge of the ridges, perhaps 2,000 feet above them—and they felt that special kind of pride of a person who in a foolish moment accepts an impossible dare—then pulls it off to perfection.

After a meal of biscuit and sledging ration they started up the snowy slope toward the east. It was tricky going in the dark, and extreme caution was needed to watch for crevasses. But off to the southwest a hazy glow silhouetted the mountain peaks. And after they had spent an hour in anxious travel, the glow rose above the ranges—the full moon, directly in their path.

What a sight it was. In its light the edges of the crevasses were now easily discernible, and every ridgeline in the snow cast its shadow. They kept on, guided by the friendly moon, until after midnight, stopping at intervals to rest, for their weariness was now becoming a real burden, relieved only by the knowledge that surely they were getting close.

At about twelve-thirty they had reached a height of perhaps 4,000 feet and the slope leveled off; then slowly it started to descend, curving slightly toward the northeast—exactly as it should toward Stromness Bay. With great expectation they turned to follow it down. The cold, however, was increasing—or perhaps they were beginning to feel it more. So at 1 A.M., Shackleton permitted a brief halt for food. They were up and moving again at one-thirty.

For more than an hour they traveled downhill, then they came in sight of the water once more. There, outlined by the moonlight, was Mutton Island, sitting in the middle of Stromness Bay. As they made their way along, other familiar landmarks came into view, and they excitedly pointed them out to one another. Within an hour or two they would be down.

But then Crean spotted a crevasse off to the right, and looking ahead they saw other crevasses in their path. They stopped—confused. They were on a glacier. Only there were no glaciers surrounding Stromness Bay.

They knew then that their own eagerness had cruelly deceived them. The island lying just ahead wasn't Mutton Island, and the landmarks they had seen were the creations of their imagination.

Worsley took out the chart and the others gathered around him in the moonlight. They had descended to what must be Fortuna Bay, one of the many coastal indentations on South Georgia lying to the west of Stromness Bay. It meant that once more they had to retrace their steps. Bitterly disappointed, they turned and began to plod uphill again.

For two miserable hours they kept at it, skirting the edge of Fortuna Bay and struggling to regain the ground they had lost. By 5 o'clock they had recovered most of it, and they came to another line of ridges similar to the ones that had blocked their way the previous afternoon. Only this time there appeared to be a small pass.

But they were tired now to the point of exhaustion. They found a little sheltered spot behind a rock and sat down, huddled together with their arms around one another for warmth. Almost at once Worsley and Crean fell asleep, and Shackleton, too, caught himself nodding. Suddenly he jerked his head up-right. All the years of Antarctic experience told him that this was the danger sign—the fatal sleep that trails off into freezing death. He fought to stay awake for five long minutes, then he woke the others, telling them that they had slept for half an hour.

Even after so brief a rest, their legs had stiffened so that it was actually painful to straighten them, and they were awkward when they moved off again. The gap through the ridges lay perhaps a thousand feet above them, and they trudged toward it, silent with apprehension of what they would find on the other side.

It was just six o'clock when they passed through, and the first light of dawn showed that no cliff, no precipice barred the way—only a comfortable grade so far as they could see. Beyond the valley, the high hills to the west of Stromness stood away in the distance.

"It looks too good to be true," Worsley said.

They started down. When they had descended to a height of about 2,500 feet they paused to prepare breakfast. Worsley and Crean dug a hole for the Primus stove while Shackleton went to see if he could learn what lay ahead. He climbed a small ridge by cutting steps in it. The view from the top was not altogether encouraging. The slope appeared to end in another precipice, though it was hard to tell for sure.

He started down—and just then a sound reached him. It was faint and uncertain, but it could have been a steam whistle. Shackleton knew it was about 6:30 A.M. . . . the time when the men at whaling stations usually were awakened.

He hurried down from the ridge to tell Worsley and Crean the exciting news. Breakfast was gulped down, then Worsley took the chronometer from around his neck and the three of them crowded around, staring fixedly at its hands. If Shackleton had heard the steam whistle at Stromness, it should blow again to call the men to work at seven o'clock.

It was 6:50 . . . then 6:55. They hardly even breathed for fear of making a sound. 6:58 . . . 6:59. . . . Exactly to the second, the hoot of the whistle carried through the thin morning air.

They looked at one another and smiled. Then they shook hands without speaking.

A peculiar thing to stir a man—the sound of a factory whistle heard on a mountainside. But for them it was the first sound from the outside world that they had heard since December, 1914— seventeen unbelievable months before. In that instant, they felt an overwhelming sense of pride and accomplishment. Though they had failed dismally even to come close to the expedition's original objective, they knew now that somehow they had done much, much more than ever they set out to do.

Shackleton now seemed possessed with urgency to get down, and though there was an obviously safer but longer route off to the left, he elected to press forward and risk the chance of a steep grade. They gathered up their gear, except for the Primus stove which was now empty and useless. Each of them carried one last sledging ration and a single biscuit. And so they hurried forward, floundering through the deep snow.

But 500 feet down they discovered that Shackleton had indeed seen a precipice at the end of the slope. And it was terrifyingly steep, too, almost like a church steeple. But they were in no humor to turn back now. Shackleton was lowered over the edge, and he cut steps in the icy face of the cliff. When he had reached the 50-foot limit of the rope, the other two descended to where he stood and the cycle was repeated over again. It was progress, but slow and dangerous.

It took them three full hours to make the descent, but finally, about ten o'clock, they reached the bottom. From here there was only an easy grade down into the valley, then up the other side.

It was a long climb, however, nearly 3,000 feet in all, and they were very, very tired. But with only one more ridge to go, they drove their weary bodies upward. At noon they were halfway there, and at twelve-thirty they reached a small plateau. Then at last, just at one-thirty, they gained the final ridge and stood looking down.

Spread out beneath them, 2,500 feet below, was Stromness Whaling Station. A sailing ship was tied up to one of the wharfs and a small whale catcher was entering the bay. They saw the tiny figures of men moving around the docks and sheds.

For a very long moment they stared without speaking. There didn't really seem to be very much to say, or at least anything that needed to be said.

"Let's go down," Shackleton said quietly.

Having got so close, his old familiar caution returned, and he was determined that nothing was to go wrong now. The terrain below demanded caution. It was a severe, ice-covered grade, like the sides of a bowl, sloping in all directions down toward the harbor. If a man lost his footing, he might plunge the entire distance, for there was almost nothing to get hold of.

They worked along the top of the ridge until they found a small ravine which appeared to offer a footing, and they started down. After about an hour the sides of the ravine were getting steeper and a small stream flowed down the center. As they made their way along, the stream increased in depth until they were wading through knee-deep water that was frigidly cold from the snowy uplands that fed it.

About three o'clock they looked ahead and saw that the stream ended abruptly—in a waterfall.

They reached the edge and leaned over. There was a drop of about 25 feet. But it was the only way. The ravine here had grown to the size of a gorge, and its sides were perpendicular and offered no way of getting down.

There was nothing to do but to go over the edge. With some trouble they found a boulder large enough to hold their weight, and they made one end of the rope fast to it. All three of them pulled off their Burberrys, in which they wrapped the adz, the cook pot and Worsley's diary, then pitched them over the side.

Crean was the first to go down. Shackleton and Worsley lowered him, and he reached the bottom gasping and choking. Then Shackleton lowered himself down through the water. Worsley was last.

It was an icy ducking, but they were at the bottom, and from here the ground was almost level. The rope could not be recovered, but they picked up the three articles that remained and started off for the station, now only a mile or so away.

Almost simultaneously, all three of them remembered their appearance. Their hair hung down almost to their shoulders, and their beards were matted with salt and blubber oil. Their clothes were filthy, and threadbare, and torn.

Worsley reached under his sweater and carefully took out four rusty safety pins that he had hoarded for almost two years. With them he did his best to pin up the major rents in his trousers.

CHAPTER 3

Mathias Andersen was the station foreman at Stromness. He had never met Shackleton, but along with everyone else at South Georgia he knew that the *Endurance* had sailed from there in 1914 . . . and had undoubtedly been lost with all hands in the Weddell Sea.

Just then, however, his thoughts were a long way from Shackleton and the ill-fated Imperial Trans-Antarctic Expedition. He had put in a long work day, beginning at 7 A.M., and it was now after four o'clock in the afternoon and he was tired. He was standing on the dock, supervising a group of his men who were unloading supplies from a boat.

Just then he heard an outcry and looked up. Two small boys about eleven years old were running, not in play but in terror. Behind them Andersen saw the figures of three men walking slowly and with great weariness in his direction.

He was puzzled. They were strangers, certainly. But that was not so unusual as the fact that they were coming—not from the docks where a ship might come in—but from the direction of the mountains, the interior of the island.

As they drew closer he saw that they were heavily bearded, and their faces were almost black except for their eyes. Their hair was as long as a woman's and hung down almost to their shoulders. For some reason it looked stringy and stiff. Their clothing was peculiar, too. It was not the sweaters and boots worn by seamen. Instead, the three men appeared to have on parkas, though it was hard to tell because their garments were in such a ragged state.

By then the workmen had stopped what they were doing to stare at the three strangers approaching. The foreman stepped forward to meet them. The man in the center spoke in English.

"Would you please take us to Anton Andersen," he said softly.

The foreman shook his head. Anton Andersen was not at Stromness any longer, he explained. He had been replaced by the regular factory manager, Thoralf Sørlle.

The Englishman seemed pleased. "Good," he said. "I know Sørlle well."

The foreman led the way to Sørlle's house, about a hundred yards off to the right. Almost all the workmen on the pier had left their jobs to come see the three strangers who had appeared at the dock. Now they lined the route, looking curiously at the foreman and his three companions.

Andersen knocked at the manager's door, and after a moment Sørlle himself opened it. He was in his shirt sleeves and he still sported his big handlebar mustache.

When he saw the three men he stepped back and a look of disbelief came over his face. For a long moment he stood shocked and silent before he spoke.

"Who the hell are you?" he said at last.

The man in the center stepped forward.

"My name is Shackleton," he replied in a quiet voice.

Again there was silence. Some said that Sørlle turned away and wept.

EPILOGUE

The crossing of South Georgia has been accomplished only by one other party. That was almost forty years later, in 1955, by a British survey team under the able leadership of Duncan Carse. That party was made up of expert climbers and was well equipped with everything needed for the journey. Even so, they found it treacherous going.

Writing from the scene in October, 1955, Carse explained that to make the crossing, two routes were available—the "high road" and the "low road."

"In distance," Carse wrote, "they are nowhere more than 10 miles apart; in difficulty, they are hardly comparable.

"We to-day are travelling easily and unhurriedly. We are fit men, with our sledges and tents and ample food and time. We break new ground but with the leisure and opportunity to probe ahead. We pick and choose our hazards, accepting only the calculated risk. No lives depend upon our success—except our own. We take the high road.

"They—Shackleton, Worsley and Crean . . . took the low road.

"I do not know how they did it, except that they had to—three men of the heroic age of Antarctic exploration with 50 feet of rope between them—and a carpenter's adze."

Every comfort the whaling station could provide was placed at the disposal of Shackleton, Worsley, and Crean. They first enjoyed the glorious luxury of a long bath, followed by a shave. Then new clothes were given them from the station's storehouse.

That night after a hearty dinner, Worsley went on board the whale-catcher *Samson* for the trip around South Georgia to Peggotty Camp where McNeish, McCarthy, and Vincent were waiting. The *Samson* arrived the following morning at King Haakon Bay. Very little is known about the meeting except that the three castaways at first failed to recognize Worsley because his appearance was so drastically altered now that he was shaved and had on fresh clothes. McNeish, McCarthy, and Vincent were taken on board the whale-catcher, and the *Caird*, too, was loaded. The *Samson* arrived back at Stromness the following day, May 22.

Shackleton, meanwhile, had arranged for the use of a large wooden whaler, the *Southern Sky*, in which to return to Elephant Island for the relief of the party there.

That evening a sort of crude reception was held in what Worsley described as a "large room, full of captains and mates and sailors, and hazy with tobacco smoke." Four white-haired, veteran Norwegian skippers came forward. Their spokesman, speaking in Norse with Sørlle translating, said that they had sailed the Antarctic seas for forty years, and that they wanted to shake the hands of the men who could bring an open 22-foot boat from Elephant Island through the Drake Passage to South Georgia.

Then every man in that room stood up, and the four old skippers took Shackleton and Worsley and Crean by the hand and congratulated them on what they had done.

Many of the whalermen were bearded and dressed in heavy sweaters and sea boots. There was no formality, no speeches. They had no medals or decorations to bestow—only their heartfelt admiration for an accomplishment which perhaps only they would ever fully appreciate. And their sincerity lent to the scene a simple but profoundly moving solemnity. Of the honors that followed—and there were many—possibly none ever exceeded that night of May 22, 1916, when, in a dingy warehouse shack on South Georgia, with the smell of rotting whale carcasses in the air, the whalermen of the southern ocean stepped forward one by one and silently shook hands with Shackleton, Worsley, and Crean.

The following morning, less than seventy-two hours after arriving at Stromness from across the mountains, Shackleton and his two companions set out for Elephant Island.

It was the beginning of a maddeningly frustrating series of rescue attempts lasting more than three months, during which the pack ice surrounding Elephant Island seemed resolutely determined that no rescue ship would get through to relieve the castaways.

The *Southern Sky* encountered ice only three days out from South Georgia, and less than a week later she was forced to return to port. Within ten days, however, Shackleton had obtained from the Uruguayan government the loan of a small survey vessel, the *Instituto de Pesca No. 1*, for a second attempt to rescue his men. She limped home six days later, severely damaged by the ice through which Shackleton had tried to push her.

A third attempt was made in a balky wooden schooner, the *Emma,* which Shackleton chartered. She was at sea for nearly three weeks, during which it was a struggle merely to keep her afloat—much less to effect a rescue. The *Emma* never approached Elephant Island closer than 100 miles.

It was now August 3, nearly three and a half months since the *Caird* had sailed for South Georgia. Throughout each failure of the subsequent rescue attempts, Shackleton's anxiety had risen to the extent that Worsley said he had never seen him so on edge.

He had consistently appealed to the government back in England to send a proper ice vessel to get through the pack. Now word came that the *Discovery*, which had originally carried Scott to the Antarctic in 1901, was finally on her way from England. But it would take weeks for her to arrive, and Shackleton was in no mood to sit idly by and wait.

Instead he appealed to the Chilean government for the use of an ancient sea-going tug, the *Yelcho*. He promised not to take her into any ice, for she was steel-hulled and her ability to weather the sea—much less any pack—was doubtful. The request was granted, and the *Yelcho* sailed on August 25. This time the fates were willing.

Five days later, on August 30, Worsley logged: "5.25 am Full speed . . . 11.10 [A.M.] . . . base of land faintly visible. Threadg: our way between lumps ice, reefs, & grounded bergs. 1.10 PM Sight the Camp to sw. . . . "

For the twenty-two castaways on Elephant Island, August 30 began like almost any other day. At sunrise the weather was clear and cold, giving promise of a fine day. But before long heavy clouds rolled in and the scene once more became, as Orde-Lees recorded, "the prevailing gloom to which we are now so inured."

As always, almost everyone tramped individually to the top of the lookout bluff to satisfy himself once more that there was no ship to be seen. By now they did so more out of habit than of hope. It was simply a ritual to which they had become accustomed, and they climbed the bluff without anticipation and returned to the hut without disappointment. It had been four months and six days since the *Caird* had left, and there was not a man among them who still believed seriously that she had survived the journey to South Georgia. It was now only a matter of time until a party was sent in the *Wills* on the perilous journey to Deception Island.

After breakfast, all hands got busy digging snow from around the hut. But later in the morning the tide was low and they decided to postpone their digging in order to gather limpets, a small crustacean which had been found in some numbers in the water off the spit. Wally How was acting as cook and he was preparing a lunch of boiled seal's backbone, a dish of which everyone had become extremely fond.

The hoosh was ready about 12:45, and they all gathered in the hut except Marston, who had gone to the lookout bluff to make some thumbnail sketches.

A few minutes later they heard his footsteps running along the path, but nobody paid much attention. He was simply late for lunch. Then he put his head inside and spoke to Wild in a tone so breathless that some of the men thought he sounded casual.

"Hadn't we better send up some smoke signals?" he asked.

For a moment there was silence, and then, as one man, they grasped what Marston was saying.

"Before there was time for a reply," Orde-Lees recorded, "there was a rush of members tumbling over one another, all mixed up with mugs of seal hoosh, making a simultaneous dive for the door-hole which was immediately torn to shreds so that those members who could not pass through it, on account of the crush, made their exits through the 'wall,' or what remained of it."

Some put their boots on—others didn't bother. James put his on the wrong feet.

Sure enough, there was a small ship, only about a mile offshore.

Macklin dashed to the lookout bluff, tearing off his Burberry jacket as he ran. There he tied it onto the halliard of the oar that served as their flagpole. But he was only able to hoist it part of the way up before the halliard jammed. (Shackleton saw the signal at half-staff and his heart sank, he later said, because he took it to be a sign that some of the party had been lost.)

Hurley gathered up all the sennegrass he could find, then poured over it some blubber oil and the two gallons of paraffin they still had. He had a hard time lighting it, and when it finally ignited—almost with an explosion—it produced more flame than smoke.

But no matter. The ship was headed toward the spit.

Wild, meanwhile, had gone to the water's edge and was signaling from there the best place to send in a boat. And How had broken open a tin of precious biscuits and was offering them around. Few men, however, stopped to have one. Even so rare a treat held little appeal in the excitement of the moment.

Macklin returned to the hut and lifted Blackboro to his shoulders, then carried him to a position on the rocks near Wild where he might better see the thrilling sight.

The ship approached to within several hundred yards, then stopped. The men ashore could see a boat being lowered. Four men got into it, followed by the sturdy, square-set figure they knew so well—Shackleton. A spontaneous cheer went up. In fact the excitement ashore was so intense that many men actually were giggling.

Within a few minutes the boat was near enough for Shackleton to be heard.

"Are you all right?" he shouted.

"All well," they replied.

Wild guided the boat to a safe place among the rocks, but because of the ice around the spit it was impossible to make a landing, so the boat was held a few feet off.

Wild urged Shackleton to come ashore, if only briefly, to see how they had fixed the hut in which they had waited four long months. But Shackleton, though he was smiling and obviously relieved, was still quite noticeably anxious and wanted only to be away. He declined Wild's offer and urged the men to get on board as quickly as possible.

Certainly no great urging was needed, and one at a time they jumped from the rocks into the boat, leaving behind them without a second thought dozens of personal little items which only an hour before had been considered almost indispensable.

One load was rowed out to the *Yelcho*, and then a second.

Throughout it all Worsley had watched anxiously from the bridge of the ship.

Finally he logged: "2.10 All Well! At last! 2.15 Full speed ahead."

Macklin wrote: "I stayed on deck to watch Elephant Island recede in the distance . . . I could still see my Burberry [jacket] flapping in the breeze on the hillside—no doubt it will flap there to the wonderment of gulls and penguins till one of our familiar [gales] blows it all to ribbons."

Acknowledgments

I could never adequately express my appreciation to all the people who contributed to this undertaking. But here, in alphabetical order, are those to whom I am particularly grateful:

William Bakewell of Dukes, Michigan.

Charles W. Ferguson of Chappaqua, New York.

Margery and James Fisher of Northhampton, England, co-authors of *Shackleton and the Antarctic*, who generously made available to me a great deal of the material they gathered in the preparation of their excellent and exhaustively researched life of Shackleton.

Charles J. Green of Hull, England.

Commander Lionel Greenstreet of Brixham, England, first of all for granting me many hours of his time, then for graciously permitting me the use of his two very detailed diaries and for answering many questions by letter.

Miss Evelyn Harvey of New York City, for her patient criticisms and advice.

Walter How of London, England.

Dr. Leonard D. A. Hussey of Chorley Wood, Hertfordshire, England, who supplied much helpful information, both in person and by letter.

355

Miss Joan Ogle Isaacs of London, who put in many long weeks of research with me.

Dr. Reginald W. James of Capetown, South Africa.

A. J. Kerr of Ilford, Essex, England.

James Marr of Surrey, England, who generously made available to me Frank Worsley's diary of the *Caird* boat journey for which I am especially grateful.

The editors of The McGraw-Hill Book Company, notably Edward Kuhn, Jr.

Dr. J. A. McIlroy of Aberystwyth, Wales.

Miss Edna O'Brien of Scarborough, New York.

Maurice T. Ragsdale of Chappaqua, New York, who read the manuscript and offered some sage advice.

The late Miss Cecily Shackleton, who, before her death, graciously granted me the use of her father's diary and many of his personal papers.

The Scott Polar Research Institute of Cambridge, England, who made available to me the following manuscripts:

1. Frank Worsley's *Endurance* diary, 1914–1916 (S.P.R.I. ms 296).
2. Frank Worsley's *James Caird* (navigational) diary, April–May, 1916 (S.P.R.I. ms 297).
3. R. W. James' diaries (S.P.R.I. ms 370).
4. T. H. Orde-Lees' draft account of the *Endurance* expedition (S.P.R.I. ms 293). Typescript.

I am particularly grateful to Harry G. R. King and Miss Ann M. Savours of the Scott Polar Research Institute for their many hours of help and the interest they took in this project.

Arnt Wegger of the Framnaes shipbuilding firm of Sandefjord, Norway, and also Lars Christensen, Aanderud Larsen, Mathias Andersen and many others in Sandefjord who provided me with blueprints, pictures and all available information concerning the *Endurance* herself, in addition to much information about South Georgia.

Sir James Wordie of Cambridge, England.

Finally, I should like to single out three individuals to whom I am especially indebted.

The first is Paul Palmer of Ridgefield, Connecticut, without whose enthusiasm, encouragement, and help this book might never have been written.

The second is Dr. Alexander H. Macklin of Cults, Aberdeenshire, Scotland, to whom I owe a debt that is difficult to express. Not only did he supply me with his own and other diaries, but he provided me with a detailed account of the boat journey to Elephant Island. His generosity, his objectivity, and most of all his patience over a period of many long months during which he painstakingly answered my numerous questions never faltered once. I called upon him for help much more than I had right to.

Finally, of my wife, I can only say that her contribution went above and beyond the call of duty.